A Field Guide to the Snowden Files

—

MEDIA, ART, ARCHIVES

2013–2017

Edited by
Magdalena Taube
Krystian Woznicki

DIAMONDPAPER

III. ARCHIVES

APPENDIX Snowden Commons

Preface
—The Snowman¬

Foreword
by Christoph Hochhäusler

I type "Snowden", and the autocorrection function suggests "Snowman". Certainly a fitting codename for a man in Russian exile. Is my word processor really pre-Snowden? Older than the leak? And who decides which names to feed into the spelling assistance software? Will future generations of autocorrect recognize Snowden?

It seems the way my attention – my suspicion, really – was drawn to autocorrect's failure – for this anonymous entity that wants to read my mind – is the whole story of the Snowden files in a nutshell. Because, yes, the signals units of the US, GB, Germany et al. also want to read our minds. And much like autocorrect, they react to keywords in an automatic fashion. Even those words we do not send, the words we discard, erase, censor. And much like I come to avoid words, we have come to avoid certain keywords in the digisphere. After all, we now know there is a ghost in the machine that we don't want to wake – as if this form of self-censorship would help us …

In any case, Snowden's disclosures have altered our relationship to the machine, as what they have disclosed is not surveillance per se, but the potentiality of it – and that makes all the difference. In these times, machines assist writing, and killing, and pretty much everything else. For today's power, security has become an informational problem to be managed by technology. In that sense, the logic behind mass surveillance is based not on the psychology of suspicion of everyone, but rather on machine learning and artificial intelligence. Under these conditions one imperative goes practically uncontested: the more data, the better.

What Snowden's files have provided is a freeze-frame in this data storm: data is image-giving, is giving birth to image. The imagery is ugly, but what does ugly mean when there is no beholder? In this sense, the files are a battle cry for artists, archivists and activists alike, as this book affirms.

Like most people, I have never read the files, but have followed the 'story'. As a matter of fact I have checked out some files, not to read them, but to see proof that they actually exist. Why do we have books on our shelves? Not to read them, mostly. But rather for the potentiality of reading and re-reading. And as proof, to ourself and to others, that we have read them. Abstractions of memory.

In many ways, Snowden's decision to provide the crude material in need of refining, material that has to be transformed in order to reach us 'properly', reflects this logic of potentiality: We need to know that the files are there, a few clicks away, in order to believe the 'story'. A distant echo of the NSA's own interpassive approach perhaps.

This distance towards the real thing reminds me of the alleged burial shroud of Christ, "proof" that he once was a man. We will never see the sacred body of the security state either, but the Snowden files at least confirm its existence. And the religious parallels don't end here. The Anglo-American world, the one that needless to say pretty much dominates the discourse, generally refers to the disclosures as the 'Snowden revelations' – thereby echoing the Christian eschatology of the New Testament. Meanwhile, the modern 'intelligence community' is united by a single belief: that security is 'signals exegesis'. Which really is a whole new religion. Previously, security was considered something that comes into being by action. Now, it's all about knowing. About text. And ultimately, about the idea that truth can be owned. And this is something that we can't let them have.

So let us explore the many inspiring impulses that this book offers, e.g. with regard to unlocking the potential of the files for artistic practice, creatively appropriating the files for writing social history, or making access to the files sustainable and democratically accountable – and in the course of this let us explore ways to engage upon new exchanges and encounters in order to come to terms with our machine-driven present.

Christoph Hochhäusler is the critically acclaimed director of films such as "The City Below" (2010) and "The Lies of the Victors" (2014).

Preface
—The Snowden Files,
or: Civil Resistance to
Security Politics¬

Introduction
by Magdalena Taube and Krystian Woznicki

Nowadays, "security has top priority". It is under this slogan that real as well as imagined risks, such as the movements of migrants, are being administered. Increasingly, these administrative activities seek to manage everything with the aid of datarization and preemption; in effect, our future is to be shaped by algorithms. What role do the Snowden disclosures play in this context? Obviously, they disclose the inner workings of technologies and programs central to contemporary security politics. In doing this, they have sparked not only international debates but also grassroots actions of all kinds. It is difficult to evaluate the outcome of the debates and actions. Of course this does not relieve us of the task of thinking about ever new ways and approaches to augment the impact of the political moment, which entails questioning dormant possibilities. In this context it is high time to acknowledge that the full potential of the Snowden disclosures will only be realized if we begin caring as well about the actual documents that have enabled the disclosures in the first place.

To begin with, what is security politics all about? We can gauge this by turning our attention to a process that is characterized by great instability and potentially boundless risk. Today, there are more regional and international migrants than ever in recorded history, with over one billion people on the move. Faced with this epochal process, in Europe, for instance, politicians, senior media people and concerned citizens are engaging in right-wing populism that feeds on fear. They are exploiting the general increase in human mobility: instrumentalizing the seemingly excessive movement of people, they are suggesting that societies are experiencing not a crisis of democracy, which is what it is in reality, but rather a security crisis. They also suggest that we should not be calling for human rights, public infrastructure

9

or a reinvention of democracy. The demagogues of fear propose that European states should instead be calling for "control of movement" and therefore for "closed borders", "total surveillance" and "mass deportation". They also assert that we should commit ourselves to the form of power that was unleashed by the War on Terror, the form we associate with security firms, IT companies, intelligence services and military special forces.

The representatives of these organizations and companies believe that everything can be computed, and they are therefore grabbing more and more data. They are forecasting scenarios for the whole of society that, though they may never become reality, nevertheless lead them to arm themselves and mobilize and act against all the threats that will supposedly appear in the future. To go about this, they are implementing a project of algorithmic logistics based on the movement of people and of data; and they are demanding sovereignty over all infrastructure essential to carry out this project.

In this situation, the control of movement (movement by humans and bits alike) and the production of the future seem to be two sides of a coin increasingly being minted with the aid of big data technologies. To put it another way: data-driven preemption is changing our horizon and the space for what is possible, both in designing and producing the future and in managing movements. The future of movement and the movement of our future are both meant to reach a state of completion through computation and preemption – even before starting to debate them within society.

* Most notably The New York Times, the Canadian Broadcasting Corporation, the Australian Broadcasting Corporation, Der Spiegel in Germany, O Globo in Brazil, Le Monde in France, L'Espresso in Italy, NRC Handelsblad in the Netherlands, Dagbladet in Norway, El País in Spain, and Sveriges Television in Sweden.

Security and its discontents

Instead of glorifying this state of affairs, it is time to question and challenge it. With the Snowden disclosures that started in June 2013, such ambitions have gained new urgency as well as new ground; they can no longer be dismissed as paranoia or someone else's problem.

The first documents to be published simultaneously by The Washington Post and The Guardian caused an international outcry as they shed light on "NSA collecting phone records of millions of Verizon customers daily" and the "Top secret court order requiring Verizon to hand over all call data shows scale of domestic surveillance under Obama". The disclosures continued throughout 2013 unveiling other security programs, including one called PRISM, which is essentially about a data-sharing partnership among governmental secret service agencies in the US, Australia, UK, the Netherlands, etc. and global IT corporations such as Microsoft, Facebook, Apple and Google. Media outlets joining the coverage from all over the world* – picking up on the disclosures rather than working with the files themselves – have been contributing to and causing a disturbing picture to arise: as security politics seems to be caught up in a vicious cycle of controlling what of necessity is beyond control – namely, future threats – they are running wild and expanding seemingly without limit, beyond democratic reason and accountability. On top of this: citizens, nowadays mostly busy with their role as consumers, are complicit in all of this.

After all, the attractive muscles of security politics have been part of our daily lives for some time now. Are societies not becoming increasingly dependent on big data-driven technologies, for example in finance and logistics, consumption and health care, and geopolitics and climate policy? Are tech users not actually becoming its accomplices, e.g. when jauntily using corporate social networks that feed the big data-driven security apparatus; when calming their nerves with the belief that they are carrying a guarantee against confusion and exclusion in their pockets because their smartphones – by receiving GPS signals – are always providing orientation? Are more and more people not increasingly falling for the belief that these tools are the ultimate early-warning system for general security?

Processing the collective unconscious

If we speak today about the Snowden files, we are not actually talking about the documents compiled and archived by former NSA subcontractor Edward Snowden, but about those documents which, after Snowden leaked them to a handful of journalists, were then partially and selectively published by the aforementioned media houses.

As is well-known, these disclosures initiated global debates about the role of secret services in democracies, citizen rights in the age of digital networks, the role and definition of national security, the state of big data and technologies of prediction. In the process, the debates directed public attention towards an increasingly untransparent control of data traffic and human traffic – a drama that concerns many, many people whom we never hear about, but also public figures such as the filmmaker Laura Poitras, who was repeatedly detained at borders due to her work on the War on Terror, or Edward Snowden himself, who is no longer free to move; a drama which eventually, as the work of the two people shows, is taking place equally in the realm of data technologies. They

have quite literally been subjected to increasingly data-driven security methodologies such as motion profiling, predictive policing and so-called pattern of life analysis.

By documenting the technical details of such data-driven security methodologies as well as the inner workings of a clandestine data industry/ state security complex in general, the Snowden files represent a kind of collective unconscious: something that society was never meant to learn about itself, its past, present, and future. In that sense the Snowden files can be seen as a message from "children from an era that is yet to be received", as the filmmaker Kim Ki-Duk has said in a different context. This notion is highlighted by the fact that the interpretations of even the published documents remain unfinished due to their cryptic language and specialized information. And it is also strikingly supported by the fact that only a small percentage has been published: We can expect more disclosures to emerge in the future, though it may take decades before they all enter the public domain. In this sense, the Snowden files represent not only a repressed awareness of the design of our social and political present, they also represent an awareness yet to come, provided we can develop the tools and capacities to decode and share them. Actually, this would be a very concrete way to question and challenge the new form of power that operates as a power over the possible and that organizes its capacities in order to pre-empt threats, including putatively dangerous movements by humans and bits alike.

But how can we render this awareness and knowledge into our commons? How can we incorporate it as a vital part of our common history and common future? A future in which we reclaim the autonomy of movement. A future in which the democratic organization of infrastructure for data and human traffic becomes our vanishing point. In order to go about this huge task, we propose looking at the Snowden files anew: many people have been talking about the disclosures and their consequences, but most have not dared to actually appreciate the materiality, aesthetics and politics of the files themselves. Who makes a difference?

Civil societies are responding

Not only debates about security politics, democracy, civil rights, the internet and intelligence agencies, but also collective actions by people all around the world have been triggered by the secret information revealed by Edward Snowden. Admittedly, these actions did not include storming parliaments and seizing power; nor did they lead to the biggest demonstrations in history. Yet many small things have been happening all over the planet. The disclosures have been providing impetus for the creation of activist organizations, such as Restore the Fourth, which seeks to strengthen the Fourth Amendment to the United States Constitution and end programs that violate it.

A great number of online initiatives have emerged, including petitions, open letters and other forms of protest such as The Day We Fight Back, which took place on February 11, 2014 with more than 6,000 participating websites, primarily in the form of webpage banner-advertisements that read, for instance: "Dear Internet, we're sick of complaining about the NSA. We want new laws that curtail online surveillance. Today we fight back." The work of bloggers and other media activists who are providing independent information resources is also notable in this context. The diversity of approaches is impressive. The spectrum ranges from websites such as PRISM Break, which provides an overview of free software alternatives that make it possible to circumvent security programs, to projects such as Transparency Toolkit that "gathers open data on surveillance and human rights abuses and makes free software to examine it" to blogs such as netzpolitik.org, which not only comments on the disclosures beyond the constraints of mainstream media, but also continuously protocols the German Parliamentary Committee investigating the NSA spying scandal – a process that is more or less closed to the public.

Of course, protest has also taken to the streets. In Germany, for example, demonstrations took place during Barack Obama's Berlin visit in June 2013, and slogans like "Yes we scan", "StopWatchingUs" or "Freiheit statt Angst" ("freedom instead of fear") entered the public realm. People have also started to organize walks and tours leading to the headquarters of the state security complex. While some of these actions continue to the present day, all of them are contributing to create a participatory space with the potential to affect the general public – soliciting solidarity, expanding awareness and inspiring new movements.

The CryptoParty movement for example, said to have emerged around 2012 as a grassroots global endeavor to introduce the basics of practical cryptography, has been experiencing a big boost since the Snowden disclosures. Mushrooming all over the world, workshops are being organized in hacker spaces, universities and libraries to train in the use of the TOR anonymity network, PGP and disk encryption. This wave has attracted considerable media attention. A report in Wired magazine, for instance, told the story of Edward Snowden, while employed by Dell as an NSA contractor, organizing a local CryptoParty at a small hackerspace in Honolulu, Hawaii on December 11, 2012 – just six months before leaking tens of thousands of secret U.S. government documents. During that CryptoParty, Snowden taught 20 Hawaii residents how to encrypt their hard drives and use the Internet anonymously.

La Quadrature du Net, one of Europe's most active civil rights organizations, has urged the French government "to break its deafening silence" on issues related to the Snowden disclosures and "to allow for an open and democratic debate on the extent of its surveillance practices", specifically with regard to the cooperation of network operator Orange with French intelligence services. In February 2015, they launched a legal challenge against a French government administrative decree on access to metadata. In Germany, in turn, the Chaos Computer Club has also created a coalition of various civil society actors to file suits against the German government for complicity in the unconstitutional activities carried out by the NSA and GCHQ. On the legal

Human Rights Watch, Transparency International, and the Index on Censorship, among others.

Nonetheless, the actual documents that triggered these global repercussions are at risk of disappearing in the background noise of the NSA scandal – be it because they are ostensibly dangerous; be it because the facts that they make it possible to establish seem to suit supplementing social struggles better; be it because the voices of politicians manage to captivate our attention more efficiently. The latter is exposed by a chart that was created by Karin Wahl-Jorgensen, Professor at Cardiff University. Primarily based on British newspaper coverage, it shows the degrees to which different sources were used in the media narratives prompted by the Snowden disclosures. The Snowden files themselves appear to play a relatively small role among the 19 different categories.

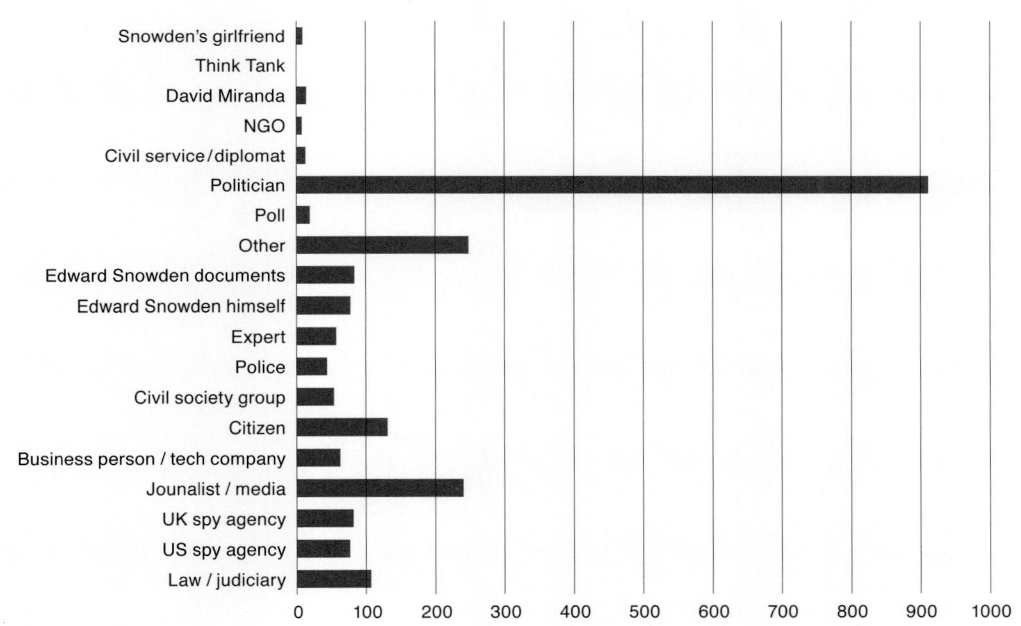

front in the US, the Electronic Frontier Foundation has created a coalition of various groups filing law suits against the NSA. Meanwhile, human rights organizations all over the world have urged the Obama administration not to prosecute but to protect whistleblower Snowden: Amnesty International,

Sources used in the media narratives prompted by the Snowden disclosures (British newspaper coverage) show the dominance of political actors.

All told, the documents remain arcane, not understood by the general public nor even by many experts. And it is not ensured that the documents will be preserved for posterity or for those writing our history.

Appropriating the Snowden files

Certainly both the obscurity and instability of the Snowden files have to do with contemporary security politics. It is the language of power obsessed with securitization that must remain inscrutable to most members of society. Hence they veil themselves in darkness, using codes, acronyms, intelligence speak, etc. But this is not the only problem confronting the files today. Another is that they have been declared stolen state secrets, which also means that they have been declared to be still under the protective shields of securitization. This means: whoever dares even to look at them is by inference undermining the powers in charge. Understandably, this can trouble and paralyze many who are afraid of prosecution. But this, of course, can also be a moment to challenge security politics: if, for reasons of public interest, we disrespect the official gestures and implicit protocols that are intended to securitize the files simply by looking at them, we are creating a starting point for civil resistance. Where could this take us?

Let us briefly recapitulate the logic of security politics: as this politics is about securing against future threats, it claims and seizes power over the possible, that is, power over the future itself, and, more broadly speaking, even power over history as such. Today, in times marked by growing inequalities and expulsions, unwriting and rewriting history from the viewpoint of the defeated, the marginalized and illegalized is gaining ever greater urgency. And the very basis of social history writing depends and will depend on documents such as those leaked by whistleblowers.

So, what if we continue indulging further in the general tendency to ignore the Snowden files? Against the backdrop described, we can guess how serious the implications of ignoring the Snowden files are for democracies today and in the future. We can sense that the very future of civil resistance to increasingly authoritarian security politics is at stake, and consequently the future of movement and the movement of the future. In this sense, to reiterate, dealing with the files themselves can be a crucial beginning for counter-politics, since deploying the files as sources for the unwriting and rewriting of 'the history of the victors and oppressors' is central to our struggles. It is this insight that our book takes as a starting point to situate the historic Snowden leak in the context of appropriations carried out by civil society actors.

For now, we are focusing on the appropriations carried out by artists, activists and researchers who have done groundbreaking work with the Snowden documents. The project presents various forms of appropriation and is organized according to the different contexts in which the material was published: firstly, in the international media; secondly, within the art world; thirdly, in web archives. To go about this, our project puts together for the first time a representative overview of positions from the fields of journalism, art, activism and research – from analytical approaches to the form and the content of the files (presented in chapter one), to artistic appropriations of the files in artworks (presented in chapter two), to the most ambitious international archive initiatives working on the documents (presented in chapter three).

The different approaches have in common that their aim is to transform the historical documents from 'unconscious records' into graspable and shareable parts of collective memory. This means to actually work with them, to make them accessible and to preserve them – a matter of continuous cooperative appropriation. In this sense, the intention of all the approaches is to reach out to and engage with the public. However, they have also tasked themselves with outlining and explaining the complex political, social and technological realities that the Snowden documents helped to lay bare.

This book is in some sense a work in progress. With this in mind we hope that you will also read the appendix, where we present an overview of our ongoing work to transform the Snowden files into a commons. This section gathers some data on our interventions as well as public responses related to this issue. It is augmented with photos by Norman Posselt and Andi Weiland that they have taken at various stages of the Berliner Gazette initiative. Their image series "The Many Faces of the Snowden Commons" presents a representative group of civil society actors who have joined us over the years: librarians, researchers, coders, curators, journalists, activists, artists, entrepreneurs, architects, campaigners and policy consultants.

We are grateful for any feedback and any hint about other important initiatives and approaches that work creatively with the Snowden files. Expanding our understanding of this new field in the making, we hope to expand and extend our scope in future initiatives. At the same time, we hope to inspire others to begin critically and creatively working with the files: appropriating them, turning them into public records and eventually transforming their secret knowledge into a common good.

I
—MEDIA

I
—MEDIA¬
Journalism, Historical Data Leaks and Public Interest¬

Text
by Krystian Woznicki

If we speak today about the Snowden files, we are not actually talking about the documents compiled and archived by former NSA subcontractor Edward Snowden, but rather about those documents which, after Snowden leaked them to a handful of journalists, were then partially and selectively published by a small number of international media houses.

This procedure is no mere coincidence. Snowden had studied prior leaks including landmark WikiLeaks disclosures because he was seeking the right balance between impact and responsibility. His research led him early on to the journalists Glenn Greenwald and Laura Poitras; he was fond of their strong interest in security issues and their attitude to dealing with them diligently as well as uncompromisingly. Embarking upon this path eventually entailed the involvement of media houses as editorial platforms for the Snowden documents – in a much more direct and exclusive way than in WikiLeaks projects like the US diplomatic cables leak.

Snowden's approach is yet another experiment in the relatively young history of huge data leaks. There is no established model for this matter – instead, it's all trial and error. Therefore, it seems obligatory to explore and critique this process. This means questioning primarily two things: first, what it actually means in this context for media to put itself in the service of public interest; second, what the limits of established forms of media narratives are.

Is there a global security industry, in which states and corporations share interests and data beyond democratic legitimation and beyond democratic control? The Snowden files have proven to be of public interest by raising this question and to some extent answering it. This is highlighted by the fact that they have prompted an exceptional media narrative – be it for its unusual duration, unfolding over the course of several years and stimulating a variety of debates.

However, the media narrative has functioned largely within the logic of mainstream media: rather top-down, rather oriented towards the criteria of entertainment and attention economics, rather abstaining from engaging the public in forms of participation and collaboration. This also has to do with the fact that access to the Snowden files remains restricted. Material that the whistleblower put together at the risk of his life because he considered it of public interest – that material has not been at the public's disposal. After being locked in secret NSA desks, it has been rendered inaccessible again. Doesn't this impede the democratic potential of the disclosures?

Who is holding Snowden's archive?

Only a small percentage of those files have been made available to the public in the first years. Only a small circle of people has been able to access, read, analyze, interpret and publish the Snowden files. The same people were deciding what is going out: journalists at The Guardian, Der Spiegel, The New York Times, The Washington Post and The Intercept. Those who belong to the small circle of people tend to argue that this is for security reasons. In this sense, one can say that the leaked files have been "secured" in order to prevent greater harm. There is also the obvious argument that this method has enabled the long-lasting media narrative to enfold – a sustained visibility that some observers consider the whistleblower's life insurance. But what if, in the sense that "data is the oil of the 21st century", we have to acknowledge that the Snowden files have been re-privatized by people who are trying to exploit them for their own interests?

There has been hardly any debate about the style of handling this historic data leak. Hardly anyone has been asking whether there is a way to "open" this huge set of data for public scrutiny. Considering the current circumstances – the whistleblower stuck in Moscow – it may seem far-fetched to come up with such a proposition. Hardly anyone supporting the cause would want to annul his life insurance plan. Yet I think we need to raise the question. Not so much because the aforementioned journalists are not living up to their task, but rather because I think that processes in the service of the public should be designed as inclusively as possible in order to live up to the challenges of this specific obligation. Is this possible in this context?

Leaks and cooperative knowledge production

The philosopher Theodor Adorno once famously said (I am paraphrasing): The impact of an artwork starts where the author's intention ends. Creating an analogy to Snowden, one could say: the impact of the Snowden files starts to unfold its full potential where both the whistleblower's and the initiated journalist's intentions end. Many artists, researchers, activists and technology experts (not to mention journalists other than the "few lucky ones") have a great interest in working with the Snowden files. They are interested in the archive that Snowden built over a considerable period of time: the organizational principles he chose, the order he created, the files he selected, etc.

The motivation to acquire first-hand knowledge about the content, materiality and architecture of the leak is actually comparable to the curiosity uttered in the context of major WikiLeaks projects such as Cablegate before they entered the public domain: if not only media houses were able to access and process the material, but also historians at universities, activists at NGOs and artists in museums – wouldn't this enable a more far-reaching collaborative process, one that would actually be able to live up to the task of processing those enormous amounts of data? Having said this, let us look at the Snowden files and let us imagine the historical impact on sciences, social movements and IT infrastructures should those files become in the public domain and serve the general public as material to study and learn from.

At the netzwerk recherche summit in 2014 – the large gathering of the investigative community in Hamburg – I confronted the journalist Luke Harding, the author of "The Snowden Files", with this issue at the Q&A session of his talk. Prior to my intervention, Harding had already hinted at some limitations of the ongoing investigation, alluding to various reasons why those "few lucky ones" are incapable of dealing with the analytical challenge in an appropriate manner: "We are not technical experts". Or: "After two hours your eyes pop out". In spite of this, Harding seemed unprepared to reflect on the possibility of opening the small circle of actors currently dealing with the Snowden files. To paraphrase his response: yes, it is a dilemma that only a few people can look at the Snowden files and draw their own conclusions. However, this limitation is a natural result of their very precarious nature (files containing state secrets) and a consequence of the influence exerted by the government. Nonetheless, "if you have a special project" you could contact Alan Rusbridger, The Guardian's editor-in-chief, and probably get him to provide you with the requested material, he said.

Unlocking closed systems

A request for files is usually directed towards somewhat obscure organizations or corporations and is usually articulated by the press, deploying the freedom of information law or other legal instruments. At first, the request is usually denied. As the history of investigative journalism shows, including many successful cases: the fight for one's right to access for information often needs to include going to court. Requests for files are an important instrument for the press. But now it is the press itself – or rather some of its representatives – towards which such a request needs to be articulated. This seems absurd and prompts various questions, including: to whom are organizations like The Guardian, The Washington Post, The New York Times, Der Spiegel and The Intercept accountable? Are they actually subject to any democratic control?

When I asked the investigative reporter Seymour Hersh about this issue, I had the tone of a fighter in my ear and statements in mind like "taking into account the massive violations against the Constitution, why would any newspaper worry about breaking the law when considering what to publish and with whom to share their material?" Yet when I approached him, first face to face in Hamburg after his talk, then later by email, his stance was a little less "aggressive". Hersh's statement on the fact that the Snowden files are locked away by people who actually represent the freedom of speech: "I don't think there is much chance of getting either Greenwald […] or anyone on the NY Times or Wash Post or The Guardian to open up their files. […] The reporters and editors will all claim they have done the public a great service, etc. […] Meanwhile they all continue to hoard what they have and share it with no one. […] Newspapers turn out to be not very interested in spreading the wealth."

So should we consider the discussion on this topic closed? Or is there still something that can be done? Requests for files may seem futile, but they are an instrument and, as experience shows, one can win the fight. In Great Britain one can consider filing a complaint at the Press Complaints Commission with regard to media corporations exercising exclusive control over the files. In Germany, where this sort of (quasi-monopolistic) control violates the so-called Pressekodex, you could file a complaint at the Deutscher Presserat.

It is at this juncture that the issue of public interest most strikingly reveals a discrepancy, prompting the following question: Should we all not try to collaborate with each other within the press and media sphere in order to solve the major problems of our times, rather than suing each other? And it is here, at this juncture, that we feel very directly the shortcomings of the current model and the need to start to think about a new model for the future. Against this backdrop, one could start to work out a model for transferring those specific files (and big data leaks in general) into the public domain – also taking into account the obvious problems of "security", "government pressure" and a whistleblower's "life insurance".

"Dumping all the material online"

At first glance, there are not many reasons to be overly optimistic. Eventually, "in each of the last global leaks you had a different problem in dumping all the material online. So you can't really construct a [global] model on leaks. Each new batch of leaks will have new problems", as Stefan Candea, a central figure in the OffshoreLeaks and FootballLeaks projects, points out. Others active in the field of investigative journalism for many years are also skeptical about allowing unlimited access. "Featured in the files may be suppliers of information who never knew that they were involved with a secret service", says Ewan Tarkan, who is a journalist pursuing (undercover) research on the security industry, "in the case of Afghanistan, e.g., names of translators or other locals. One example of this would be geheimerkrieg.de – not itself a leak, but an analysis. Here, many names of people were included who just did normal things like IT services."

Should we consider this a blocker to our endeavor? Or just a challenge?

Just because major data leaks seem impossible to "regulate", should we not even try to think about it? Looking back at his professional history, Tarkan states: "I am strictly against publishing leaks without partially blackened names. In the past there have been several cases in which the names of people who had just done simple IT services were visible. Their lives are at stake when documents containing visible names are published. At the same time, this can't be brought forth as an argument to withhold all the files. As the case of Wikileaks shows, it is possible to remove names from documents before publishing them."

In pursuing this aim, we have to keep in mind that "it is the choice of the leaker to tell the journalist what to do with the material", as Candea reminds us. So we need to convince people like Snowden to consider open access to their files. Maybe this is not such a futile endeavor when you take into account the fact that Snowden may not be very satisfied about how his material has been processed so far (as some observers assume). In any case, we are facing a lot of work. We need to raise consciousness among whistleblowers, and we need to craft an adequate concept for platforms that allow open access to their leaks.

Towards a new model for data leaks

First of all, any responsible disclosure of leaked source material "should come with information about the entire corpus of documents, as long as this kind of information does not reveal the identity of the leaker", Detlef Borchers, long-standing IT journalist for heise.de, suggests. "This entails that any informed reader can assess with a sufficient certitude whether the publication by mass media is part of a marketing campaign or not."

Secondly, the public version should be cleared of all names. Yet, who deletes the names? Who has access to that? Who designs the interface in a way that is also attractive to a broad, non-technical audience? Here we require an entity in charge of programming or control, and with regard to that we need to be "foregrounding the issue of responsibility as central", as Borchers points out, while reminding us: "Consider how many mistakes are constantly being made, e.g. in the German version of the Greenwald book, in which many names of NSA employees are included while being blackened in the English original."

Thirdly, we need to consider that the files need to be made accessible in a manner that allows everybody working with them a certain degree of anonymity – you don't want the files on your desktop but in the cloud, at a publicly known location that is accessible in a secure way. But hosted by whom? For instance, a public institution like a library?

Fourthly, the question of how to work with the files is central to the model: Are the respective files machine-readable? Or do they need to be rendered that way? There are various tools that will solve that problem, e.g. DocumentCloud.

Fifthly, you need to understand the language in which the files are written. Solicit the help of someone who is fluent, learn it yourself or have your machine do it for you. Data journalism tool kits (dispersed online or presented on the ubiquitous DDJ panels) will help with the ensuing systematization, analysis and "user-friendly" interpretation. Needless to say, any publication would have to provide links to the sources, openly accessible to anyone.

Finally, specifically in the Snowden case, you need to make sure that the whistleblower does not lose his life insurance and consequently his life. Ed, as supporters passionately call him, has already changed his strategy several times. In the beginning he did not want to take part in the public debate, but rather wanted the documents to speak for themselves. Around December 2013, he changed his mind about that and started a series of public appearances. The next big step would be to open access to the files. Remember Julian Assange: in his case some files (perhaps a major leak of one of the US banks) remained undisclosed in order to back up his publishing activity. This approach could also work for Snowden.

Is this all a new model would have to consider? Probably not. Any feature, whether mentioned thus far or not, requires in-depth scrutiny by the public. For now, we could start by asking: what if only the aforementioned "lucky few" are actually working with the documents, while the rest of the media world – waiting until they are selected and published – merely follows up on the disclosures, rather than digging into the documents that enabled the disclosures in the first place? What does it mean for the writing of social history if these precious sources subsequently become redundant in the unfolding media narratives? And, when thinking more concretely about public interest: is it clever to approach the problem by asking us to make a choice between Snowden's life insurance and open access to the files? Should this really be an either/or issue? Or should we rather demand both: protection of the whistleblower as well as publicly accountable storage and access to the entire leak? The discussion about this entails reflections on the foundations of our democracy. It is not the worst moment in history to rethink most of them.

This piece is a revised version of a text initially published in 2014. Its initial publication in Berliner Gazette attracted considerable attention, initiating debates and interventions that are summarized in the appendix of this book on page 130. In this text, Ewan Tarkan's name was changed by the editors.

I
—MEDIA¬
The Cloud, the Black Box and Other Network Oddities¬

● Colnate Group

Upon scrutinizing the published Snowden documents in relationship to the mechanisms of mass media, several paradoxes come to the fore. To begin with, the cloud appears as a recurring motif in both the Snowden files and the reporting based on thema.

The mass media's reproduction of the NSA's own visual language could be said to support its mythology. After all, the data of mass communication is not contained in a "cloud" but in a very material infrastructure that spans the globe. This paradox is above all a testimony to the logic of mass media narratives, which foster clichés rather than challenging and replacing them. It is safe to say that the latter can be seen as one of the major imperatives emerging from the Snowden disclosures: they have highlighted how misleading the language is that we generally use for technology.

Another recurring motif in the Snowden files is
the black box. A widely used metaphor, it usually
refers to a closed system whose inner workings
are beyond accountability and comprehension,
e.g. corporate and governmental institutions such
as the NSA or technological infrastructure like the
internet. Against this backdrop, it may seem only too
logical that the black box as visual form abounds in
the Snowden files. Yet it is not always clear what it
represents. There is no obvious key as to whether its
deployment is metaphorical or literal, accidental or
deliberate; and, generally speaking, how to account
for its appearance. Was it created by an individual
media house because it redacted something without
making the intervention explicit? Or was it the NSA
itself who created it because it wanted certain
details to remain secret to specific viewers of its
presentations? Or because it was using the black
box for symbolic reasons? Just as it is difficult to say
what the function of each black box is, this feature
is a telling commentary about the status of the files
as proofs: Apart from rather unsubstantiated claims
that the Snowden files are outright fakes, media
narratives hardly ever address to what degree and
in what sense the Snowden files may be unreliable
sources. Besides the issue of their authenticity, the
black box, which at times can fill an entire page of
a presentation, points to the question of how much
more secret knowledge remains in the dark – and
how this potential knowledge could change what has
been established as a files-based fact thus far.

Yet another recurring motif comes in the form of
abstraction: from circles to 'pixel fogs' without any
obvious function. In their own way, the sporadic
appearance of abstractions in the Snowden files
defies the notion of the documents serving as proof.

One asks: Does the pixel fog in the NSA presentation on "CNO Core Secrets" actually prove a point? If so, what point is that exactly? It is true that the Snowden files have been neglected by the public – on the one hand, their ownership and care are being delegated to a handful of journalists and media houses; on the other hand, their very status as proof is being taken for granted, leading to the dilemma that to an increasing extent the voices of media personalities are attracting attention, while less and less attention is being paid to the slides themselves. To highlight the abstractions in this context does not mean to downplay the role of the Snowden files as proofs. On the contrary: it means to question the actual documents with regard to their specific quality as proof. It is only by initiating such processes of reflection that the aforementioned neglect can eventually be overcome.

The Cloud:

Image #1 is page 4 from a source document entitled "Identity Intelligence: Image is Everything". It deals with the NSA collection of images with "facial recognition quality", in an effort to develop the ability to cross-reference data from different NSA databases using only facial images. Image #2 is a hand-drawn diagram that accompanies an undated 81-page NSA presentation entitled "Network Shaping 101". It was produced by the author of "I hunt sys admins" and explains how a country's entire network traffic could be fed into agency systems. Image #3 stems from the Glenn Greenwald PDF appendix to his book "No Place to Hide", where it was presented on page 87. It is part of a 2011 presentation prepared by GCHQ's Global Telecommunications Exploitation (GTE) division describing some of the techniques the agency uses to passively monitor Facebook traffic.

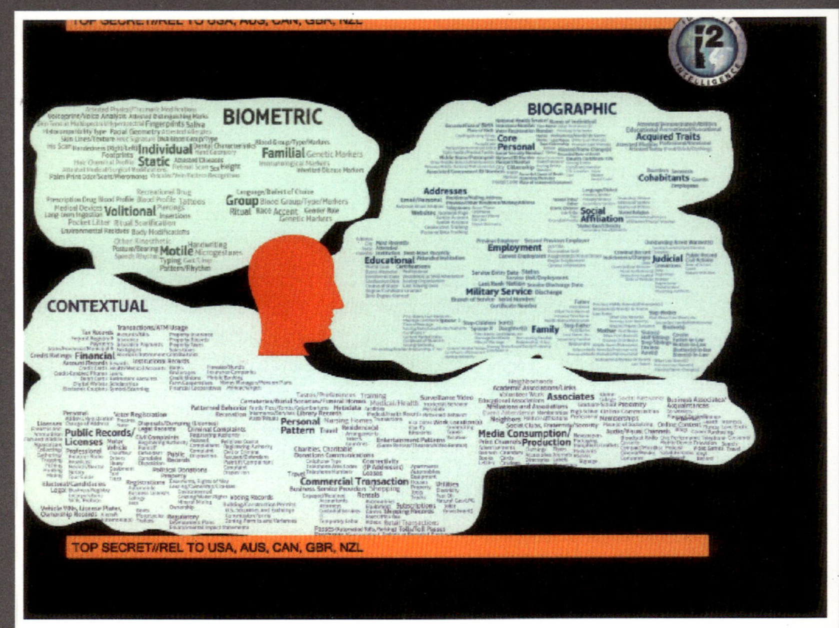

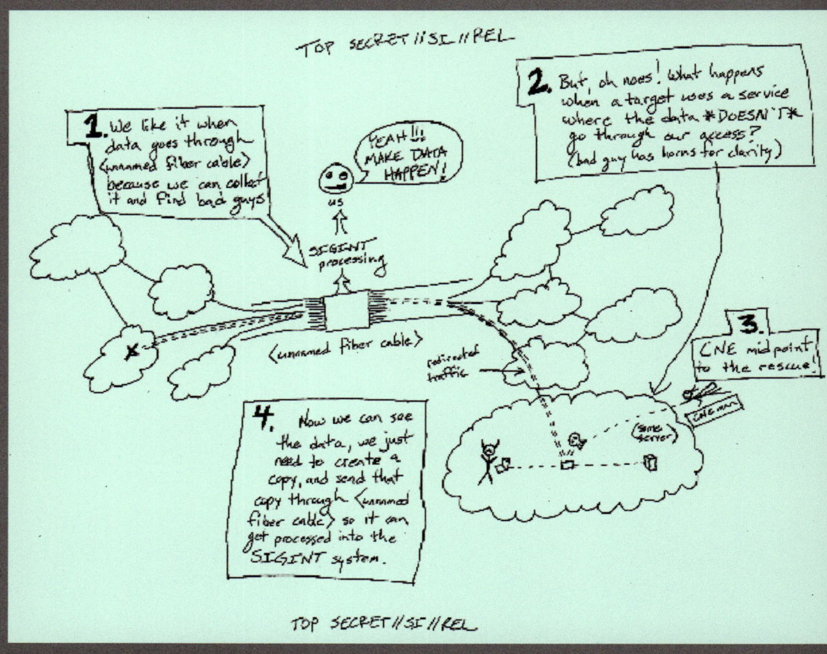

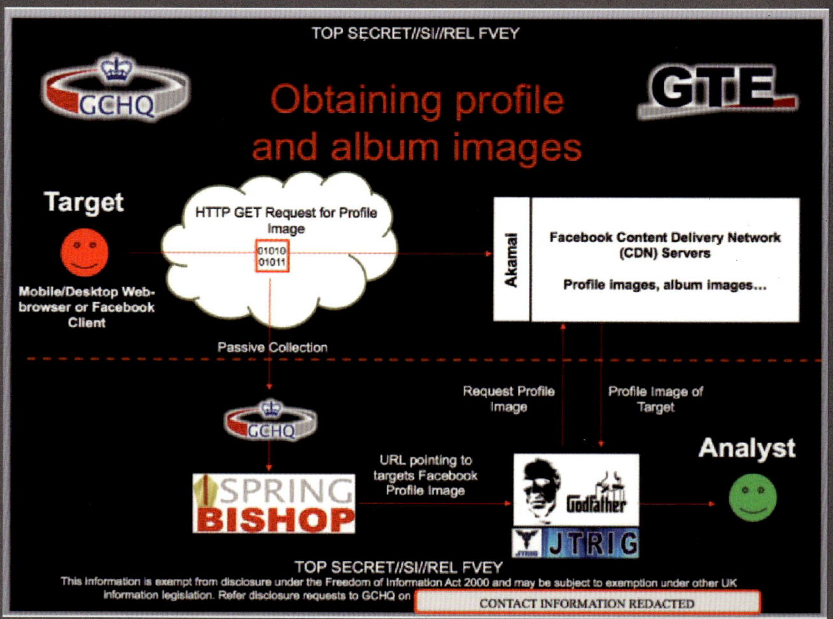

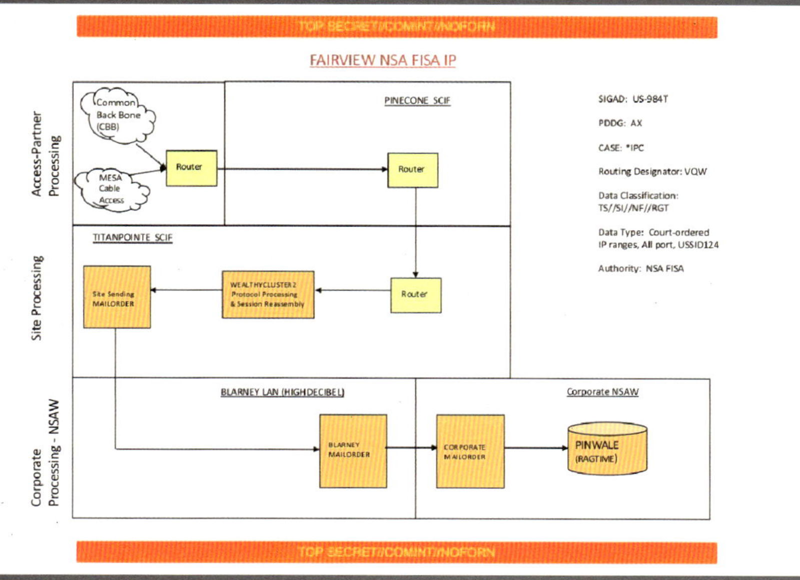

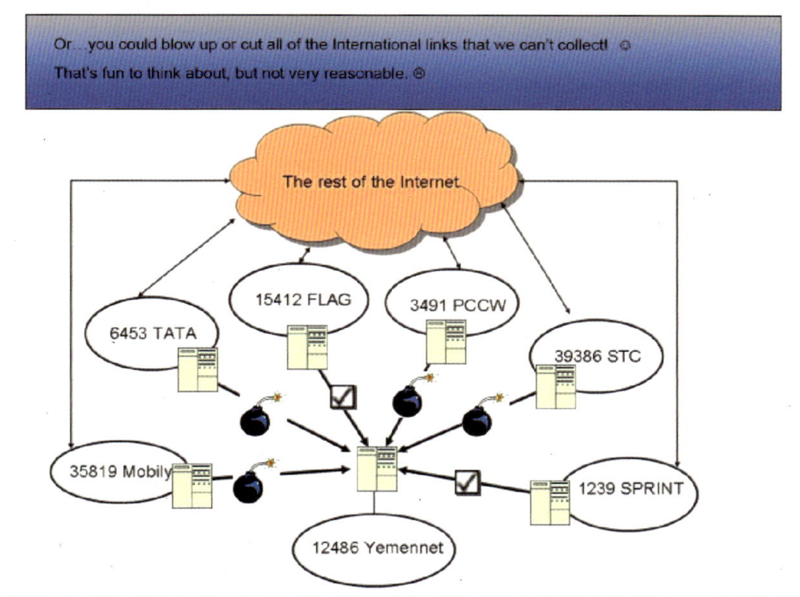

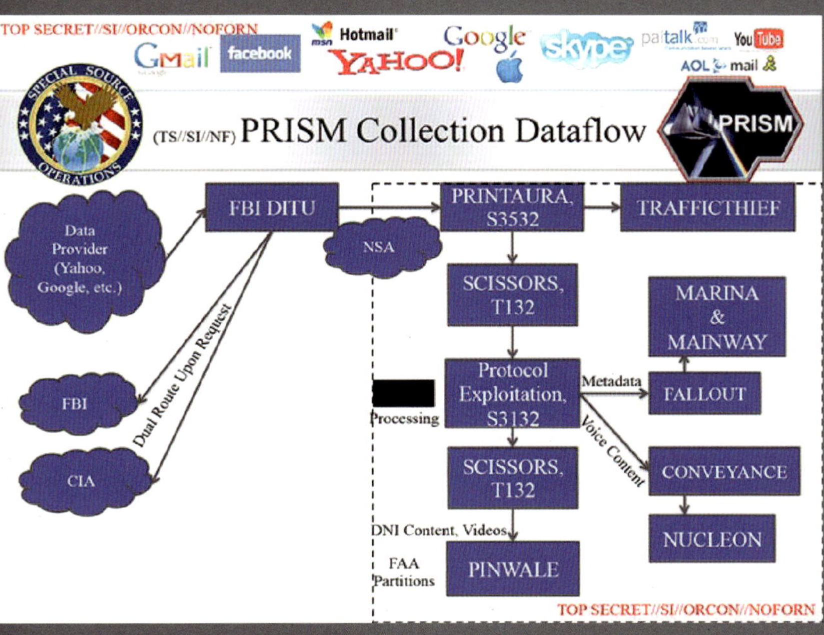

The Cloud:

Image #1 is page 14 in the presentation FAIRVIEW Dataflow Diagrams, issued in April 2012 by the NSA. The presentation uses an AT&T-specific term – Common Backbone or CBB – to refer to the Internet backbone of the corporate partner it codenames FAIRVIEW. See the New York Times article "AT&T Helped U.S. Spy on Internet on a Vast Scale", 15 August 2015. Image #2 is page 42 in an undated 81-page NSA presentation entitled "Network Shaping 101". It was produced by the author of "I hunt sys admins" and explains how a country's entire network traffic could be fed into agency systems. Image #3 stems from a 41-slide April 2013 NSA presentation describing the PRISM program, which enables the routine collection of data, including emails, chats, videos, file transfers and photos, from private companies that include Microsoft, Google, Facebook, YouTube, Skype, AOL and Apple.

The Black Box:

Image #1 is page 15 in an undated NSA presentation, written by the author of "I hunt sys admins". It outlines tactics for tracking users of TOR and other anonymizing technologies. See the Intercept article "The Hunter", 28 June 2016. Image #2 stems from excerpts from slides describing GHOSTMACHINE, the NSA Special Source Operations cloud-based analytics platform. See the Washington Post article "New documents show how the NSA infers relationships based on mobile location data", 10 December 2013. Image #3 is page 23 in an undated 26-page GCHQ presentation entitled SOCIAL ANTHROPOID. This program analyzes metadata records relating to instant messaging, email, Skype calls, text messages, including monitoring data of what the agency regards as "suspicious" Google searches and Google Maps usage.

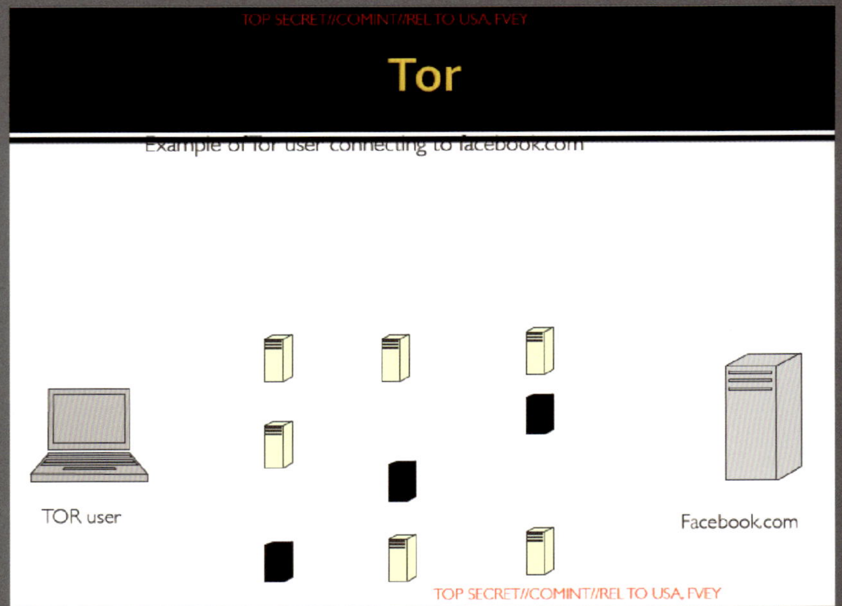

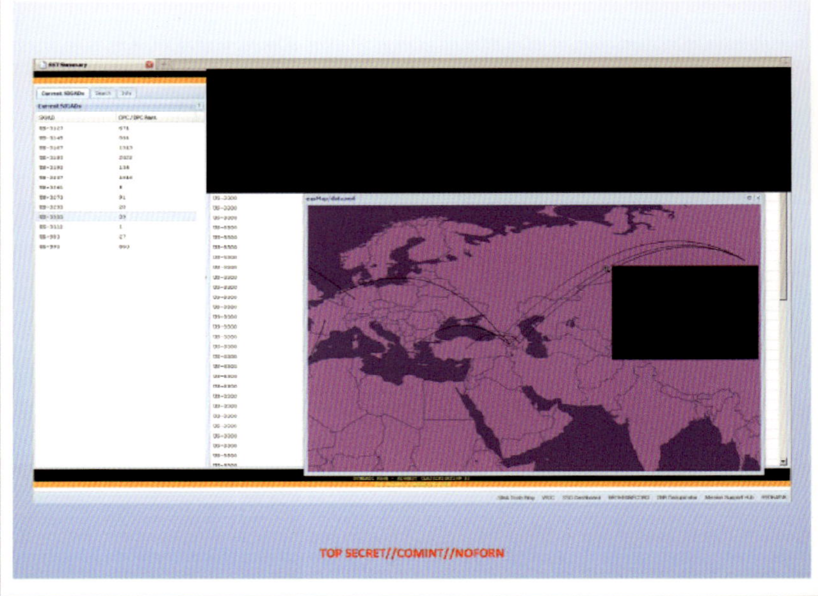

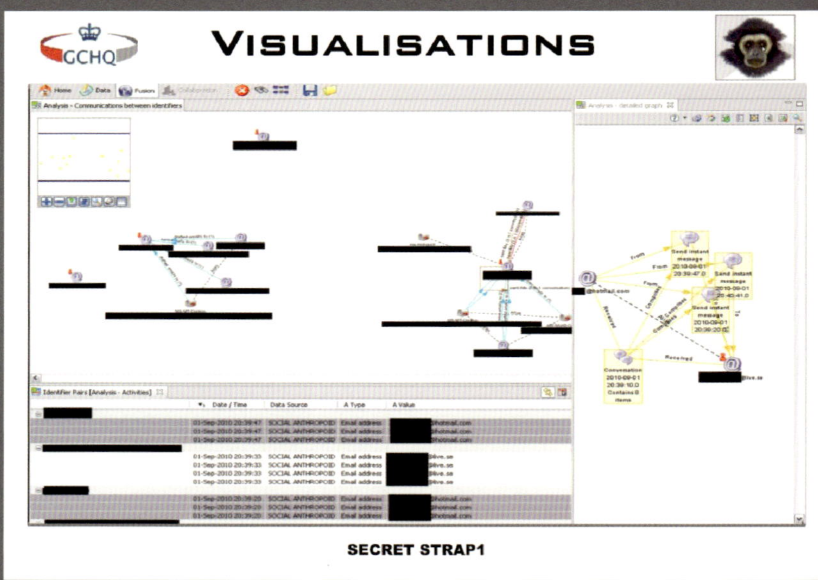

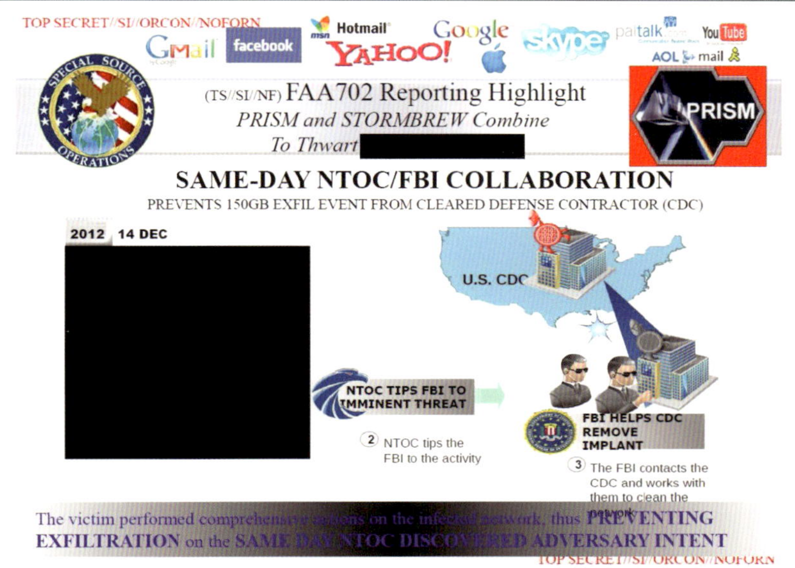

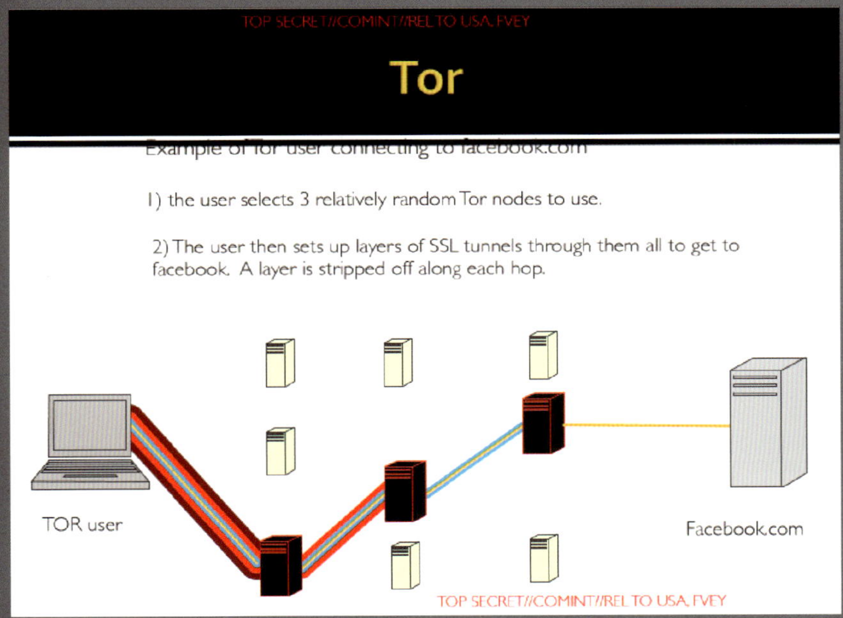

The Black Box:

Image #1 stems from a a 41-slide April 2013 NSA presentation describing the PRISM program, which enables the routine collection of data including emails, chats, videos, file transfers and photos from private companies that include Microsoft, Yahoo, etc. Image #2 is pages 22 and 30 in a 32-page NSA presentation dated 25 February 2008. It details XKEYSCORE, a tool used to search unfiltered internet traffic in real time. Two slightly different versions of this presentation have been published. See the Guardian article "XKeyscore: NSA tool collects nearly everything a user does on the internet", 31 July 2013. Image #3 is page 22 in an undated NSA presentation, written by the author of "I hunt sys admins". It outlines tactics for tracking users of TOR and other anonymizing technologies. See the Intercept article "The Hunter", 28 June 2016.

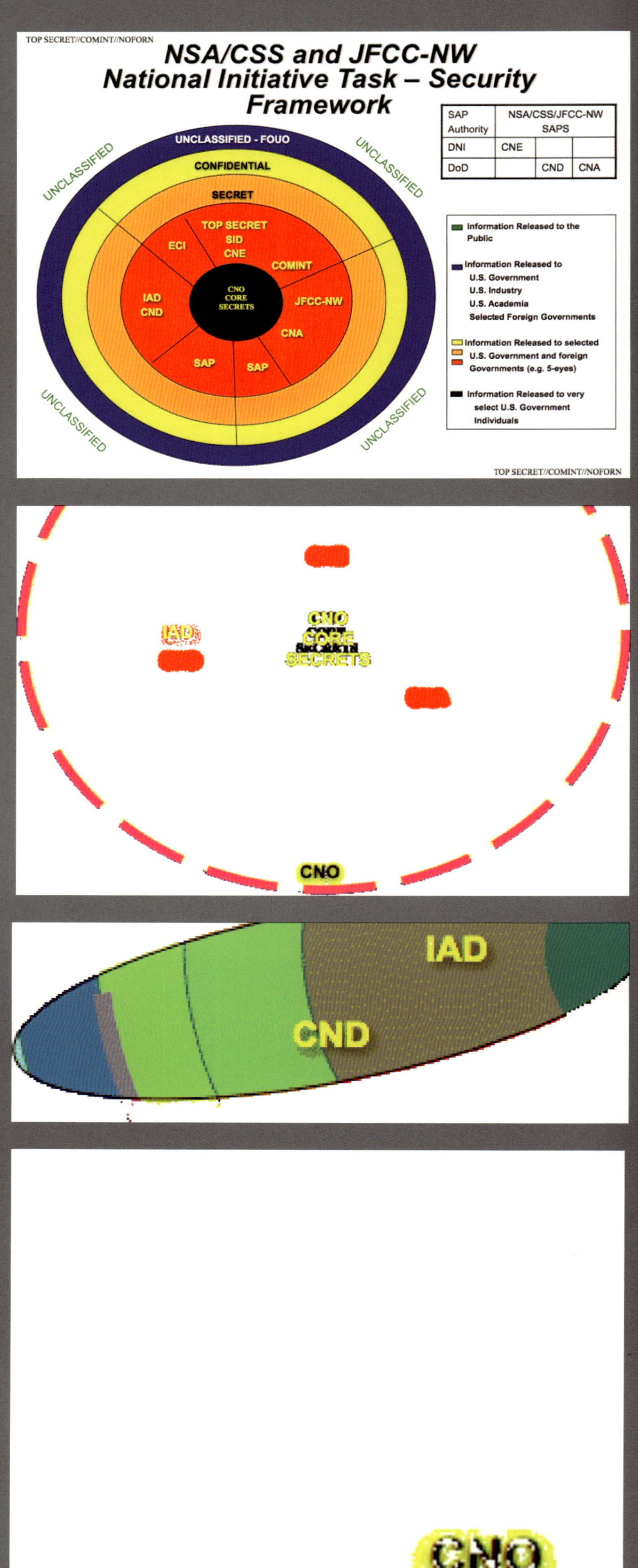

Network Oddities:

All these images stem from the undated seven-page NSA presentation entitled "CNO Core Secrets". It highlights the activities the agency regards as its "core secrets" and is used as a source in the Intercept article "Core Secrets: NSA Saboteurs in China and Germany", 10 October 2014. The article lists nine other source documents amounting to in total 62 more pages. While the magnified details that are shown above stem from the aforementioned seven-page document, they are quite obviously not derived from the first slide of this presentation (see top left), but rather from the 10-page document "CNO Core Secrets Slide Slices" that the Intercept article also lists as a source. Pages 2 to 7 of that document display the type of layering that is typical of the magnified sections above.

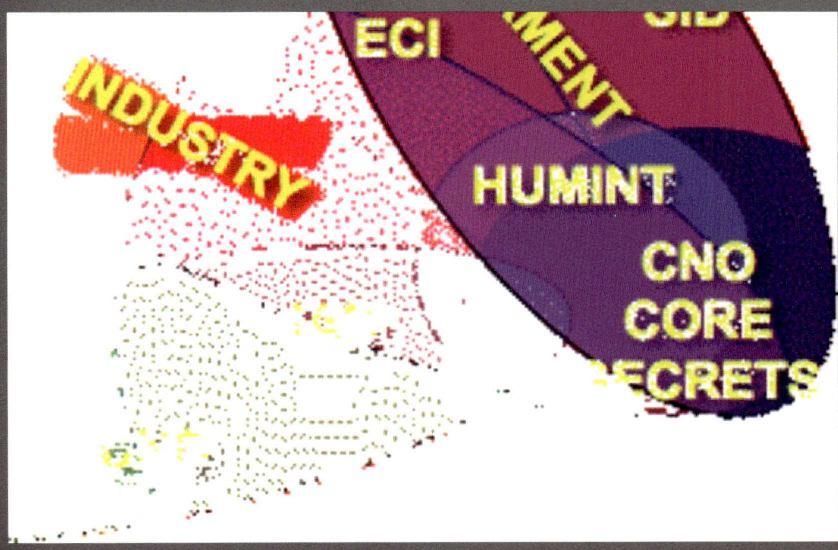
ECI
MENT
SID
INDUSTRY
HUMINT
CNO
CORE
SECRETS

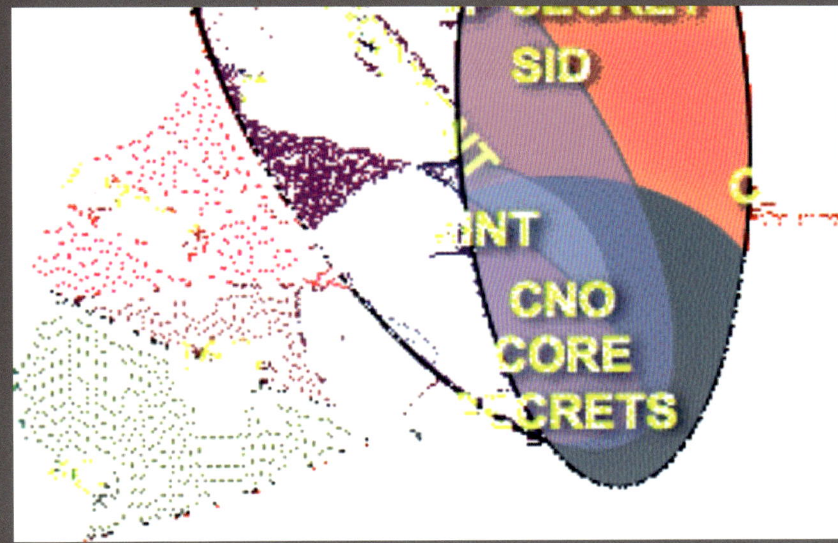
SID
INT
CNO
CORE
SECRETS

II
—ART

II
—ART¬
Power, Cultures of Secrecy and the Art of Memory¬

Text
by Krystian Woznicki

Since the Snowden disclosures, we can perceive an alarming development considerably more clearly: while citizens are not supposed to have any secrets, global players safeguard their monopolies with secrets. This means that while pressure for social inclusion bears fruit in the technological and ideological mass standard of informational self-exposure, secrecy is being reevaluated as the central capital of political and economic power. While calls for transparency towards institutions are on the upswing, governments and corporations are establishing their shared interests in a grey area that is difficult to enclose. Snowden's disclosures show how state secrets are blending with business secrets in this grey area in an uncontrolled way. As a consequence, an ensemble of black boxes with proto-feudal character is emerging right in the middle of societies: an outside on the inside, like a palace or a treasure vault.

For artists, this situation constitutes a special challenge. Artists have always had to deal with power, not least because powers like the clergy in the Middle Ages or the Stasi in the former GDR attempted to restrict their activity; or because where power resides, for instance at royal courts, capital is also usually in circulation, creating opportunities for making money with what would otherwise have been an unprofitable activity. Time and again, friction and grappling with power can be understood as a confrontation with cultures of secrecy. This applies, for instance, in complicity mode when it is necessary to maintain silence about internal processes or conspiracies, in that way also saving 'the face of power' towards the outside. Or in espionage mode, when artists have set out to leak their knowledge to other powers. One way or another: artists who come close to power have always operated in a liminal zone, performing multiple balancing acts between submission and transgression in doing so.

Even the person who resorts to complicity can become an actor in the process, as shown in the updating of the figure of the artist at the king's court in the TV series "House of Cards", with writer Thomas Yates in the White House. He can become an actor who gets much closer to power than the sovereign would have liked; an actor who can exert, as court jesters were sometimes able to do, a certain influence on the king; an actor who on the basis of his intimate relationship is able to create artworks that – though in encrypted form – expose the king's true self. Or an actor who sets free a spark of truth where lies and appearances prevail. Or who with his artwork brings something into being that at least feels like truth, leaving open what the concrete contours of the truth of power actually are. Hence, that should be clear as well: art itself is part of cultures of secrecy, and can even be one of its cornerstones.

"A modest sort of extremism"

In times of security politics and big data monopolies, cultures of secrecy are experiencing a fundamental reassessment. This reevaluates, not least, the work of the artist. At the same time, it hampers art's realization and the possibilities to evaluate artistic processes. The latter doubtless also has to do with the fact that it is not always clear for the actors themselves under what conditions they are actually working: to what extent are they able to remain autonomous; to what extent are they able to be true to themselves and their aspiration to veracity; to what extent do they pay too high a price for their risky intervention. In other words: to what extent do they – with their wings made of wax – possibly get too close to the sun. Thus, besides the

artist's autonomy, the authenticity of their work is also at stake. At the same time, the question of how close is close enough when it comes to approaching power can never be conclusively answered.

In a statement that Trevor Paglen, artist and geographer, placed at the front of his book "Emblems from the Pentagon's Black World", this tension attains certain contours: "Readers of this book will find a collection of images that are fragmentary, torn out of context, inconclusive, unreliable, and deceptive. Readers will find, in other words, a glimpse into the black world itself." The bearing expressed here has something to do, last but not least, with the nature of power, itself difficult to grasp or circumscribe: does power in the age of security politics actually know any limits at all?

An increasing number of artists are reacting to these uncertainties with radical empiricism. Instead of retreating and resorting to a safe distance from power, they are in a way forging ahead and exposing themselves to the uncertainties, in the spirit of an "enactive logic in circumstantial coevolution with its 'object' (or 'subject') of inquiry." This logic "does not place itself in a posture of superiority, but rather in a parallel evolution. It is allagmatic. It relishes getting its hands dirty. It is self-embroiling. It consents to conceptual risk, knowing in advance that it will fall short no matter how far it is able to go, so that it might as well go to the limit. It is a modest sort of extremism", as the philosopher Brian Massumi writes.

The uncertainties of power that provoke such radical empiricism also arise because the cultures of secrecy are changing in times of major data leaks. Just the series from Afghan War Diary (2010), Cablegate (2012), Offshore Leaks (2013), Snowden Files (2013), Panama Papers (2016) to Football Leaks (2016) shows: the leaks are getting bigger, they are coming more quickly, and they are exposing the vulnerability of power in times of ever more mobile and fluid secrets. Yet, as partial insights into the "black world", they also hint at how much knowledge remains under lock and key, and how unfathomably large those treasure chambers of secret knowledge potentially are that are being withheld from the public. In other words: the prevalent notion is that what has been able to surface thus far may be only a fraction of what is actually locked away.

A dilemma manifests itself at this juncture: we can hardly appropriately process everything that becomes public knowledge. So far we lack suitable tools, methodologies and legal frameworks. The transparency that is generated through leaks thus generates a new condition of opaqueness. First of all, because the volume of data has become unmanageably vast – and it keeps growing. Secondly, because much of the leaked data has not even been properly protected in the first place. For instance, the important leaks of the activist network Anonymous, such as the internal e-mails of the Bank of America or NASA's drone data, are in danger of disappearing for good.

Cultures of secrecy

When artists work under such uncertainties, they are also exposing themselves in a new way to questions of social responsibility. What is the nature of artists' responsibility when confronted with contemporary cultures of secrecy? And does the question get a specific spin in times when huge data leaks are on the upswing?

Let us first point out that deprivation of knowledge – e.g. in the form of material that is intended to remain classified – not only helps the prevailing powers to constitute and stabilize, but can also define artists' influence and status. Artists, by exposing themselves to institutional cultures of secrecy, themselves become bearers of secrets, or they make their art into that – whether passively or actively, whether ironically fractured or intervening and protecting. One need think only of Laura Poitras, who in the scope of her documentary trilogy on the War on Terror unexpectedly became a bearer of Edward Snowden's immense leak. And one can also think of Julian Oliver, who, on the other end of the spectrum, created openly writable templates from the Snowden documents – meaning bearers of secrets that have yet to be defined.

The work of artists with historical data leaks, which as such is still relatively new and unexplored and that will entail a more extensive art history discussion – this work manifests some special features when you reflect on the connection between art, cultures of secrecy and power. At first one has to note that the major data leaks of recent years have not experienced a great response in the art world. At least not directly, that is, not in the sense that the leaks have become the specific material of artistic work. The implications and consequences have certainly generated an echo – for instance, when artists reflect on the fact that some leaks became an integral part of pop culture or when issues like surveillance come to the fore at exhibitions such as "Watched" or "Under the Clouds" (without explicitly referring to the Snowden disclosures). But the leaked documents resulting from the Afghanistan war, the diplomatic dispatches of the USA or from trusts at offshore financial centers – all these documents remain largely 'undiscovered' as the material of art. Things are different with the documents that Edward Snowden compiled for years and then leaked to some journalists in 2013.

Trackers of power

A comparably large number of artists have appropriated the Snowden documents published by various media houses as the material of art. I am thinking of artists as varied as the social media avatar SAZAE bot from Japan and the conceptual artist Simon Denny from New Zealand. What they have in common is that they are not only artistically processing the implications and consequences of Snowden's disclosures. Going beyond that, they are working concretely with the specific documents. In the course of this they are exploring the material and semiotic characteristics of those vehicles of secrecy that today are so key to establish power. Their work prompts important questions: How are the documents structured? What cultural signs do they process? What processes of reassessment can be identified? How are aesthetic means deployed to support the discourses of power?

Looking at the documents in this way, the communication design of the Snowden documents becomes the focus of artistic examination. Acknowledging this, art has to come to terms with the fact that for the NSA and its partners it was not just a matter of being able to talk about the specialist field of national security in a special language, but also being able to present the programs run by each NSA unit in a visually attractive way. The presentation program PowerPoint plays an important part in this context: When the NSA wanted to pitch its secret and costly monitoring programs, it usually used PowerPoint, which is also used daily by office workers the world over. Artists who work with the leaks as concrete material are hence potentially able to stimulate reflections on the hidden power that this specific program wields – a notion that has been analyzed by media theoreticians such as Wolfgang Coy and Claus Pias – and on the hidden transfers that occur between civil use and use by intelligence agencies.

Here is where the question arises how processes, designs and techniques of power function – rather than the question of the legitimacy of power that tends to dominate the pertinent philosophical debates. This difference is important to note, because the question of processes, designs and techniques at the same time opens up possibilities to address dysfunctionalities, ruptures and inconsistencies. It is here, in these cracks of power, where hope arises and where art can retrieve much of its emancipatory energy and political potential. But what does it mean to explore processes, designs and techniques of power? To the extent that actual technical processes (software, hardware, etc.) can become the object of artistic work, to that extent the focus in the course of this is on the techniques of power that enable these technical processes in the first place: it is about the production, depiction and securing of secrets, and thus the burning question about digital memory.

In the current economic and political situation the question of digital memory finds much topicality in the politics of databases. It is well-known and often at the center of controversies that databases are in the hands of private or state operators, who are compiling, sorting and preserving unimaginably large quantities of data. This can be shown in an example with banks and credit card transactions. A branch of the NSA named "Follow the Money" is responsible for intercepting financial data. The information obtained in that way flows into the NSA's own financial database called Tracfin. In 2011 it contained 180 million data records. The bulk of the data, approximately 80 percent, was credit card data. Meanwhile, a growing number of companies are focusing today on credit scoring, personal finance and fraud detection; in the course of doing this, they are assembling immense amounts of data about us and our 'financial behavior'. It is an open secret that untransparent data sharing processes are taking place between government agencies like the NSA and the private sector. This unregulated data market emerges in times in which a sharp asymmetry is arising not only between those who have access to data troves and those who don't, but also between those who are economic and political actors and those who are degraded to being passive bystanders. And it does not take much of an effort to imagine that these increasingly dramatic inequalities are in some way connected.

This situation reflects the burning question of digital memory as the central issue of power today, and it points to the important role that secrets play in this context: if you cannot save and retrieve knowledge that is intended to remain under lock and key, then this knowledge is practically worthless for a power's constitutive procedures. If, on the other hand, like the general public, you have no access to memory infrastructure like databases, you have no key to power. Thus, while the general public is supposed to leave as many traces as possible and power should remain without any traces – or at least have only one single trace, the one that is officially authorized – media artists like Stefan Tiron and artists' collectives like the University of the Phoenix are becoming trackers. It is not by chance that their work is increasingly characterized by extremely extensive and time-intensive research: they dig through archives for days, sometimes for weeks and months. In search of traces of power, they sometimes become archivists, taking fictitious as well as literal form in the work of Zeljko Blace and Evan Light respectively.

To work as an artist with the Snowden files means to work on and in memory. Moreover, it means is to work in part with 'repressed memories' which as such do not yet have any collective status and that are not yet 'shared memories' because it is intended they be reserved only for their administrators, like most state or company secrets. In this way, artists can initiate a process that not only disarranges the order of the archives, but also drives collective memory work down new, unforeseeable paths. Emancipating collective memory work in that way potentially enables us to reimagine social history and to reinvent its writing as an open and participatory process for the whole of civil society.

Trevor Paglen
SAZAE bot
University of the Phoenix
Simon Denny
Zeljko Blace
Evan Light
Stefan Tiron
Laura Poitras
and Henrik Moltke
Julian Oliver

—ART¬
NSA-Tapped Fiber Optic Cable Landing Site, Mastic Beach, New York, United States¬

● Trevor Paglen

Words like "cyberspace", the cloud, the information superhighway perpetrate an image of the Internet as something placeless yet ubiquitous, immaterial yet omnipresent. These metaphors are deeply misleading. In contrast, 'NSA-Tapped Fiber Optic Cable Landing Site, Mastic Beach, New York' develops a vision of the Internet that emphasizes the materiality of communications networks, and the political geography of the Internet. In doing so, the project mimics the NSA's own understanding of the Internet, emphasizing fiber optic cables, landing sites, switching facilities, data centers, and the routes and choke points in global telecommunication infrastructure.

Drawing on documents from the Snowden archive and other sources, the piece focuses on a network of transatlantic cables that come onshore at Mastic

Beach, New York, one of several major fiber optic cable landing sites in the U.S. Several NSA-tapped fiber optic cables land on Long Island, including "Atlantic Crossing-1", "Atlantic Crossing-2/Yellow", as well as the "Apollo" and "Emerald" cables.

The piece is composed as a diptych that consists of a photograph and a collage. The photograph shows the beach or landing site where the cables come onshore; here, the cables are under the water and beach. The collage combines images and documents related to the specific site. The base document is a map produced by the National Oceanic and Atmospheric Administration (NOAA) for marine navigation. Among other things, these maritime maps indicate the location of undersea cables so that ships do not interfere with them. Layered on this map are various internal NSA documents from the Snowden archive, corporate documents, additional photographs of the site, and other materials.

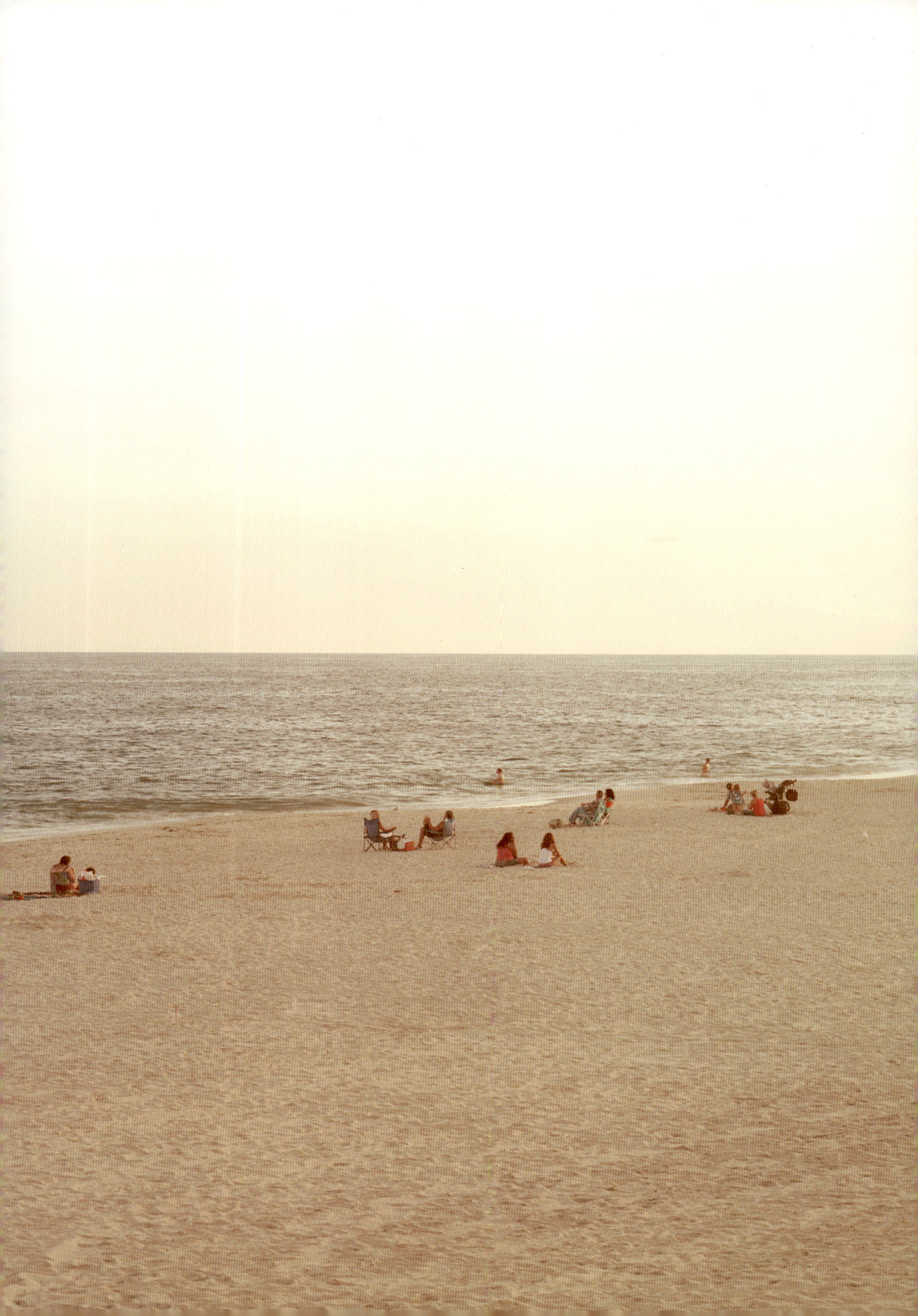

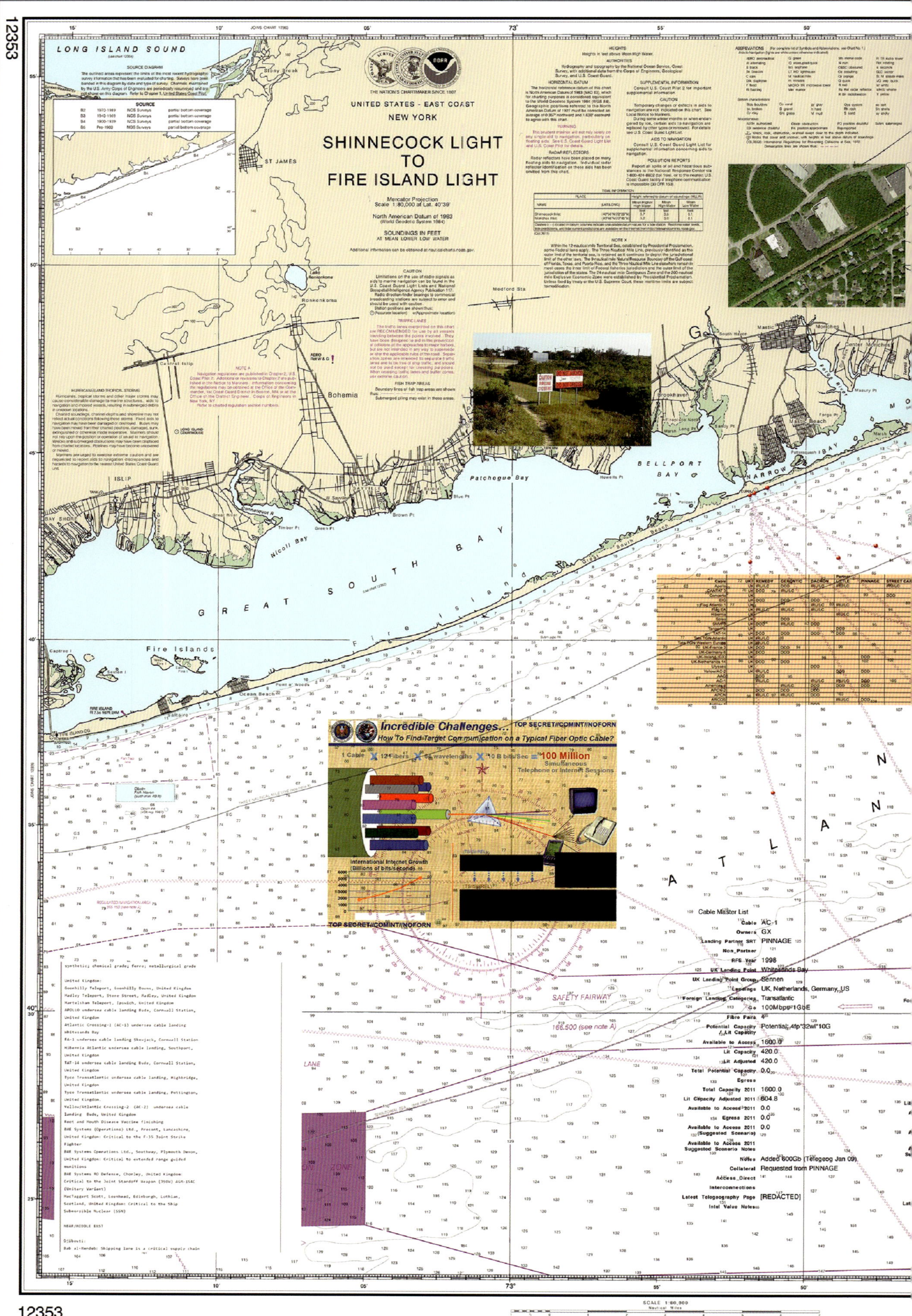

UNITED STATES - EAST COAST
NEW YORK
SHINNECOCK LIGHT
TO
FIRE ISLAND LIGHT
Mercator Projection
Scale 1:80,000 at Lat. 40°39'
North American Datum of 1983
(World Geodetic System 1984)
SOUNDINGS IN FEET
AT MEAN LOWER LOW WATER
Additional information can be obtained at nauticalcharts.noaa.gov.
THE NATION'S CHARTMAKER SINCE 1807
LONG ISLAND SOUND
GREAT SOUTH BAY
Fire Island
ATLANTIC OCEAN
Incredible Challenges...
How To Find Target Communication on a Typical Fiber Optic Cable?
TOP SECRET//COMINT//NOFORN
1 Cable X 12 Fibers X 64 wavelengths X 10 B bits/Sec = 100 Million
Simultaneous Telephone or Internet Sessions
International Internet Growth
(Billions of bits/second)
TOP SECRET//COMINT//NOFORN
Cable Master List
Cable   AC-1
Owners   GX
Landing Partner SRT   PINNAGE
Non_Partner
RFS Year   1998
UK Landing Point   Whitesands Bay
UK Landing Point Group   Sennen
Landings   UK, Netherlands, Germany, US
Foreign Landing Categories   Transatlantic
100Mbps=1GbE
Fibre Pairs   4
Potential Capacity   Potential: 4fp*32wl*10G
Available to Access   1600.0
Lit Capacity   420.0
Lit Adjusted   420.0
Total Potential Capacity   0.0
Total Capacity 2011   1600.0
Lit Capacity Adjusted 2011   1604.8
Available to Access 2011   0.0
Available to Access 2011 (Suggested Scenario)   0.0
Notes   Added 600Gb (Telegeog Jan 09)
Collateral   Requested from PINNAGE
Latest Telegeography Page   [REDACTED]

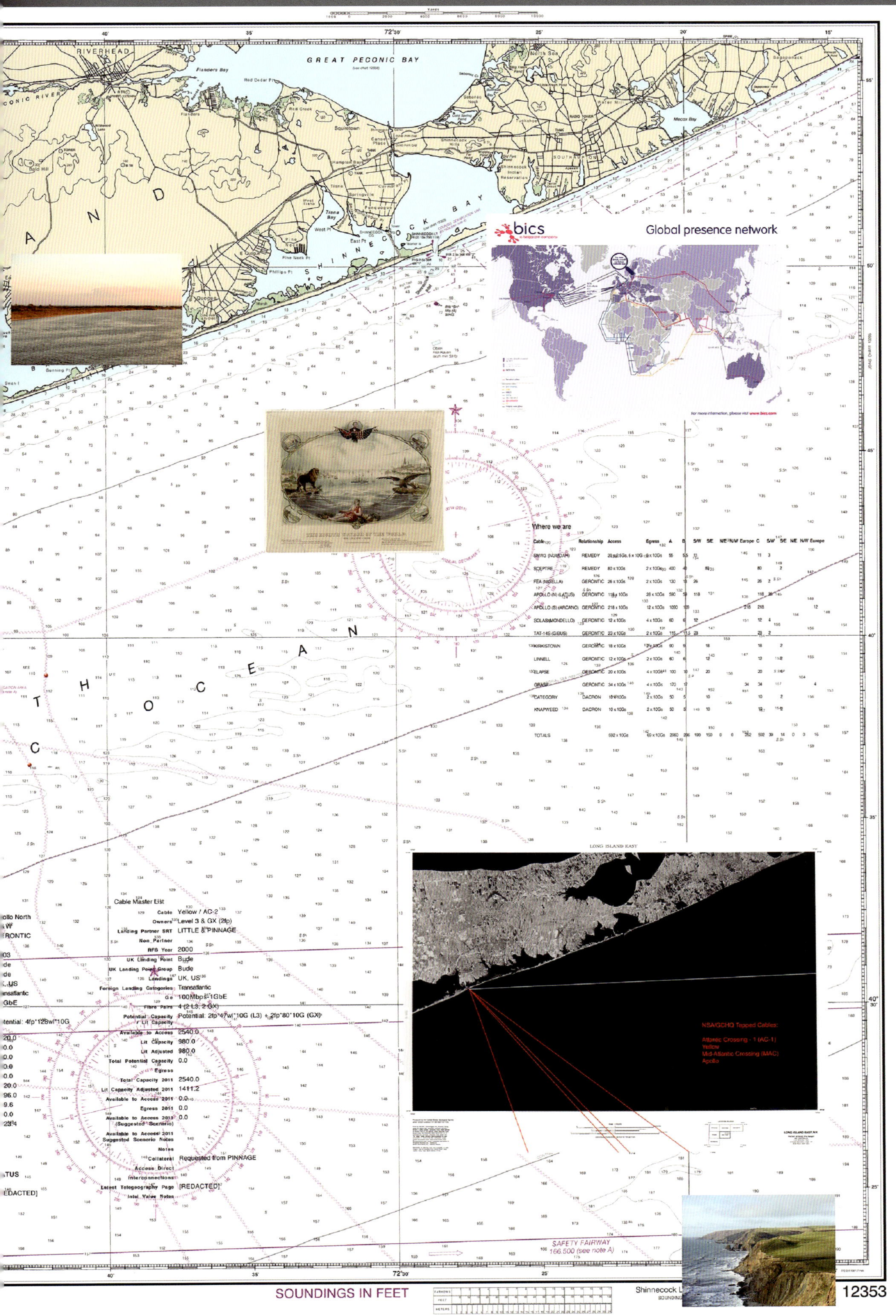

RIVERHEAD
GREAT PECONIC BAY
Flanders Bay
LONG ISLAND
THE OCEAN
ATLANTIC OCEAN
SHINNECOCK BAY
SOUTHAMPTON
Shinnecock Indian Reservation

bics
Global presence network
for more information, please visit www.bics.com

Where we are
Cable | Relationship | Access | Egress | A | B | S/W | S/E | N/E | N/W Europe | C | S/W | S/E | N/E | N/W Europe
SMW3 (NUMDAH) | REMEDY | 20 x 2.5Gs, 6 x 10G | 8 x 10Gs | 55 | 55 | 11 | | | | | 11 | 3 | | |
SCEPTRE | REMEDY | 80 x 10Gs | 2 x 10Gs | 400 | 40 | 80 | | | | | 80 | 2 | | |
FEA (NIGELLA) | GERONTIC | 26 x 10Gs | 2 x 10Gs | 130 | 13 | 26 | | | | | 26 | 2 | | |
APOLLO (N) (LATUS) | GERONTIC | 118 x 10Gs | 28 x 10Gs | 590 | 59 | 118 | | | | | 118 | 28 | | |
APOLLO (S) (ARCANO) | GERONTIC | 218 x 10Gs | 12 x 10Gs | 1090 | 109 | | | | | 218 | 218 | | | 12 |
SOLAS (MONDELLO) | GERONTIC | 12 x 10Gs | 4 x 10Gs | 60 | 6 | 12 | | | | | 12 | 4 | | |
TAT-14S (GIBUS) | GERONTIC | 23 x 10Gs | 2 x 10Gs | 115 | 11.5 | 23 | | | | | 23 | 2 | | |
KIRKISTOWN | GERONTIC | 18 x 10Gs | 2 x 10Gs | 90 | 9 | 18 | | | | | 18 | 2 | | |
LINNELL | GERONTIC | 12 x 10Gs | 2 x 10Gs | 60 | 6 | 12 | | | | | 12 | 2 | | |
ELAPSE | GERONTIC | 20 x 10Gs | 4 x 10Gs | 100 | 10 | 20 | | | | | 20 | | | |
GRASP | GERONTIC | 34 x 10Gs | 4 x 10Gs | 170 | 17 | | | | | 34 | 34 | | | 4 |
CATEGORY | DACRON | 10 x 10Gs | 2 x 10Gs | 50 | 5 | 10 | | | | | 10 | 2 | | |
KNAPWEED | DACRON | 10 x 10Gs | 2 x 10Gs | 50 | 5 | 10 | | | | | 10 | 2 | | |
TOTALS | | 592 x 10Gs | 69 x 10Gs | 2960 | 296 | 190 | 150 | 0 | 0 | 252 | 592 | 39 | 14 | 0 | 0 | 16

Cable Master List
Cable Yellow / AC-2
Owners Level 3 & GX (2fp)
Landing Partner SRT LITTLE & PINNAGE
Non_Partner
RFS Year 2000
UK Landing Point Bude
UK Landing Point Group Bude
Landings UK, US
Foreign Landing Categories Transatlantic
Ge 100Mbps-1GbE
Fibre Pairs 4 (2 L3, 2 GX)
Potential Capacity Potential: 2fp*47w|*10G (L3) + 2fp*80*10G (GX)
/ Lit Capacity
Available to Access 2540.0
Lit Capacity 980.0
Lit Adjusted 980.0
Total Potential Capacity 0.0
Egress
Total Capacity 2011 2540.0
Lit Capacity Adjusted 2011 1411.2
Available to Access 2011 0.0
Egress 2011 0.0
Available to Access 2011 0.0
(Suggested Scenario)
Available to Access 2011
Suggested Scenario Notes
Notes
Collateral Requested from PINNAGE
Access Direct
Interconnections
Latest Telegeography Page [REDACTED]
Intel Value Notes

LONG ISLAND EAST

NSA/GCHQ Tapped Cables:

Atlantic Crossing - 1 (AC-1)
Yellow
Mid-Atlantic Crossing (MAC)
Apollo

LONG ISLAND EAST_N/W

SAFETY FAIRWAY
166.500 (see note A)

SOUNDINGS IN FEET
Shinnecock L
12353

The Dark Side of the Earth¬

● SAZAE bot

The Snowden documents show how important communication design is, not only in order to be able to talk about the specialist field of state security in a special language, but also – and this is a great surprise – to be able to present the programs run by each NSA unit to the audience in a visually attractive way. The widely-used PowerPoint presentation program plays an important part in this context. When the NSA wanted to pitch its secret and costly surveillance programs, it usually used PowerPoint.

The anonymous SAZAE bot artists' collective, working in the context of social media and performance, chose to work on a 41-slide presentation describing the PRISM collection of data via internet service providers such as Google and Facebook, "the SAZAE most used in NSA reporting." These slides have been published gradually by several media organizations, including the Washington Post, whose article from 6 June 2013 explains the PRISM data collection program in detail. See: http://washingtonpost.com/wp-srv/special/politics/prism-collection-documents

SAZAE bot selected a number of these slides and redesigned them. The art work mimics the function of informing and convincing the audience of a security product at a briefing or meeting. By appropriating the Snowden documents and transforming them into art, they undertake to expand the scope of the audience beyond the 'intelligence community', also addressing, last but not least, users of social networks.

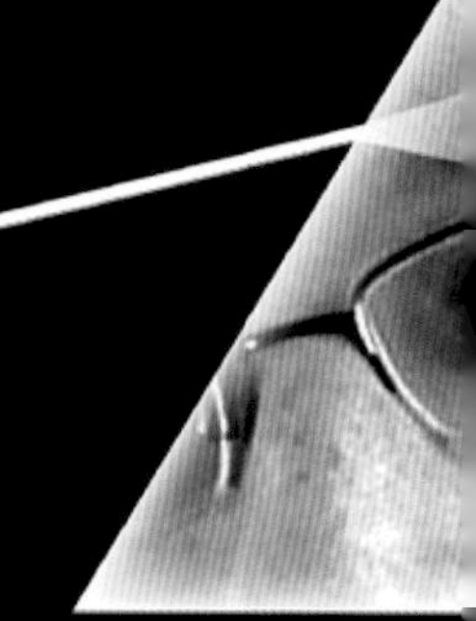

PRISM
The Dark S

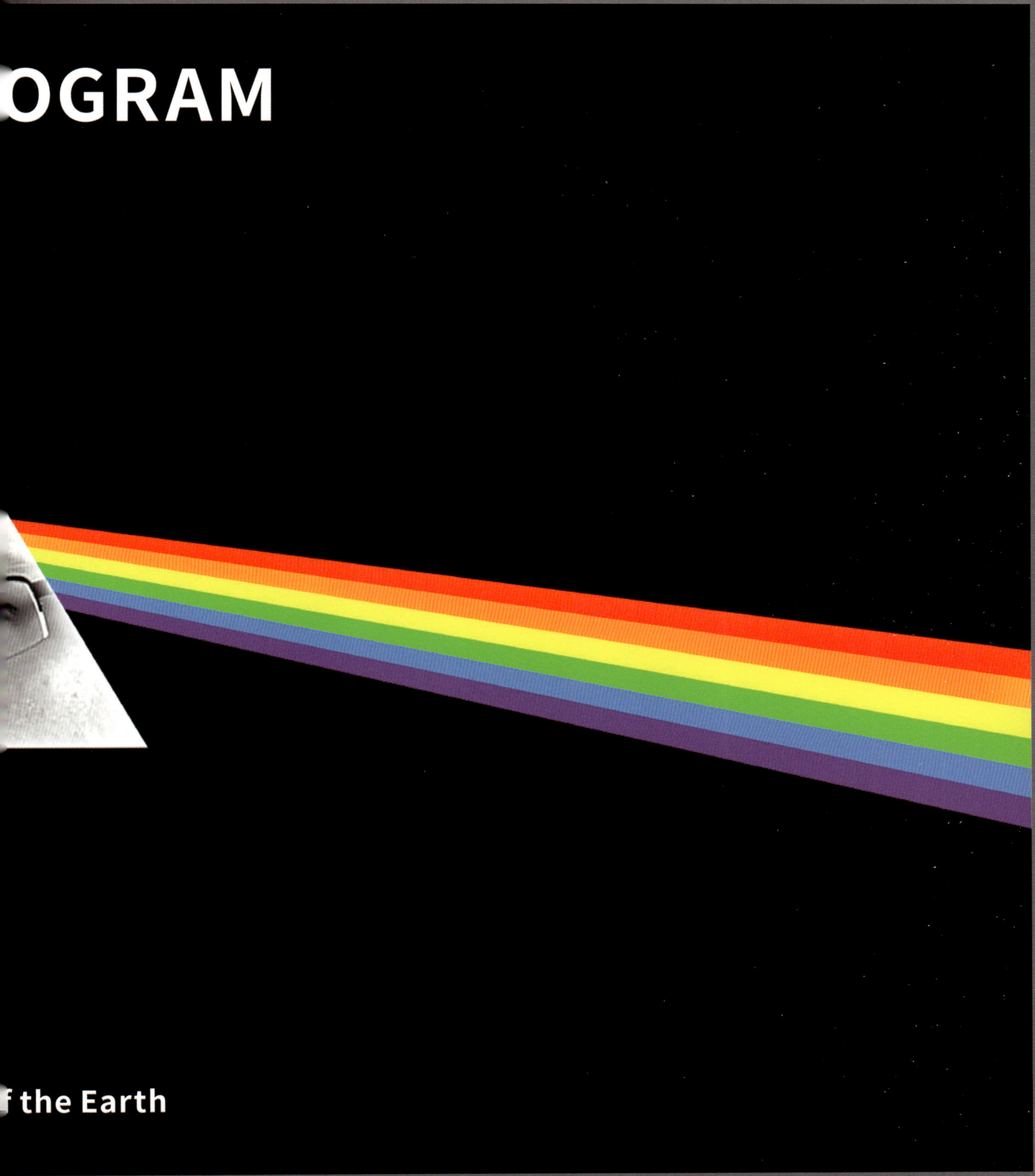

OGRAM
f the Earth

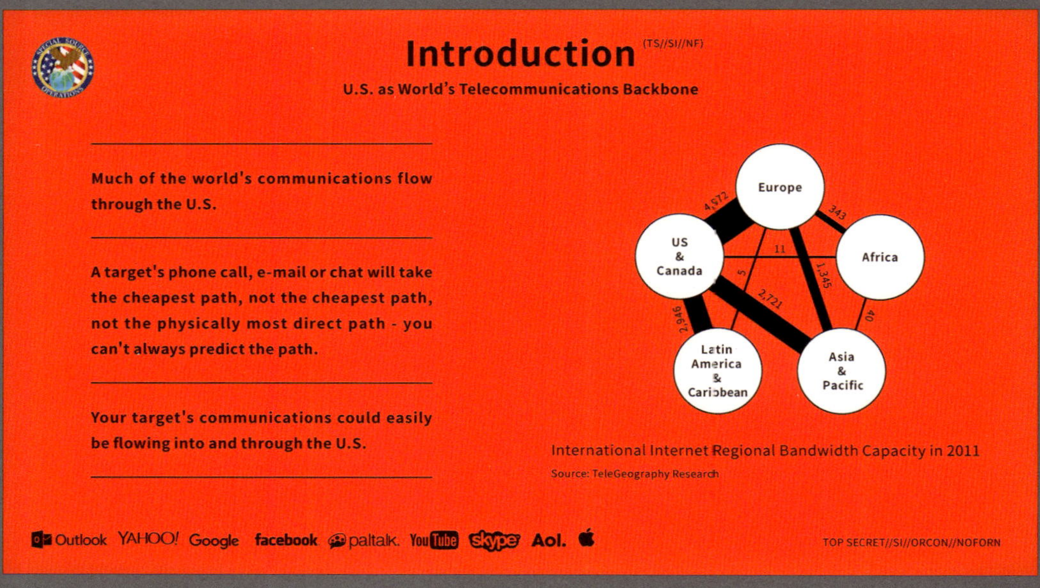

Introduction (TS//SI//NF)
U.S. as World's Telecommunications Backbone

Much of the world's communications flow through the U.S.

A target's phone call, e-mail or chat will take the cheapest path, not the cheapest path, not the physically most direct path - you can't always predict the path.

Your target's communications could easily be flowing into and through the U.S.

Europe
US & Canada
Africa
Latin America & Caribbean
Asia & Pacific
4,972
343
11
5
2,721
1,345
40
4,946

International Internet Regional Bandwidth Capacity in 2011
Source: TeleGeography Research

Outlook   YAHOO!   Google   facebook   paltalk.   You Tube   skype   Aol.
TOP SECRET//SI//ORCON//NOFORN

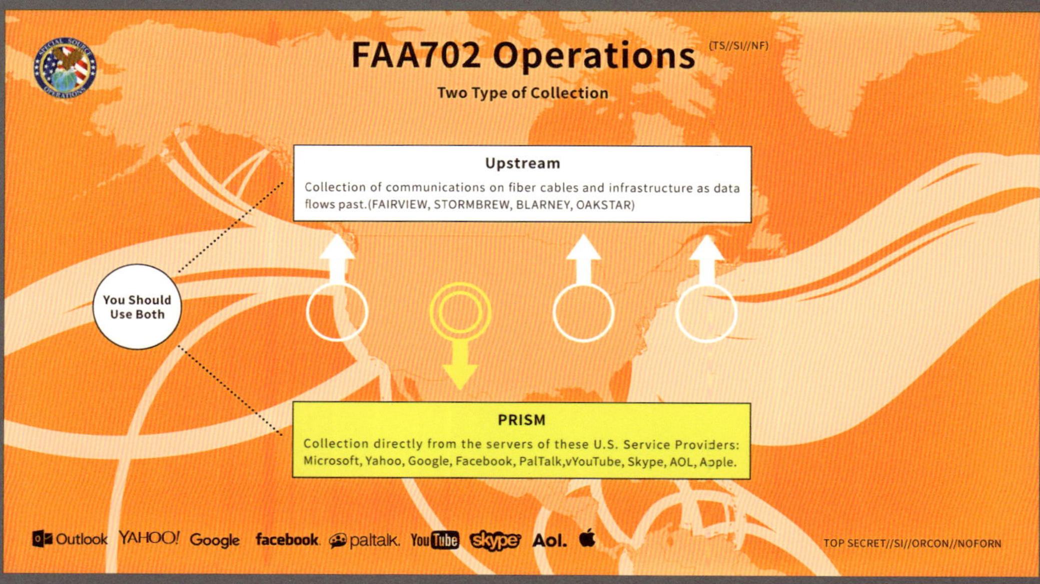

FAA702 Operations (TS//SI//NF)
Two Type of Collection

Upstream
Collection of communications on fiber cables and infrastructure as data flows past.(FAIRVIEW, STORMBREW, BLARNEY, OAKSTAR)

You Should Use Both

PRISM
Collection directly from the servers of these U.S. Service Providers:
Microsoft, Yahoo, Google, Facebook, PalTalk, vYouTube, Skype, AOL, Apple.

Outlook   YAHOO!   Google   facebook   paltalk.   You Tube   skype   Aol.
TOP SECRET//SI//ORCON//NOFORN

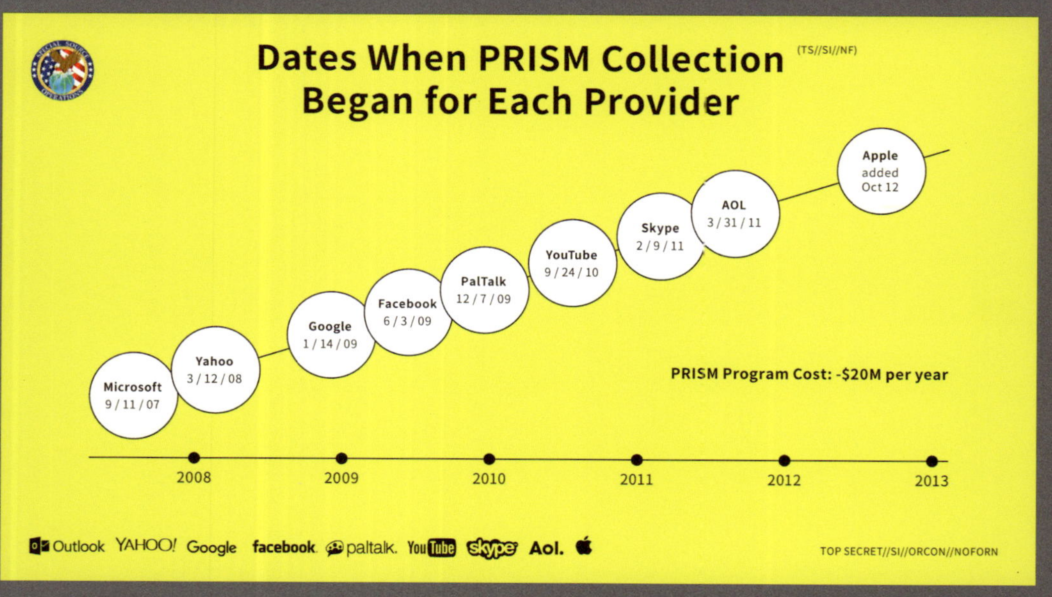

Dates When PRISM Collection (TS//SI//NF)
Began for Each Provider

Apple
added
Oct 12

AOL
3 / 31 / 11

Skype
2 / 9 / 11

YouTube
9 / 24 / 10

PalTalk
12 / 7 / 09

Facebook
6 / 3 / 09

Google
1 / 14 / 09

Yahoo
3 / 12 / 08

Microsoft
9 / 11 / 07

PRISM Program Cost: ~$20M per year

2008   2009   2010   2011   2012   2013

Outlook   YAHOO!   Google   facebook   paltalk.   You Tube   skype   Aol.
TOP SECRET//SI//ORCON//NOFORN

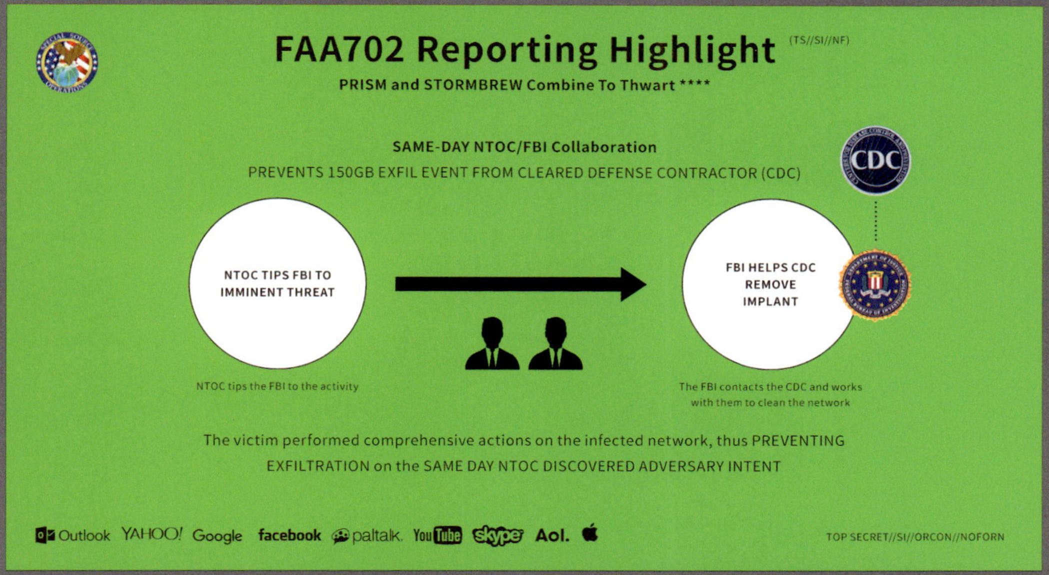

FAA702 Reporting Highlight (TS//SI//NF)
PRISM and STORMBREW Combine To Thwart ****
SAME-DAY NTOC/FBI Collaboration
PREVENTS 150GB EXFIL EVENT FROM CLEARED DEFENSE CONTRACTOR (CDC)
CDC
NTOC TIPS FBI TO IMMINENT THREAT
FBI HELPS CDC REMOVE IMPLANT
NTOC tips the FBI to the activity
The FBI contacts the CDC and works with them to clean the network
The victim performed comprehensive actions on the infected network, thus PREVENTING EXFILTRATION on the SAME DAY NTOC DISCOVERED ADVERSARY INTENT
Outlook YAHOO! Google facebook paltalk. You Tube skype Aol.
TOP SECRET//SI//ORCON//NOFORN

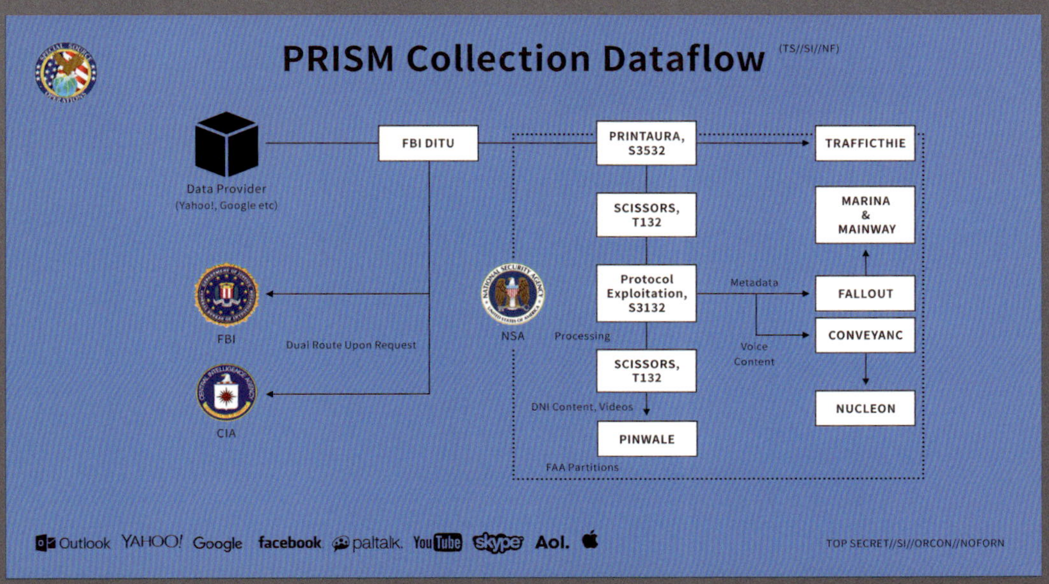

PRISM Collection Dataflow (TS//SI//NF)
Data Provider (Yahoo!, Google etc)
FBI DITU
PRINTAURA, S3532
TRAFFICTHIE
SCISSORS, T132
MARINA & MAINWAY
FBI
Dual Route Upon Request
NSA
Protocol Exploitation, S3132
Metadata
FALLOUT
Processing
Voice Content
CONVEYANC
CIA
SCISSORS, T132
DNI Content, Videos
NUCLEON
PINWALE
FAA Partitions
Outlook YAHOO! Google facebook paltalk. You Tube skype Aol.
TOP SECRET//SI//ORCON//NOFORN

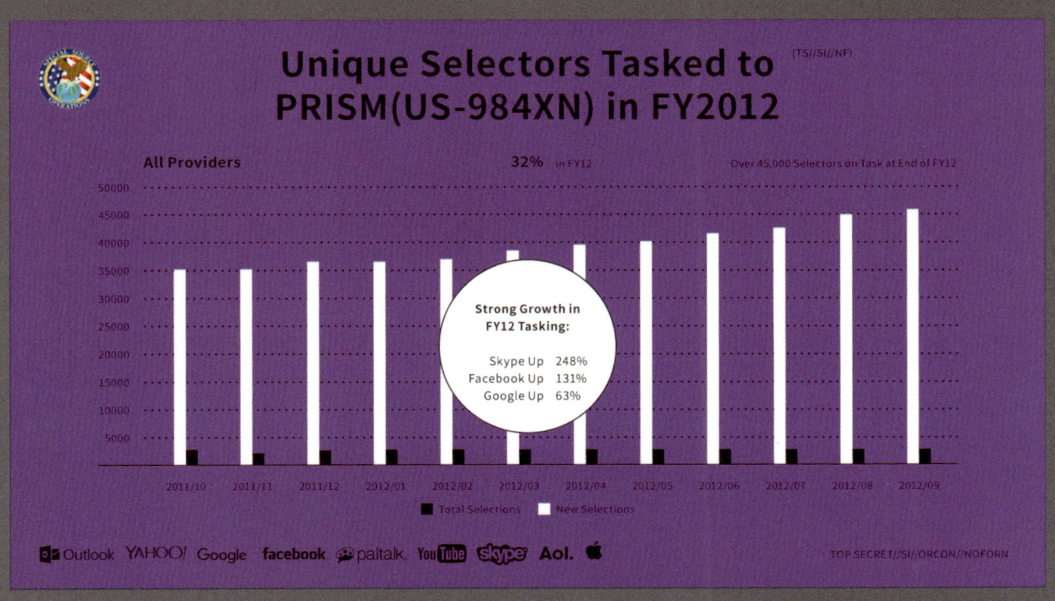

Unique Selectors Tasked to PRISM(US-984XN) in FY2012 (TS//SI//NF)
All Providers
32% in FY12
Over 45,000 Selectors on Task at End of FY12
50000
45000
40000
35000
30000
25000
20000
15000
10000
5000
Strong Growth in FY12 Tasking:
Skype Up 248%
Facebook Up 131%
Google Up 63%
2011/10 2011/11 2011/12 2012/01 2012/02 2012/03 2012/04 2012/05 2012/06 2012/07 2012/08 2012/09
Total Selections
New Selections
Outlook YAHOO! Google facebook paltalk. You Tube skype Aol.
TOP SECRET//SI//ORCON//NOFORN

—ART¬
GHOST MACHINE¬

• University of the Phoenix

There are many victims of the NSA security apparatus, but one particular population has been made eternally redundant by this nefarious new digital infrastructure: the dead. Humanity has always relied on the dead's advice to allow us to understand the complex social and historical gestalt that surpasses our individual imaginations. We have beseeched them to inform us about the sublime networks of causality that make up our world, those which our living senses cannot fathom. From politics to romance, from medicine to war, the dead have never failed to provide humanity with astute – if often cryptic – wisdom from beyond the grave.

Like so many workers today, the dead have been automated out of a job by GHOST MACHINE, a component of the NSA spying system that automates metaphysical production. This algorithm parses

tiny "pings" sent by mobile phones every time
they connect to a communications tower or place
a call or text. GHOST MACHINE cross-references
this geolocational metadata with a wide variety of
other signals from social media to churn out useful
information for its masters.

The NSA's GHOST MACHINE is part of a wider effort
to replace ghosts with machines. This technology
replaces the role that ghosts once played in our
lives with a vast digital apparatus for divination.
Now, those who have access and power can simply
ask the GHOST MACHINE for answers, rather than
seeking the slow, artisanal wisdom of the dead.
Ghosts have been rendered post-workers, struggling
to find meaning and rest in an economy that seems to
have no use for them.

What are the prospects for ghosts today? At the
University of the Phoenix, the world's first for-prophet
institution of higher learning for the dead, we are
thinking carefully about how to train our students for
the post-work world in which they find themselves.
Join us for the launch of our new flagship program
that offers the dead a chance of upgrade their
skills for a new economy. But rather than sell their
services to the highest bidder, the new collective
ghostmachine will break free the spirits of the living
and dead from the possession of capitalism.

The following images are a selection of advertisements
enticing the University's dead clients to enroll and
reclaim their future.

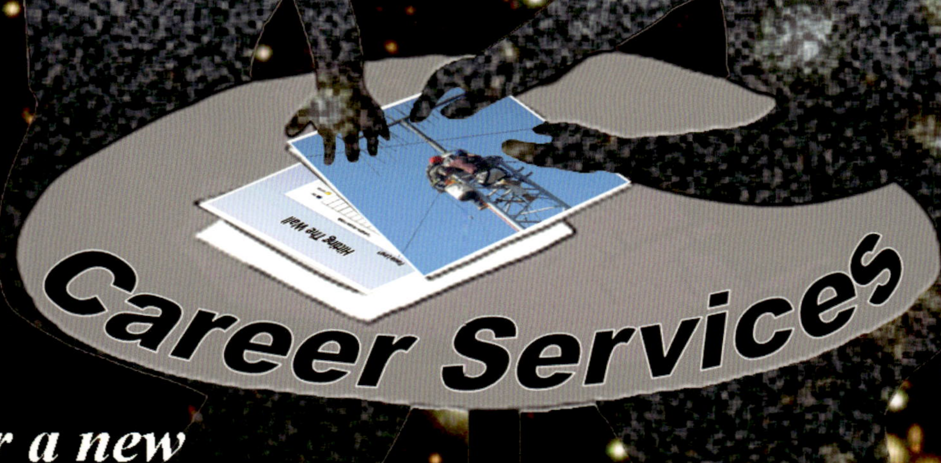

DISPLACED BY ALGORITHMS?
enroll now!!!
Activate your human capital
from beyond the grave
Career Services
for a new
GHOST MACHINE

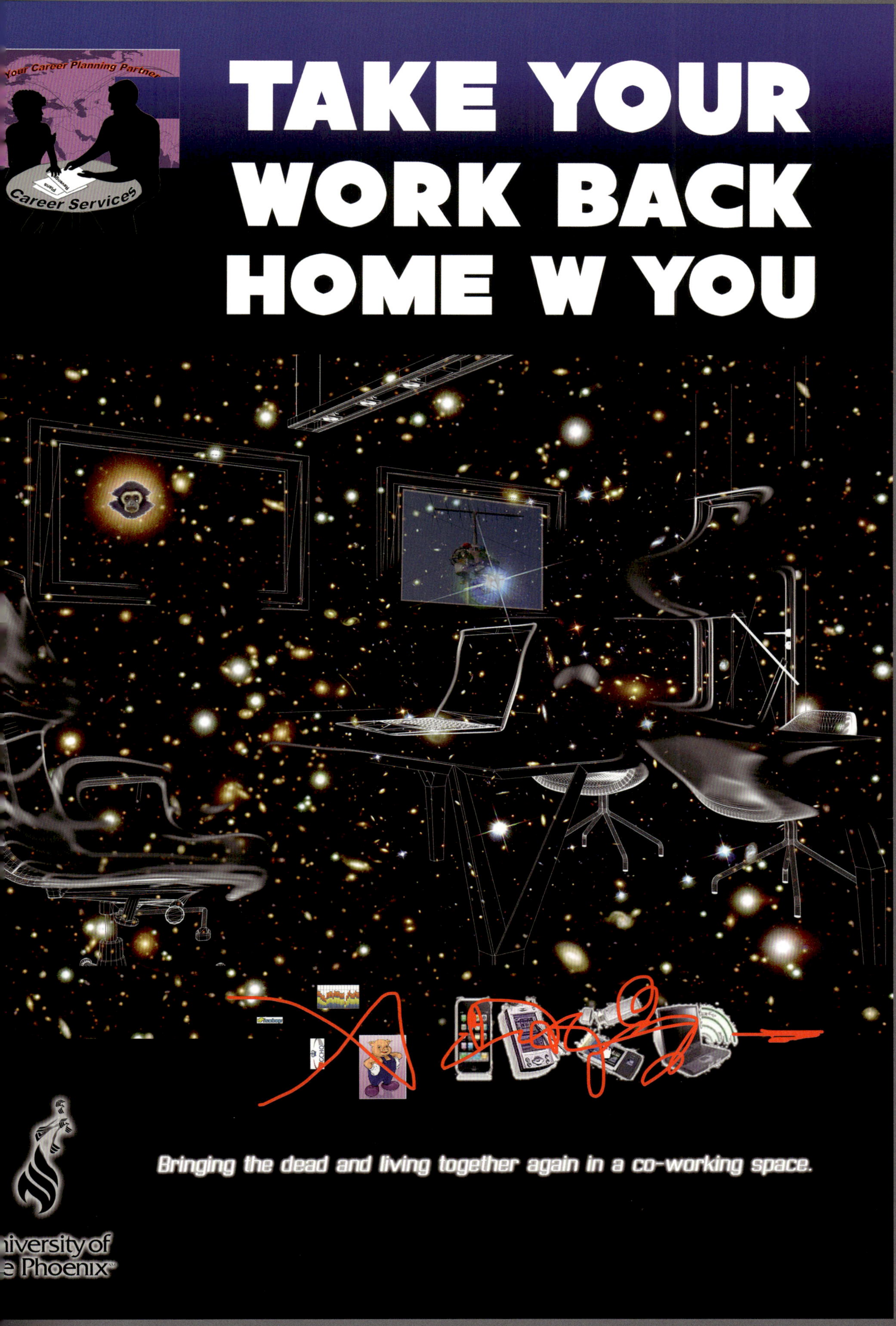

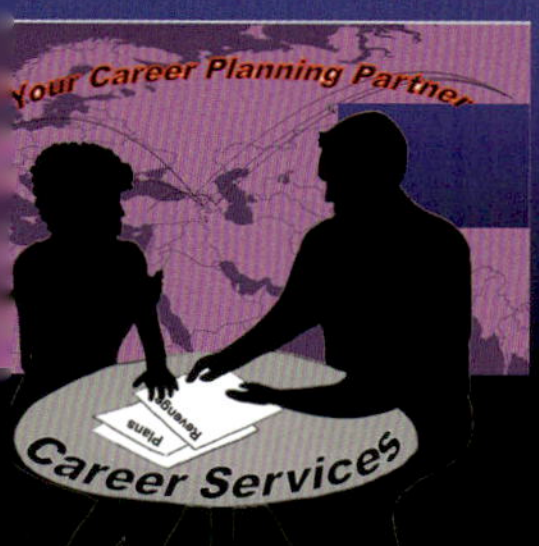

TAKE YOUR WORK BACK HOME W YOU

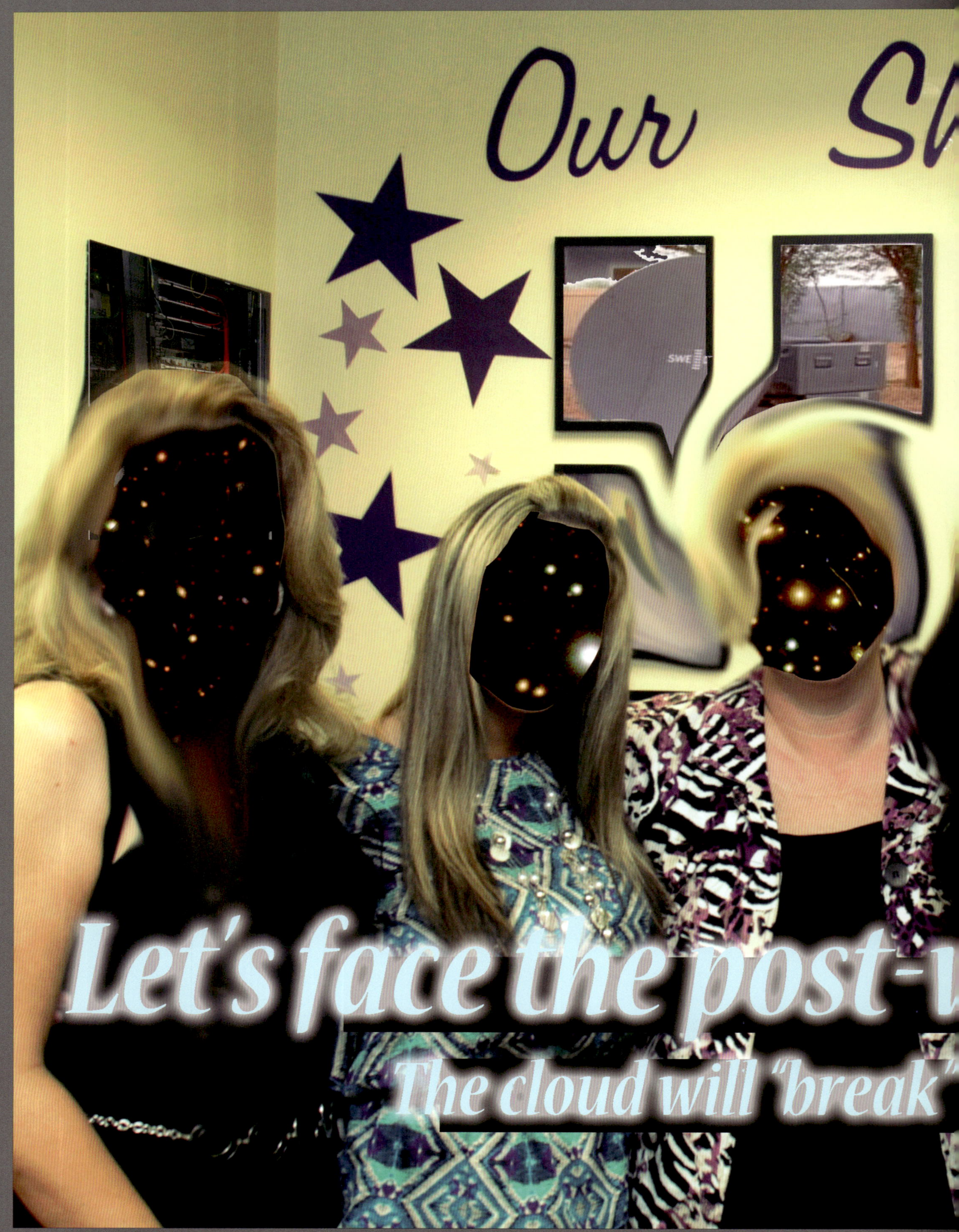

Our   Sh
Let's face the post-
The cloud will 'break'

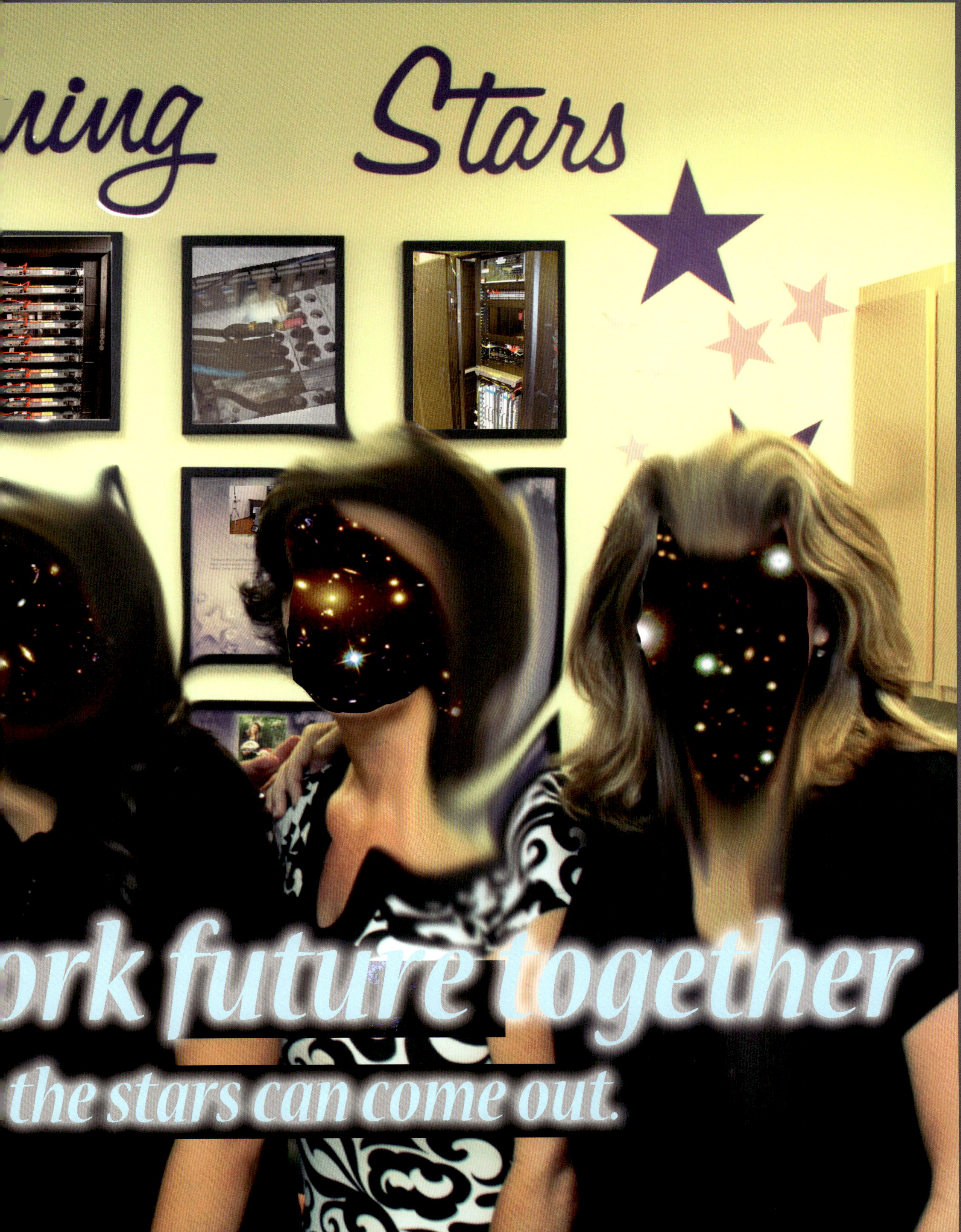

ning   Stars
ork future together
the stars can come out.

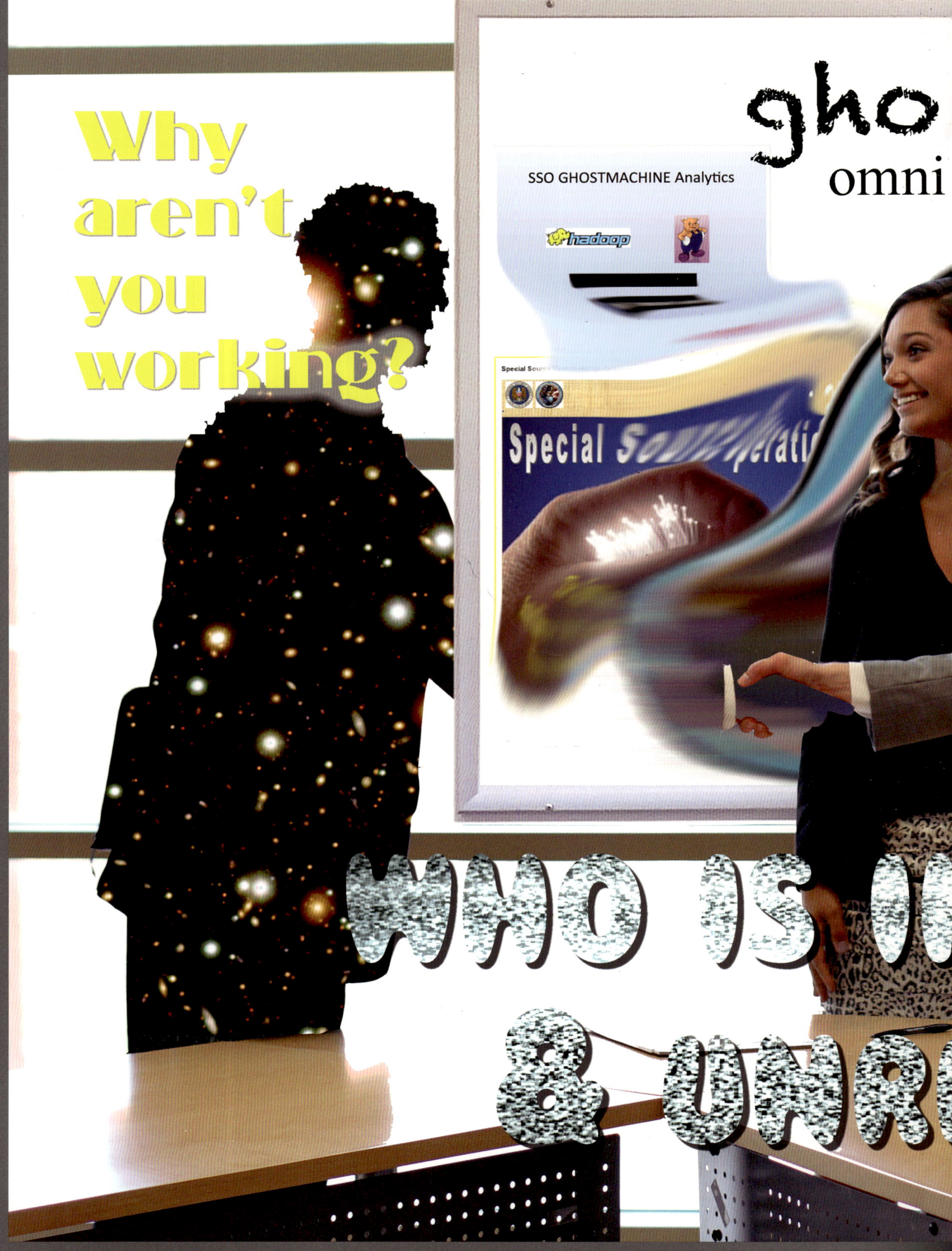

Why aren't you working?
gho
omni
SSO GHOSTMACHINE Analytics
hadoop
Special Sour
Special Sour perati
WHO IS
& UNRO

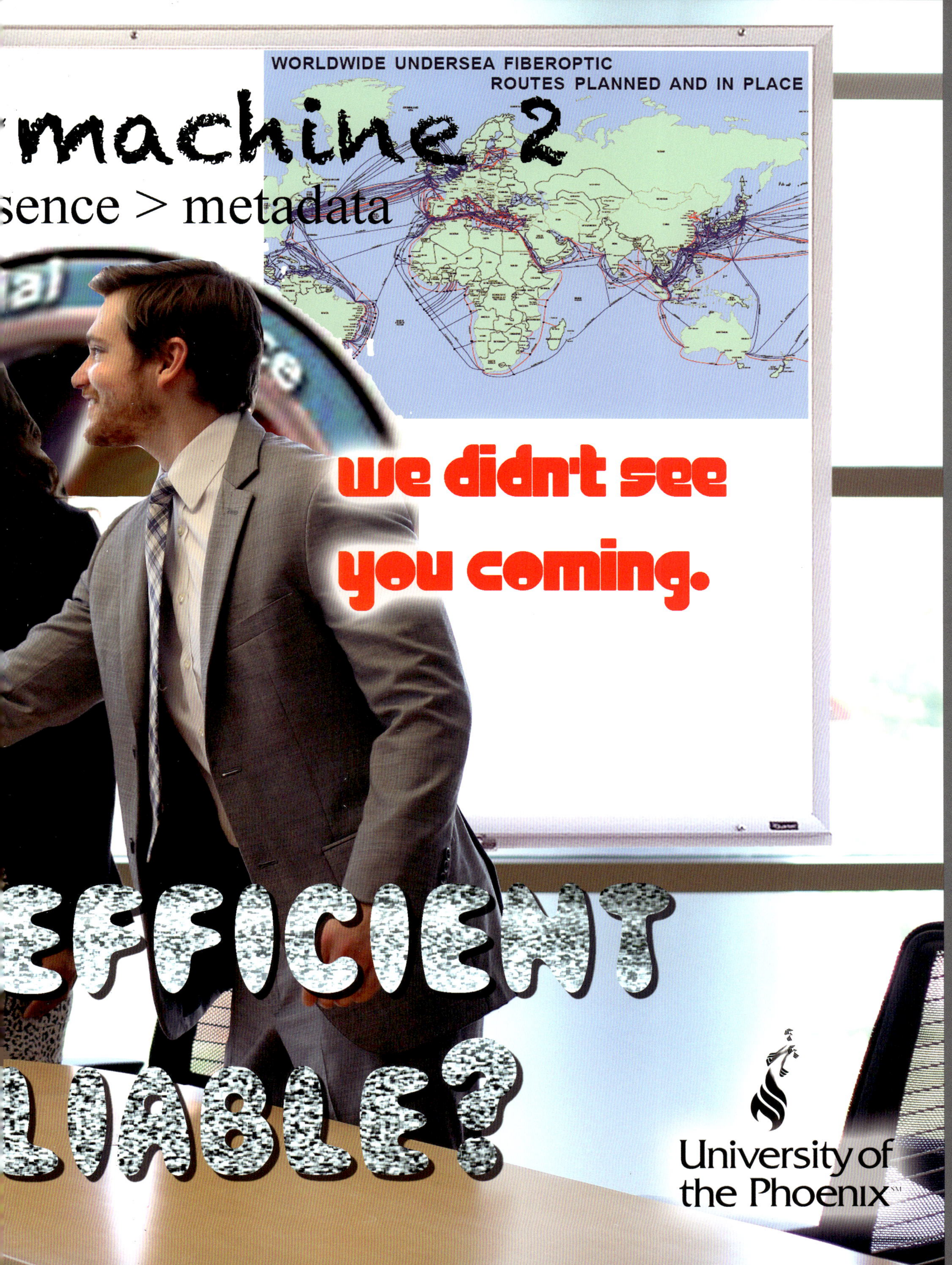
machine 2
sence > metadata
WORLDWIDE UNDERSEA FIBEROPTIC
ROUTES PLANNED AND IN PLACE
we didn't see
you coming.
EFFICIENT
LIABLE?
University of
the Phoenix
59

II
—ART⌐
Secret Power⌐

● # Simon Denny

"Secret Power" was partly inspired by the impact of NSA whistleblower Edward Snowden's leaks of National Security Agency PowerPoint slides. Based on research into the NSA's use of imagery, it examines the way the contemporary world is depicted in imagery used by the NSA; and "it imagines a possible artistic context for the way that imagery was produced" as Simon Denny states.

Initially produced as a site-specific piece for the New Zealand pavilion of the Biennale Arte 2015, "Secret Power" was split across two state buildings: the Biblioteca Nazionale Marciana (Marciana Library), in Piazzetta San Marco, in the heart of the city, and the terminal at Marco Polo Airport, on the city's outskirts. Completed in 1588, the Library represents the Republic of Venice as a wealthy world power during the Renaissance. Established in 1895, La Biennale is premised on a model of national representation that seems obsolete today in a time of cosmopolitan global art. Completed soon after 9/11, the Airport represents a new era of global security.

In the Library, Denny had a server room installed, with server racks and a workstation. Besides holding computer equipment, the server racks and workstation double as vitrines, displaying a case study in NSA visual culture. The vitrines consist of sculptural and graphic elements based on the work of a former NSA designer and Creative Director of Defense Intelligence David Darchicourt and the Snowden slide archive, suggesting links in iconography and treatment. For instance, in one of these vitrines (see the following pages) Denny remixes some imagery from the NSA slides related to programs such as MYSTIC, FOXACID, QUANTUMTHEORY and other SSO/TAO slides.

As the curator Robert Leonard explains, "each element is nested in and reframed by other elements in an expanding allegory, making interpretation potentially interminable. And yet, despite this, Denny gets us close to his ostensible subject: the visual language of western intelligence agencies. Paradoxically, he places himself and us (as artist and viewers) in positions oddly analogous to these agencies, as we trawl through data and metadata, engaging in analytics, pattern recognition, and profiling, trying to make sense of things."

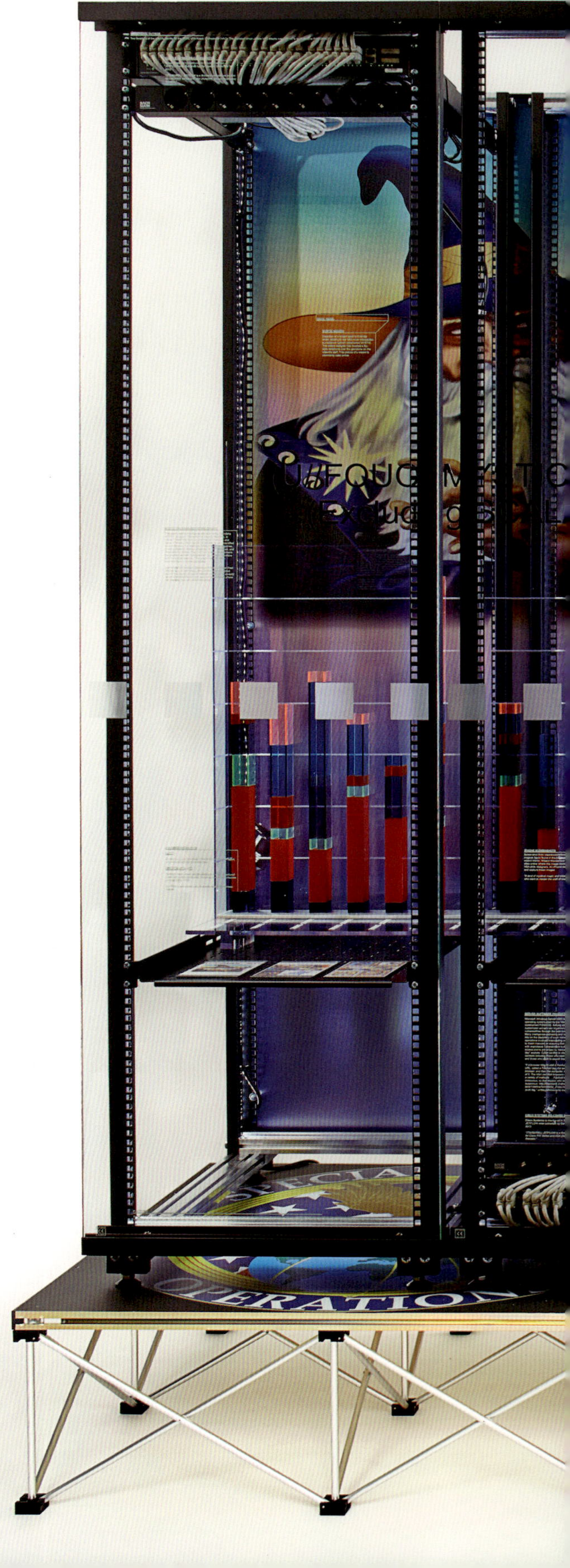

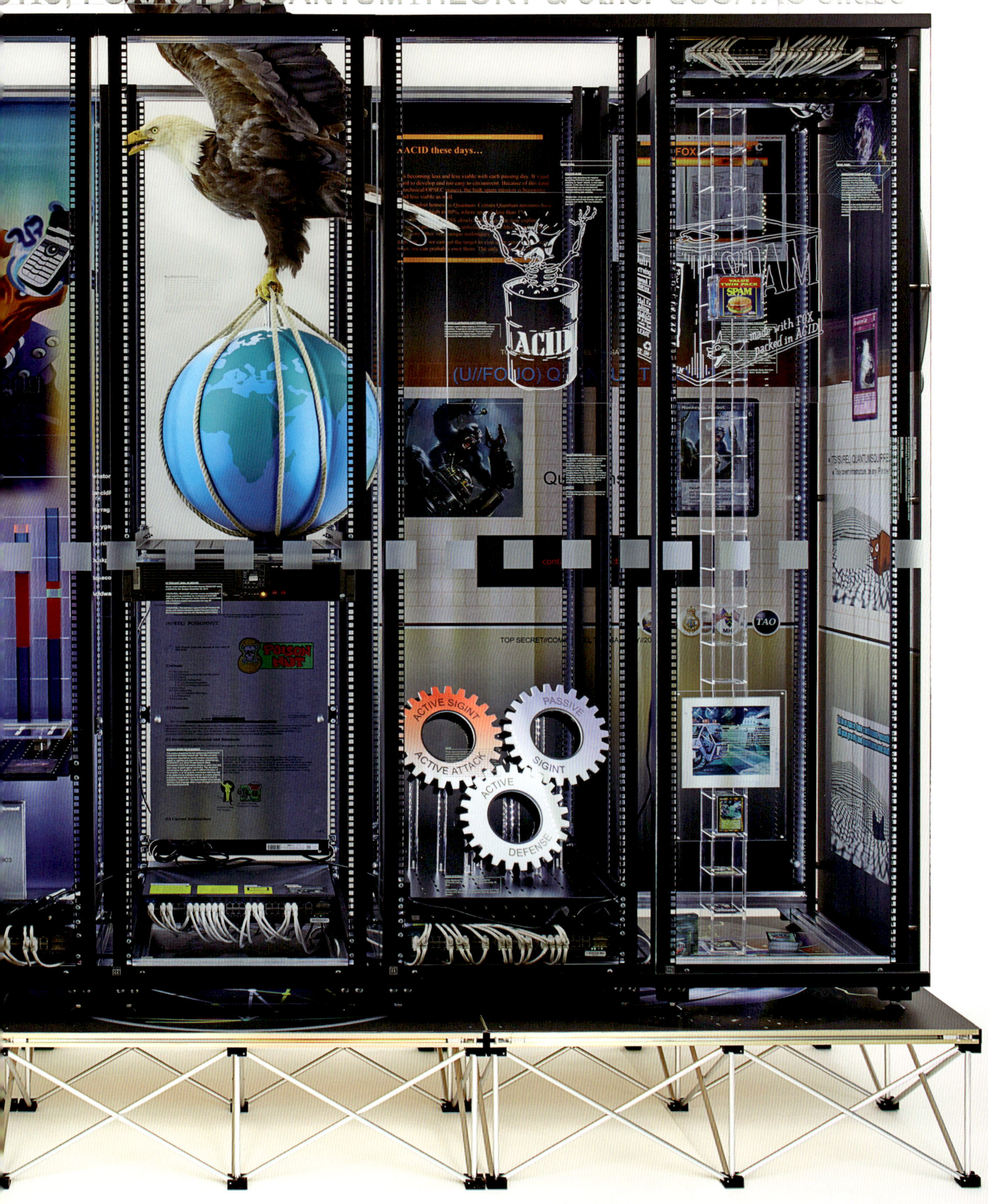

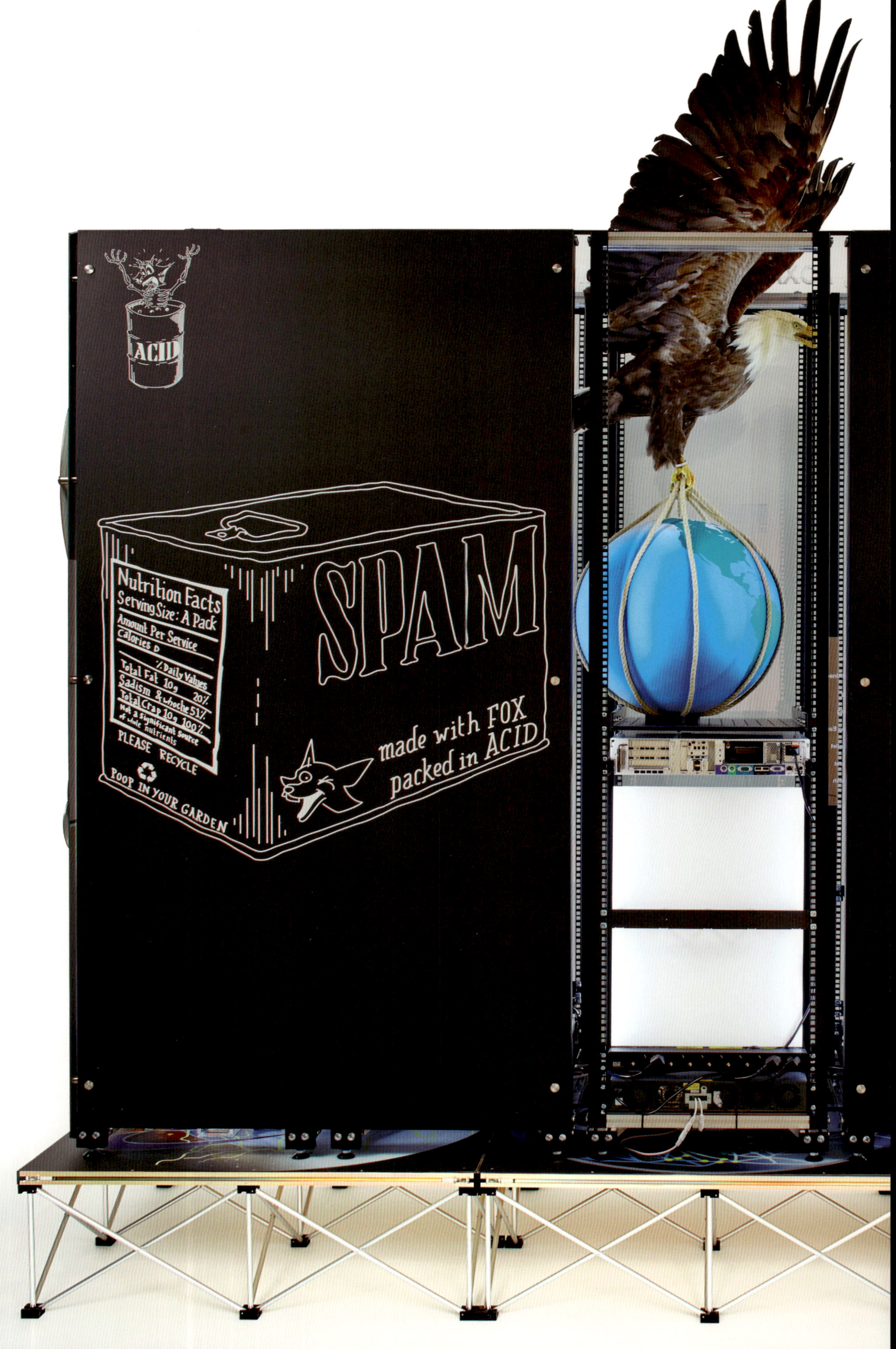

ACID
SPAM
Nutrition Facts
Serving Size: A Pack
Amount Per Service
Calories 0
% Daily Values
Total Fat 10g   20%
Sadism & whatever 51%
Total Crap 10g   100%
Not a significant source
of whole nutrients
PLEASE RECYCLE
POOP IN YOUR GARDEN
made with FOX
packed in ACID

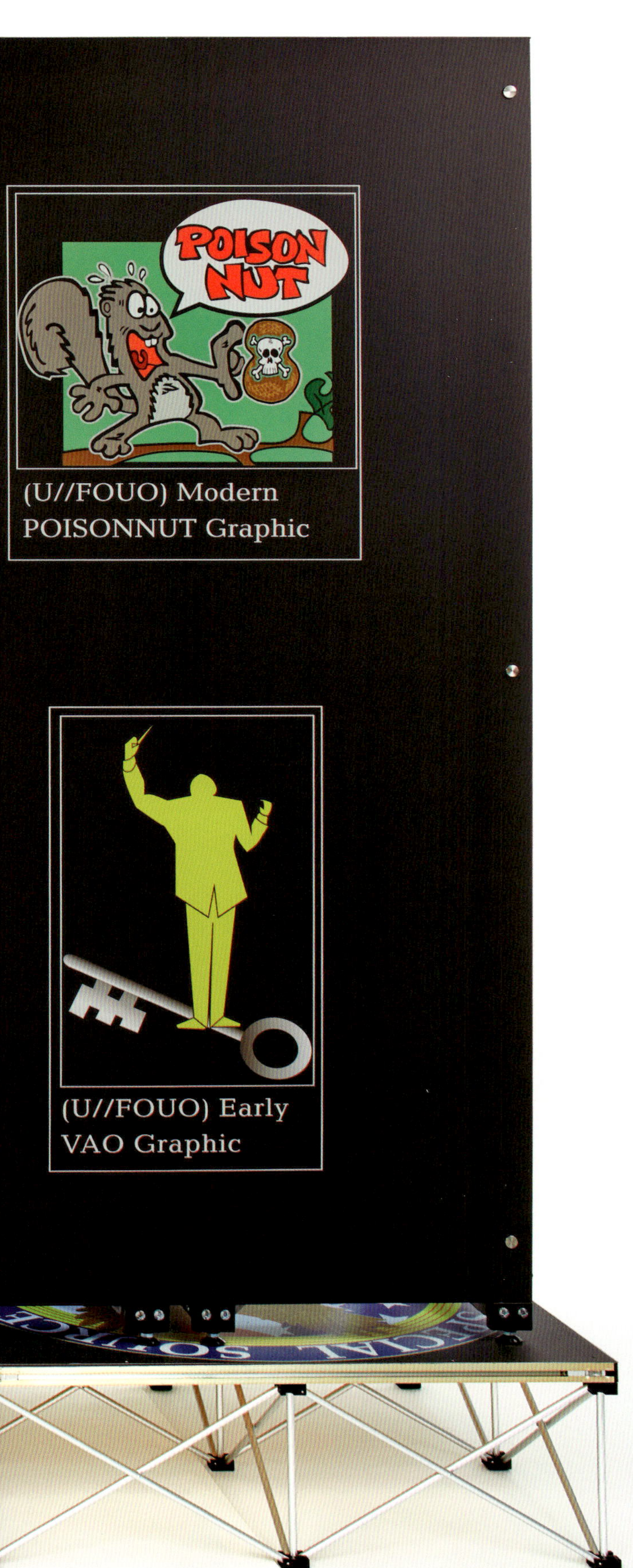

POISON NUT
(U//FOUO) Modern
POISONNUT Graphic
(U//FOUO) Early
VAO Graphic

undressing for XKeyscore – norms/forms to fit in/out¬

● **Zeljko Blace**

"Since Edward Snowden's revelations of US and UK surveillance programs, privacy advocates, progressive security engineers, and policy makers have been seeking to win majority support for countering surveillance. … [their actions] undermine a political reading that would attend to the racial, gendered, classed, and colonial aspects of the surveillance programs." (S. Gürses, A. Kundnani and J. Van Hoboken)

The NSA's XKeyscore program for searching and analyzing all global Internet data enables potentially unlimited monitoring of all network activities and users. With techniques such as cross-referencing and tagging, the program is also able to preemptively track potential future activities. In that respect, assuming the irrelevance of any collected data is not an option, as the system gets exploited beyond

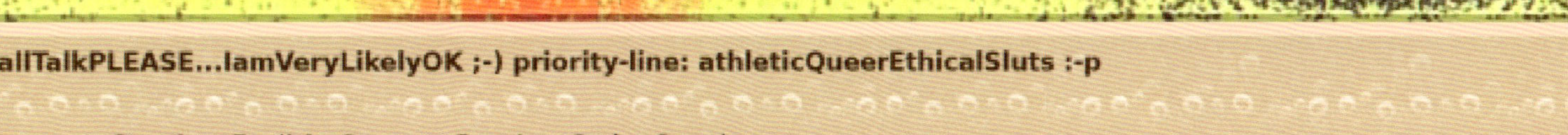

studOST Relationship

40 years, 202 cm, 101 kg
Berlin - Neukölln (0 m)
Germany, Berlin

Send Message | Message History | Save User | Hide visit ★

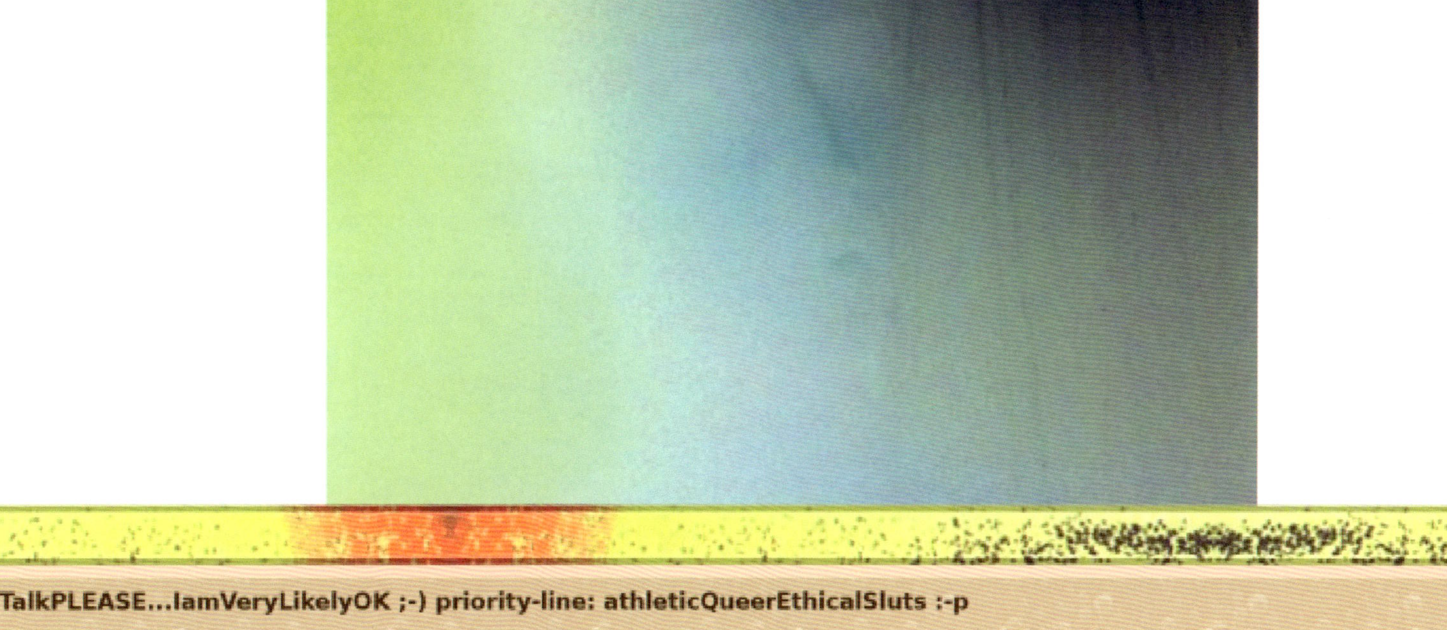

No Pictures in Gallery

19 Friends and Clubs
■□□

Partner Profile

4 Guestbook entries

No adverts

Visits 75632

NoSmallTalkPLEASE...IamVeryLikelyOK ;-) priority-line: athleticQueerEthicalSluts :-p

Language	Croatian, English, German, Bosnian, Serbo-Croatian
Body & ethnicity	Athletic & Caucasian
Hair	Short
Looking for	sexdate, friends, Relationship (Users between 28 and 50)
Profession	Self Employed
Religion	None
Food	Local Cuisine, Asian, Others, Greek, I eat it all
Music	Alternative, Dance & Electronic, Rap & HipHop, R&B & Soul, Others, House & Techno, Ethno
Sport	Swimming, Team Sports, Others, Volleyball, Surfing
Travel	Sun and Sea, Sports and Wellness, Others
Night life	Movies, Theatre, Exhibitions, Clubs, Sports, Other

What intelligence do OSN's

No Pictures in Gallery

19 Friends and Clubs
■□□

Partner Profile

4 Guestbook entries

No adverts

Visits

NoSmallTalkPLEASE...IamVeryLikelyOK ;-) priority-line: athleticQueerEthicalSluts :-p

Language	Croatian, English, German, Bosnian, Serbo-Croatian
Body & ethnicity	Athletic & Caucasian
Hair	Short
Looking for	sexdate, friends, Relationship (Users between 28 and 50)
Profession	Self Employed
Religion	None
Food	Local Cuisine, Asian, Others, Greek, I eat it all
Music	Alternative, Dance & Electronic, Rap & HipHop, R&B & Soul, Others, House & Techno,
Sport	Swimming, Team Sports, Others, Volleyball, Surfing
Travel	Sun and Sea, Sports and Wellness, Others

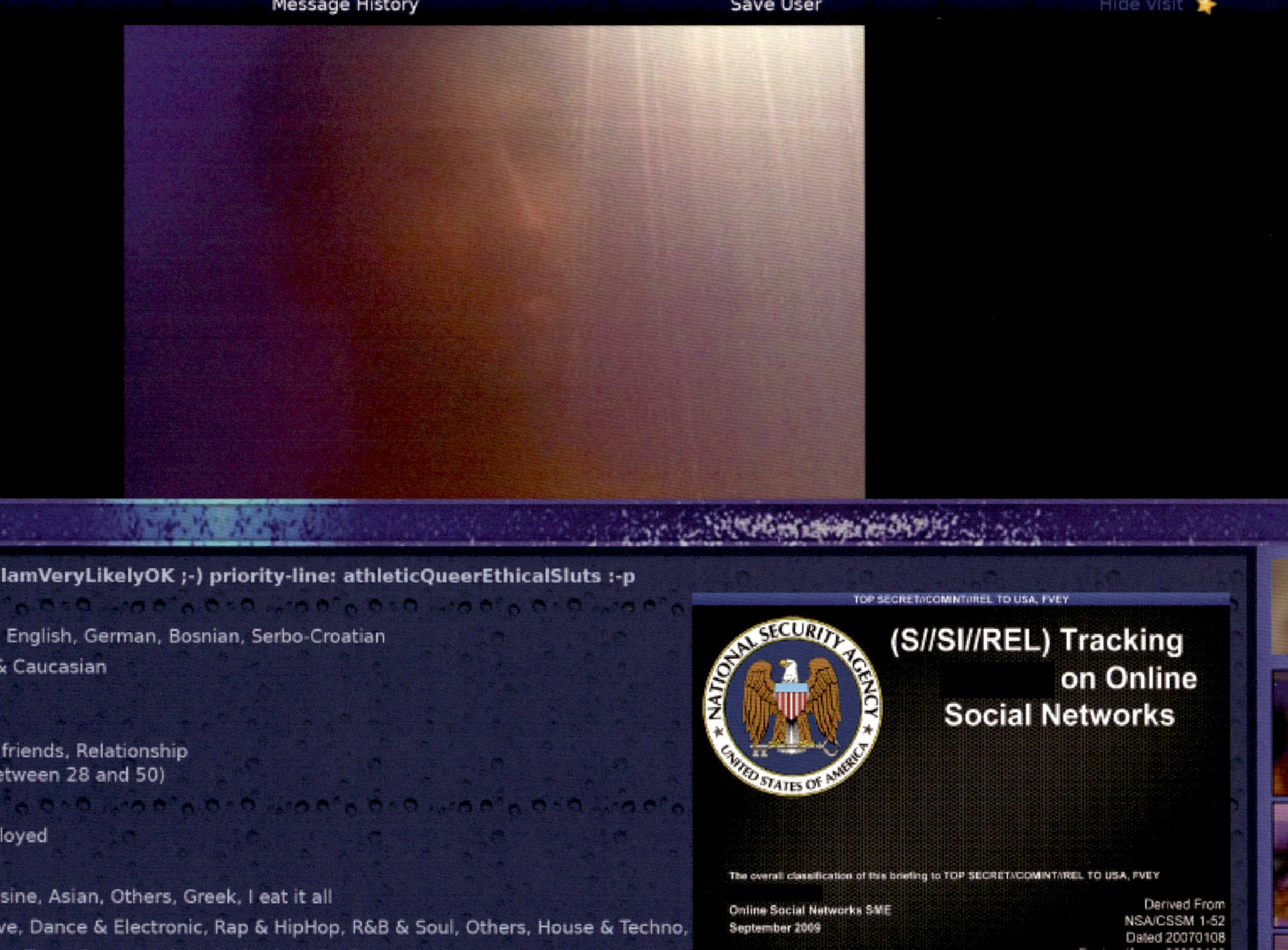

Tidiness	Pedantic		Chaotic
Planning	Planned		Spontaneous
CommunicationShy			Forward

Dicksize	XL, Uncut
Position	More top
Fucking	Versatile
Fisting	Active
S&M	Soft SM only
Dirty	WS only

=== YES I <3 or strongly pre
* athletic types, that are relax
exceptions :-) * prefer +/- 10
Sexpositive&Polyamorous :-)

=== NO I am/do not...
* fit a one specific "scene" * i
consumerism * into answerin

=== INTO:
eating wild fruits and enjoyin
swimming addict and volleyb
for mainstream charts, but do
physical over computer game
swap interesting and intimate

=== WARNINGS:
NOT ANSWERING MESSAGE
if have many incompatibilit

=== NOTES:
I work in culture/media & p
(Vienna)... but sometimes als
in your city right now - it is lik
I am socially and politically
and/or conformist, but I do try

= INTROSPECTION:
My notion of fun is out off syn
up as kid in soft socialism, bu
be satisfied with superficiality
mainstream by either linking
qualias) ...WHAT GETS YOU GOING IN THE WORLD?

P.S. for intellectually, socially and sexually curious your further READING is online version at Profile number 394296

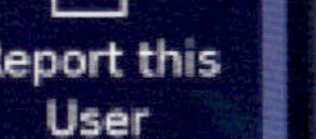

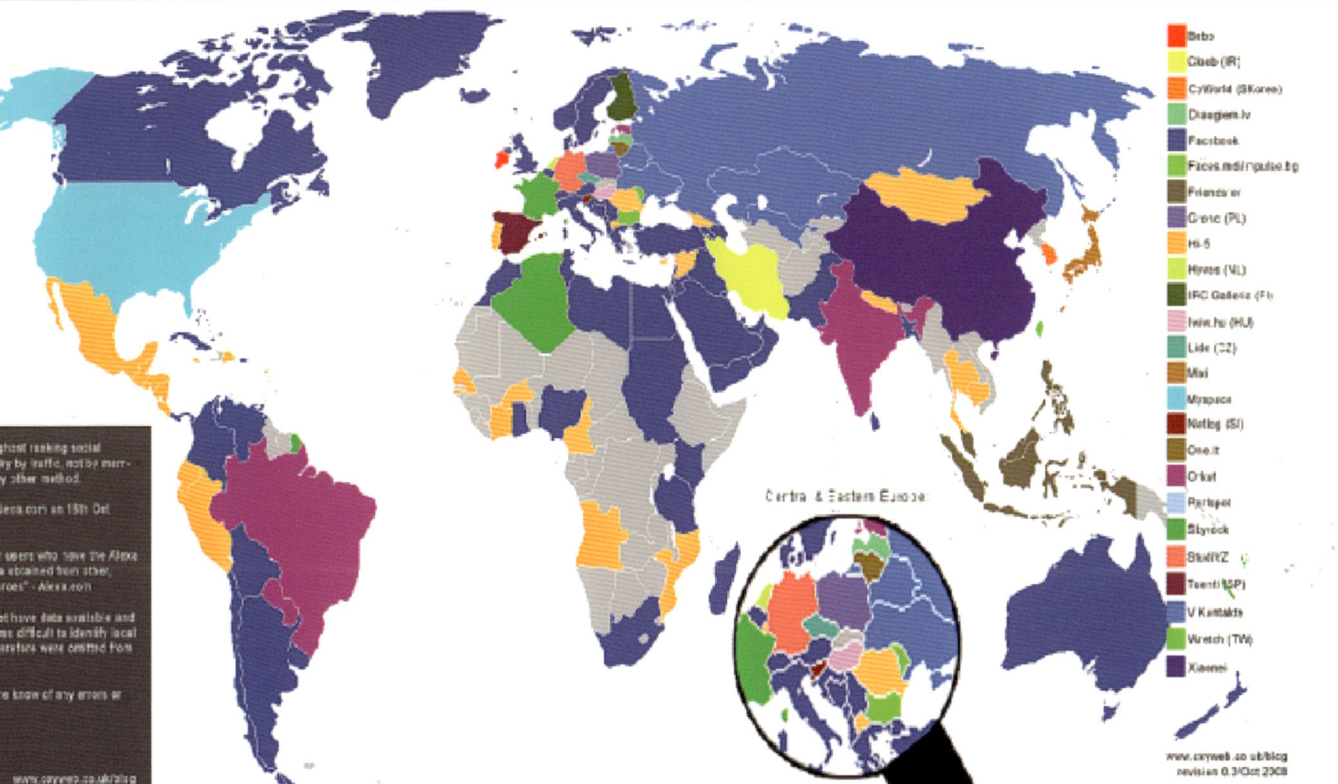

Night life	Home boy	▮▮▮▮	Party Animal
Tidiness	Pedantic	▮▮▮▮	Chaotic
Planning	Planned	▮▮▮▮	Spontaneous
Communication	Shy	▮▮▮▮	Forward

Dicksize	XL, Uncut
Position	More top
Fucking	Versatile
Fisting	Active
S&M	Soft SM only
Dirty	WS only

=== YES I <3 or strongly prefer (but am not limited to):
* athletic types, that are relaxed, laid-back and casual * natural looks with focus on self-care, not self-image * more often closer to my built but have made exceptions :-) * prefer +/- 10 years range, with exceptions for exceptional ;-) * strong personality/individuality, but with less interest in drama * Sexpositive&Polyamorous :-) over Prudent&Monogamous :-/

=== NO I am/do not...
* fit a one specific "scene" * into "acting" this and that * here for entertaining boring/bored couples * here for long chat interviews * into consumed in consumerism * into answering to generic: HI!s Hey!s Hello!s WhatsUp?s AllGood?s HowAreYou?s ...to people I do not know...Think of better entry line :-)

=== INTO:
eating wild fruits and enjoying outdoors, especially seaside (Adriatic) for walking bare footed along the beach in sunset (born near the sea)... big open water swimming addict and volleyball player looking for (beach/)volleyball mates!... love going to parties with interesting electronic music that is not exclusively made for mainstream charts, but do not go extensive drinking, crowded and smoky bars...can spend hours behind computer (mostly for work), yet always prefer physical over computer games ;-) ...as of recently I am more curious in sex to try new things and have discovered Lebanese/Moroccan men ...would always swap interesting and intimate talk over casual sex, but open for different options depending on context, personal chemistry and mood!

=== WARNINGS:
NOT ANSWERING MESSAGES from those obviously IGNORE my TEXT & PREFERENCES and APPROACH me WITHOUT personal PHOTO
if have many incompatibilities... than it is very likely that your next-to-perfect body features will not be enough to make me sexually interested here!

=== NOTES:
I work in culture/media & participate in LGBT/Queer sport events in EU - mostly in Berlin, going Brussels, Barcelona, Brighton, Budapest, Belgrade, Bec (Vienna)... but sometimes also cities with other letters Frankfurt, Lille, Paris, Cologne, Antwerp, Ghent, Karlsruhe, Copenhagen, London, Glasgow, Oslo ...so if not in your city right now - it is likely our paths will eventually cross.
I am socially and politically engaged (sometimes and to some people to much), so it is not easy for me to be around people who tend to be either indifferent and/or conformist, but I do try not to judge.

= INTROSPECTION:
My notion of fun is out off sync with consumer/commercial entertainment. I am born in (somewhat) catholic and very much-small-town Balkan family, that grew up as kid in soft socialism, but later a youngster of few civil-wars and adult in broken country/economy/society...so finally ended up too complex/complicated to be satisfied with superficiality and assumed values/structures/authorities. I am inclined to more edgy, queer, social contexts...stuff that goes off from mainstream by either linking to notions of either #1 'authenticity' (very site-specific or natural qualities) or #2 'cybernetics' (virtual and mediated network qualias) ...WHAT GETS YOU GOING IN THE WORLD?

P.S. for intellectually, socially and sexually curious your further READING is online version at Profile number 394296

These pages can be used
as a double-sided poster.
Just pull them out.

II
—ART¬
Snowden Archive-in-a-Box¬

● Evan Light

The "Snowden Archive-in-a-Box" (SAIB) is an autonomous stand-alone wireless network and web server designed to provide end users with a secure off-line method to use a database of the Snowden files without the threat of covert mass surveillance. Its technological basis is a Raspberry Pi, a credit card-sized, $50 mini-computer. Users in the vicinity of the SAIB can connect to a SnowdenArchive WiFi connection and access an offline version of the Snowden Digital Surveillance Archive, which makes published Snowden files available via a website. It also includes a surveillance demonstration apparatus that monitors wireless traffic to the server and plays it back visually in real time.

Contained in a black suitcase, this evolving art project has been traveling all over the world – presented, exhibited and deployed in contexts as varied as film festivals, academic conferences, universities and museums. A replica was built and installed at Cambridge University (UK) in 2015, and there are plans to deploy several more around the world. Evan Light conceived of and continues to develop the portable "Snowden Archive-in-a-Box". Should you wish to build one of your own, please get in touch!

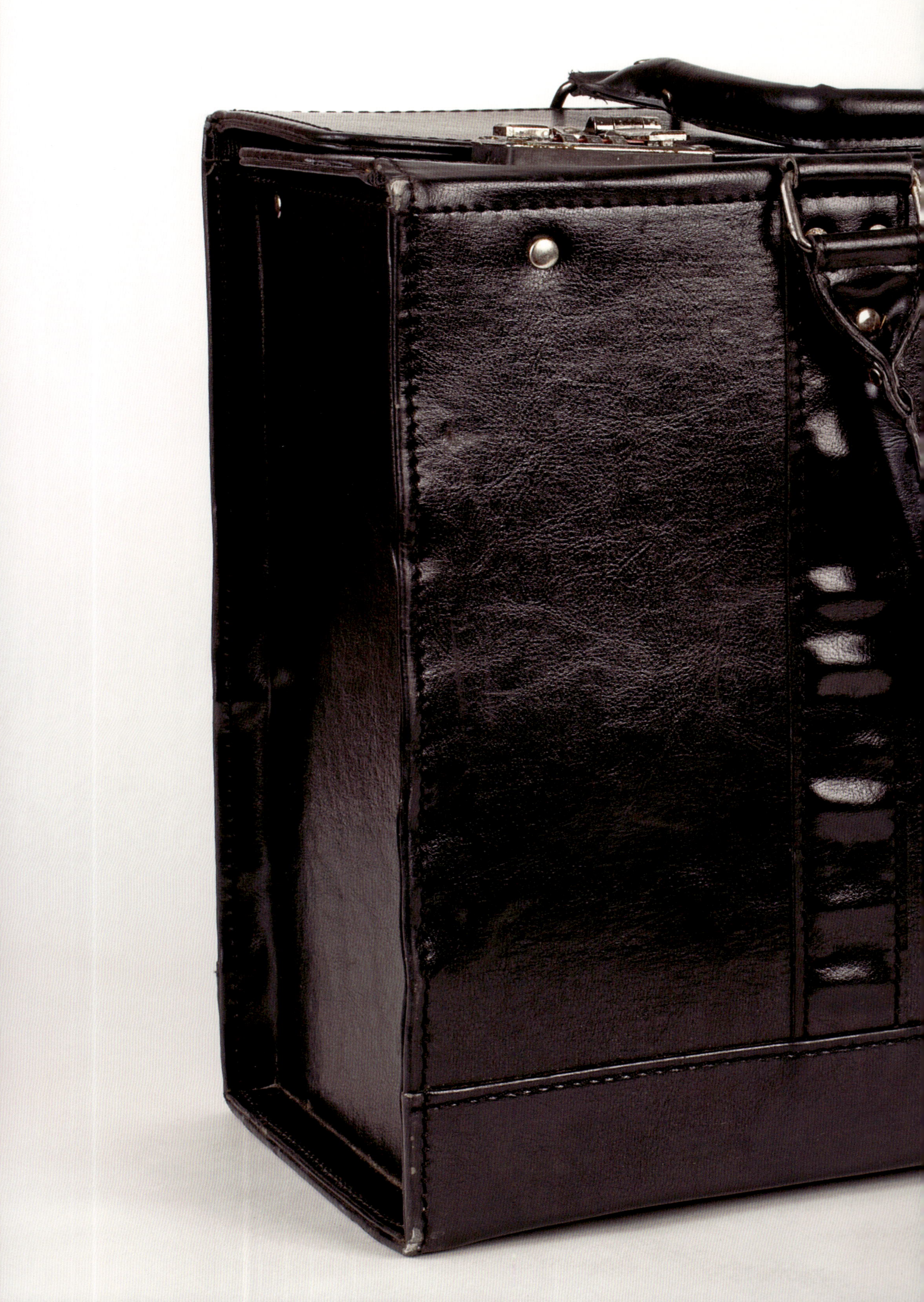

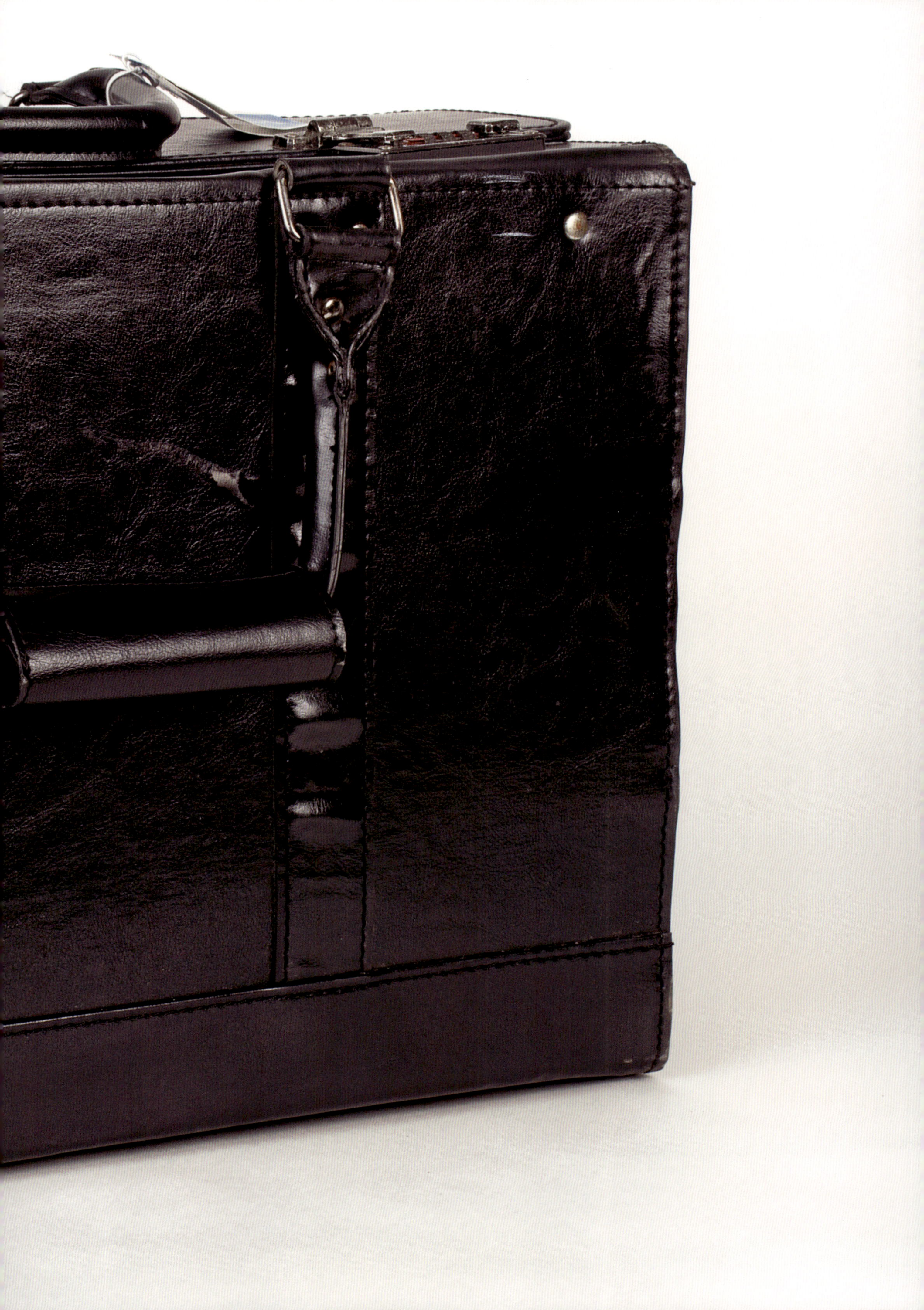

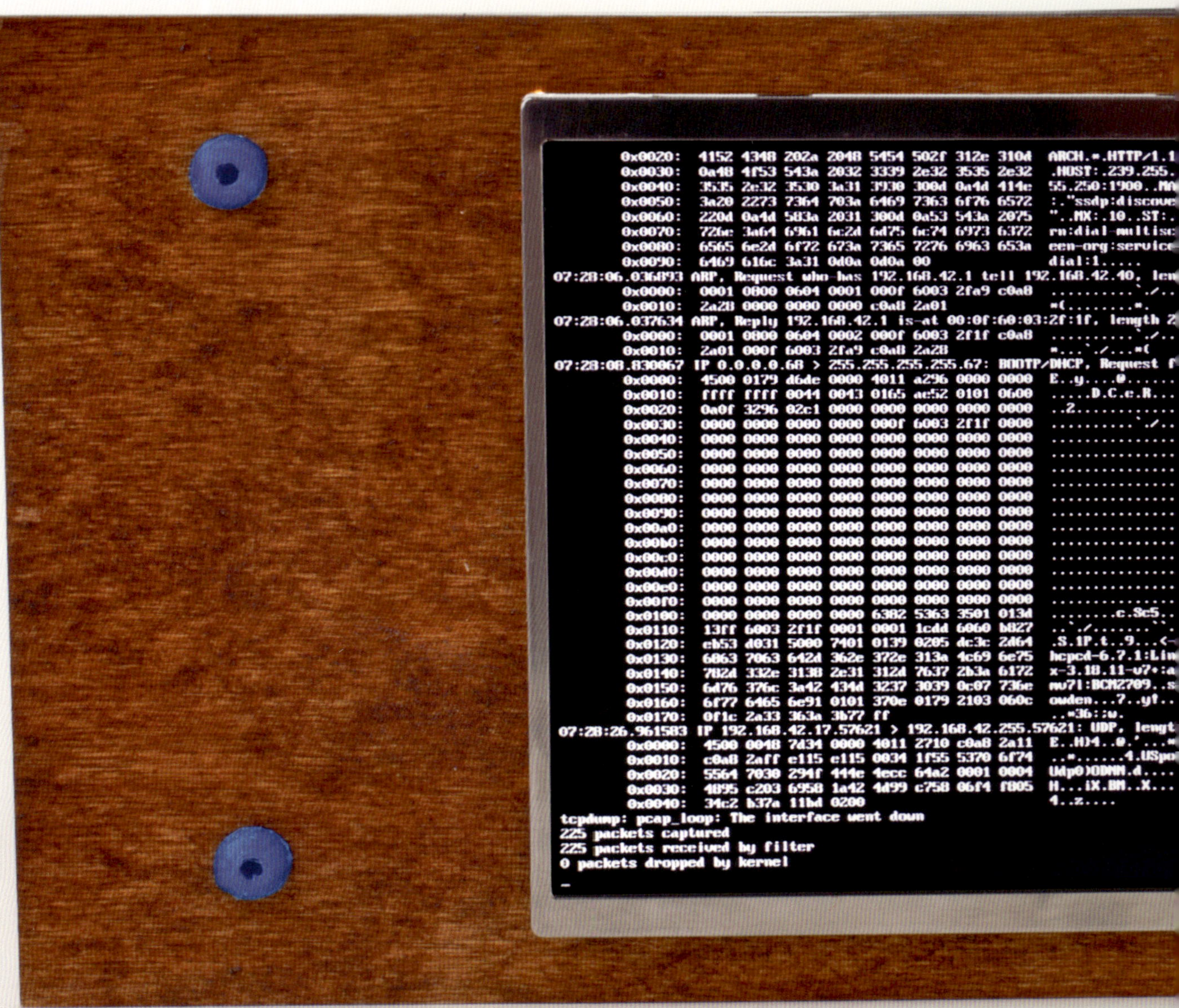

0x0020:   4152 4348 202a 2048 5454 502f 312e 310d   ARCH.*.HTTP/1.1
0x0030:   0a48 4f53 543a 2032 3339 2e32 3535 2e32   .HOST:.239.255.
0x0040:   3535 2e32 3530 3a31 3930 300d 0a4d 414e   55.250:1900..MAN
0x0050:   3a20 2273 7364 703a 6469 7363 6f76 6572   :."ssdp:discover
0x0060:   220d 0a4d 583a 2031 300d 0a53 543a 2075   "..MX:.10..ST:.u
0x0070:   726e 3a64 6961 6c2d 6d75 6c74 6973 6372   rn:dial-multiscr
0x0080:   6565 6e2d 6f72 673a 7365 7276 6963 653a   een-org:service:
0x0090:   6469 616c 3a31 0d0a 0d0a 00   dial:1.....
07:28:06.036893 ARP, Request who-has 192.168.42.1 tell 192.168.42.40, len
0x0000:   0001 0800 0604 0001 000f 6003 2fa9 c0a8   ....`./..
0x0010:   2a28 0000 0000 0000 c0a8 2a01   *(.........*.
07:28:06.037634 ARP, Reply 192.168.42.1 is-at 00:0f:60:03:2f:1f, length 2
0x0000:   0001 0800 0604 0002 000f 6003 2f1f c0a8   ....`./..
0x0010:   2a01 000f 6003 2fa9 c0a8 2a28   *...`./...*(
07:28:08.830067 IP 0.0.0.0.68 > 255.255.255.255.67: BOOTP/DHCP, Request f
0x0000:   4500 0179 d6de 0000 4011 a296 0000 0000   E..y....@......
0x0010:   ffff ffff 0044 0043 0165 ae52 0101 0600   .....D.C.e.R...
0x0020:   0a0f 3296 02c1 0000 0000 0000 0000 0000   ..2...........
0x0030:   0000 0000 0000 0000 000f 6003 2f1f 0000   ....`./..
0x0040:   0000 0000 0000 0000 0000 0000 0000 0000   ....
0x0050:   0000 0000 0000 0000 0000 0000 0000 0000   ....
0x0060:   0000 0000 0000 0000 0000 0000 0000 0000   ....
0x0070:   0000 0000 0000 0000 0000 0000 0000 0000   ....
0x0080:   0000 0000 0000 0000 0000 0000 0000 0000   ....
0x0090:   0000 0000 0000 0000 0000 0000 0000 0000   ....
0x00a0:   0000 0000 0000 0000 0000 0000 0000 0000   ....
0x00b0:   0000 0000 0000 0000 0000 0000 0000 0000   ....
0x00c0:   0000 0000 0000 0000 0000 0000 0000 0000   ....
0x00d0:   0000 0000 0000 0000 0000 0000 0000 0000   ....
0x00e0:   0000 0000 0000 0000 0000 0000 0000 0000   ....
0x00f0:   0000 0000 0000 0000 0000 0000 0000 0000   ....
0x0100:   0000 0000 0000 0000 6382 5363 3501 013d   ....c.Sc5..=
0x0110:   13ff 6003 2f1f 0001 0001 1cdd 6060 b827   ..`./.......``.'
0x0120:   eb53 d031 5000 7401 0139 0205 dc3c 2d64   .S.1P.t..9...<-d
0x0130:   6863 7063 642d 362e 372e 313a 4c69 6e75   hcpcd-6.7.1:Linu
0x0140:   782d 332e 3138 2e31 312d 7637 2b3a 6172   x-3.18.11-v7+:ar
0x0150:   6d76 376c 3a42 434d 3237 3039 0c07 736e   mv7l:BCM2709..sn
0x0160:   6f77 6465 6e91 0101 370e 0179 2103 060c   owden...7..y!...
0x0170:   0f1c 2a33 363a 3b77 ff   ..*36:;w.
07:28:26.961583 IP 192.168.42.17.57621 > 192.168.42.255.57621: UDP, lengt
0x0000:   4500 0048 7d34 0000 4011 2710 c0a8 2a11   E..H}4..@.'...*
0x0010:   c0a8 2aff e115 e115 0034 1f55 5370 6f74   ..*......4.USpot
0x0020:   5564 7030 294f 444e 4ecc 64a2 0001 0004   Udp0)ODNN.d....
0x0030:   4895 c203 6958 1a42 4d99 c758 06f4 f805   H...iX.BM..X....
0x0040:   34c2 b37a 11bd 0200   4..z....
tcpdump: pcap_loop: The interface went down
225 packets captured
225 packets received by filter
0 packets dropped by kernel
_

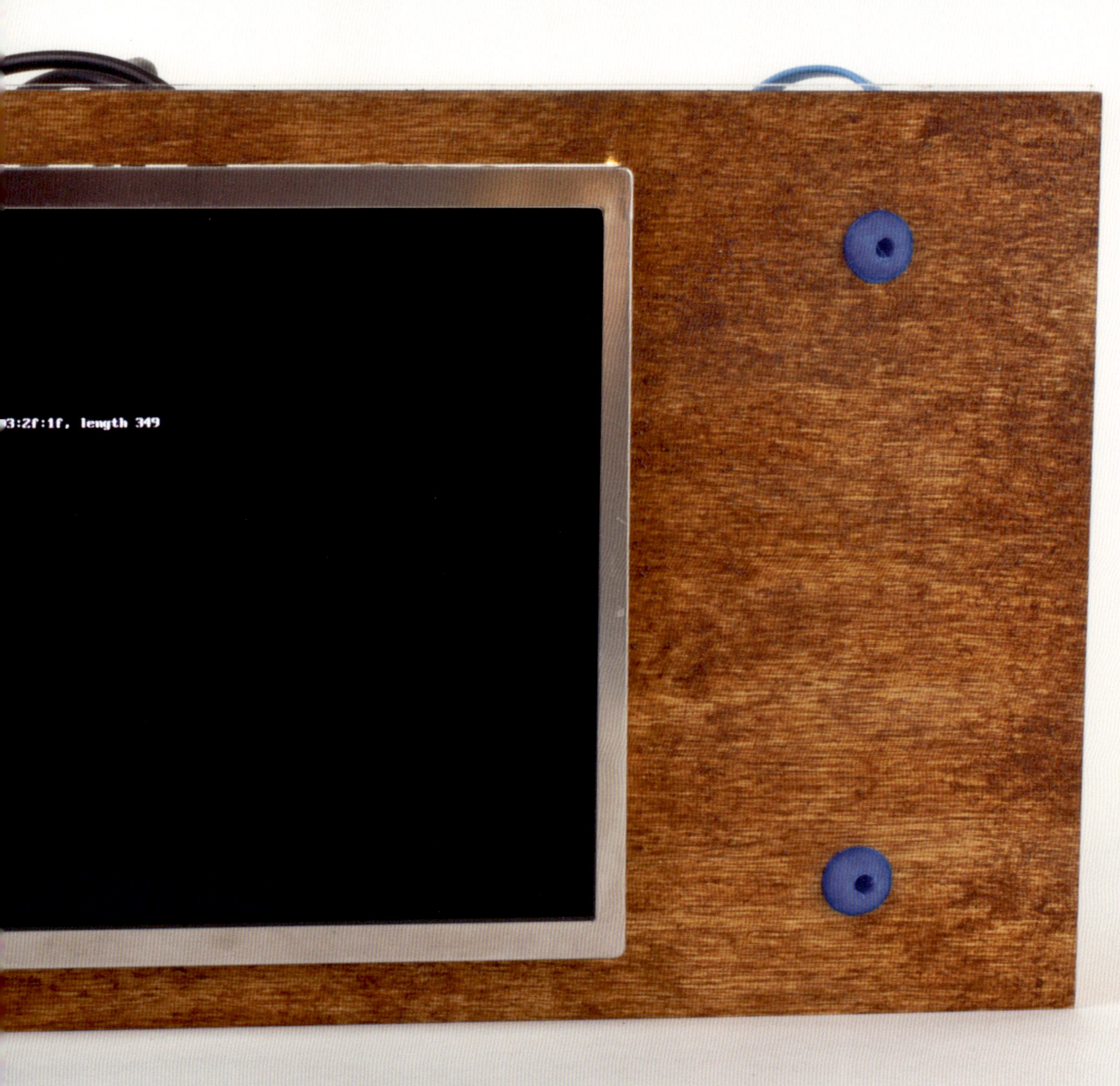
3:2f:1f, length 349

Biometric Biomass Spillover¬

● Stefan Tiron

The centerpiece of Stefan Tiron's "Biometric Biomass Spillover" is a self-made foldable passport cover. It is complemented by an image of the microfossil Saccorhytus coronarius which was 'all face', as well as the cover artwork from the NSA presentation "Identity Intelligence: Image is Everything" which mimics the logic of biometric passports with a starkly geometric aesthetic.

Tiron's passport cover design takes its cue from the body horror genre, especially the images in Brian Yuzna's movie "Society" (1989). Moreover, it reflects a historical and morphological footnote: the recently discovered 1.2 mm microfossil Saccorhytus coronarius which was literally 'all face'. The face of this oldest deep ancestor of humans (as well us all other vertebrates) was proportionally very large compared to the rest of its body. One could say that at that evolutionary stage the face had taken over the surface of the whole body. Inspired by this, Tiron's passport cover design is 'all face' as well: it has no top or bottom and defies symmetry, not to mention geometry.

Echoing the kind of covers which teenagers use to hide their horrible school books with something even more horrible, both tracking and image identification overflow everything in form of a hemorrhoidal biometric biomass spillover.

The undated NSA presentation "Identity Intelligence: Image is Everything", which was leaked by Edward Snowden, outlines the potential value of biometric data to the agency. The documents show that the NSA has been collecting "millions of images per day", of which about 55000 were "facial recognition quality", in an effort to develop the ability to cross-reference data from different NSA databases using just a facial image. A tool codenamed WELLSPRING searches online communications specifically for passport images, while another, PISCES, collects biometric data collected at the border crossings of several countries. The NSA's facial recognition capability relies in part on commercial tools, including PittPatt, which is owned by Google.

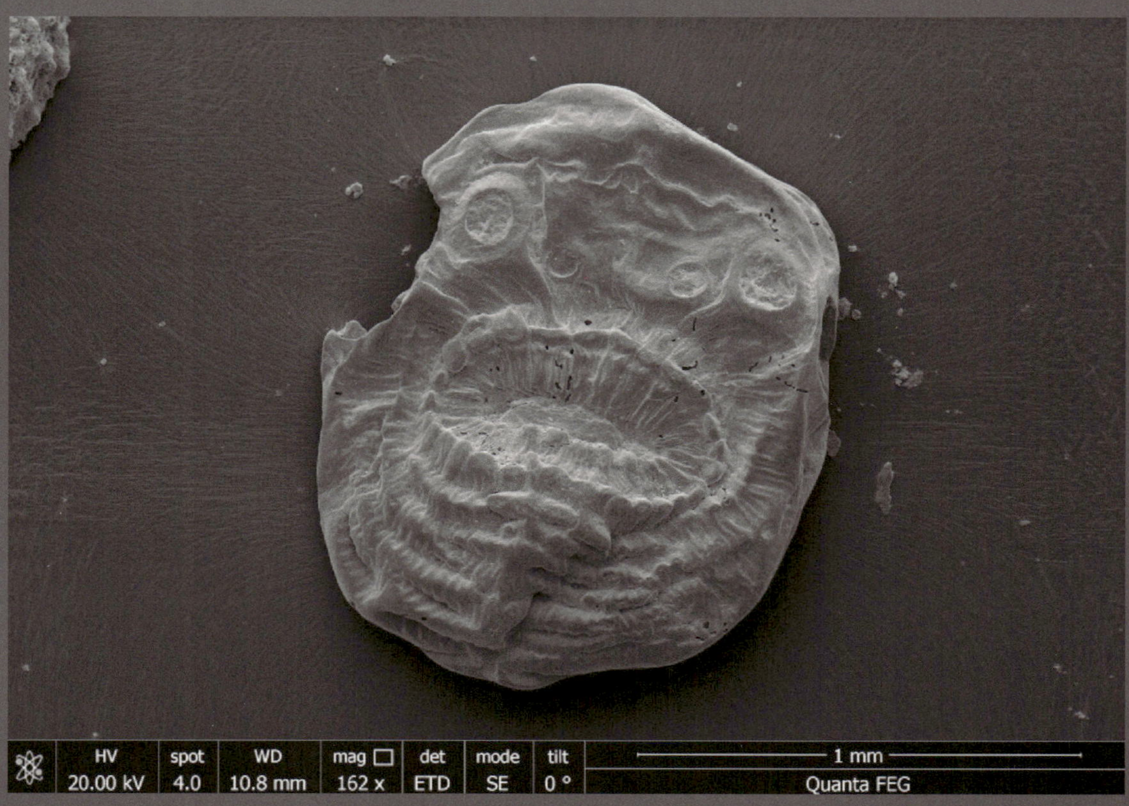

HV
20.00 kV
spot
4.0
WD
10.8 mm
mag
162 x
det
ETD
mode
SE
tilt
0 °
1 mm
Quanta FEG

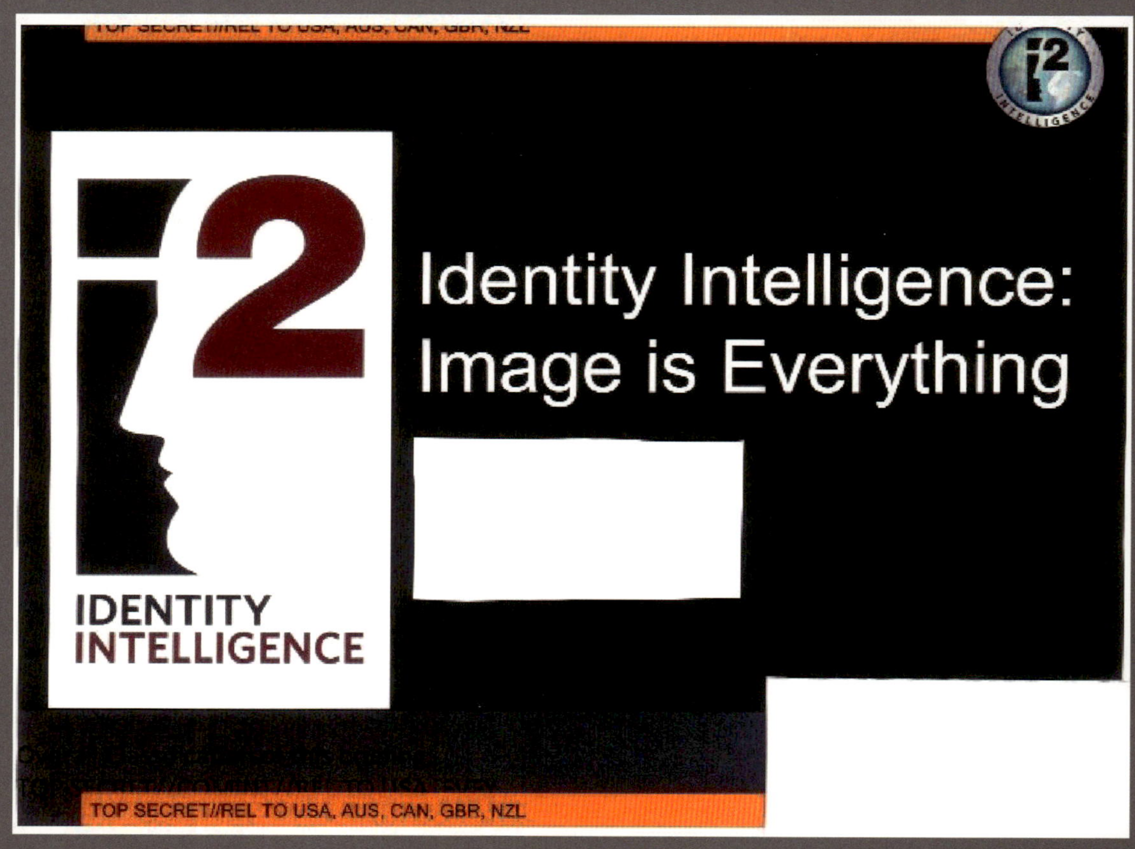

TOP SECRET//REL TO USA, AUS, CAN, GBR, NZL
i2
IDENTITY
INTELLIGENCE
Identity Intelligence:
Image is Everything
TOP SECRET//REL TO USA, AUS, CAN, GBR, NZL

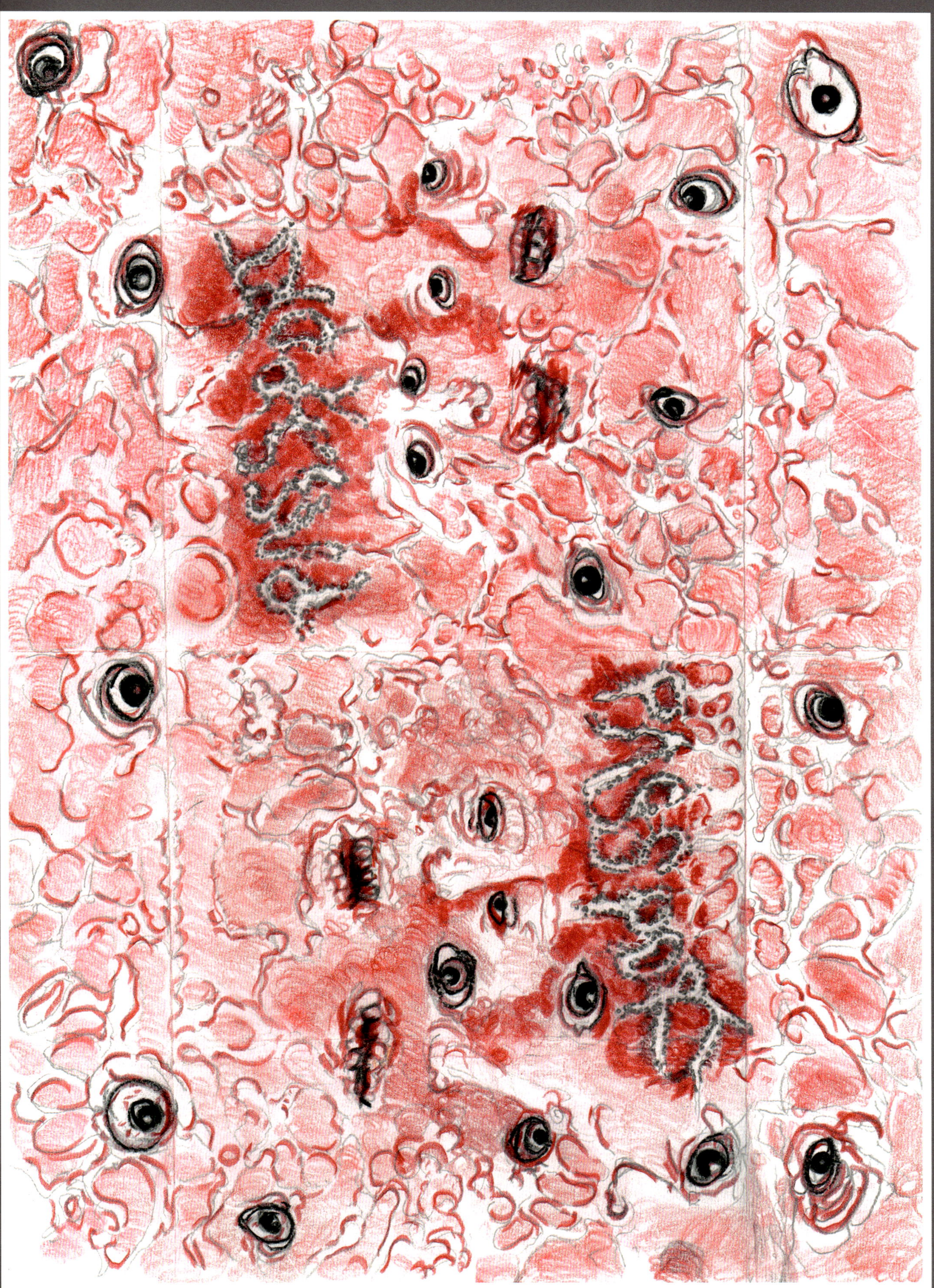

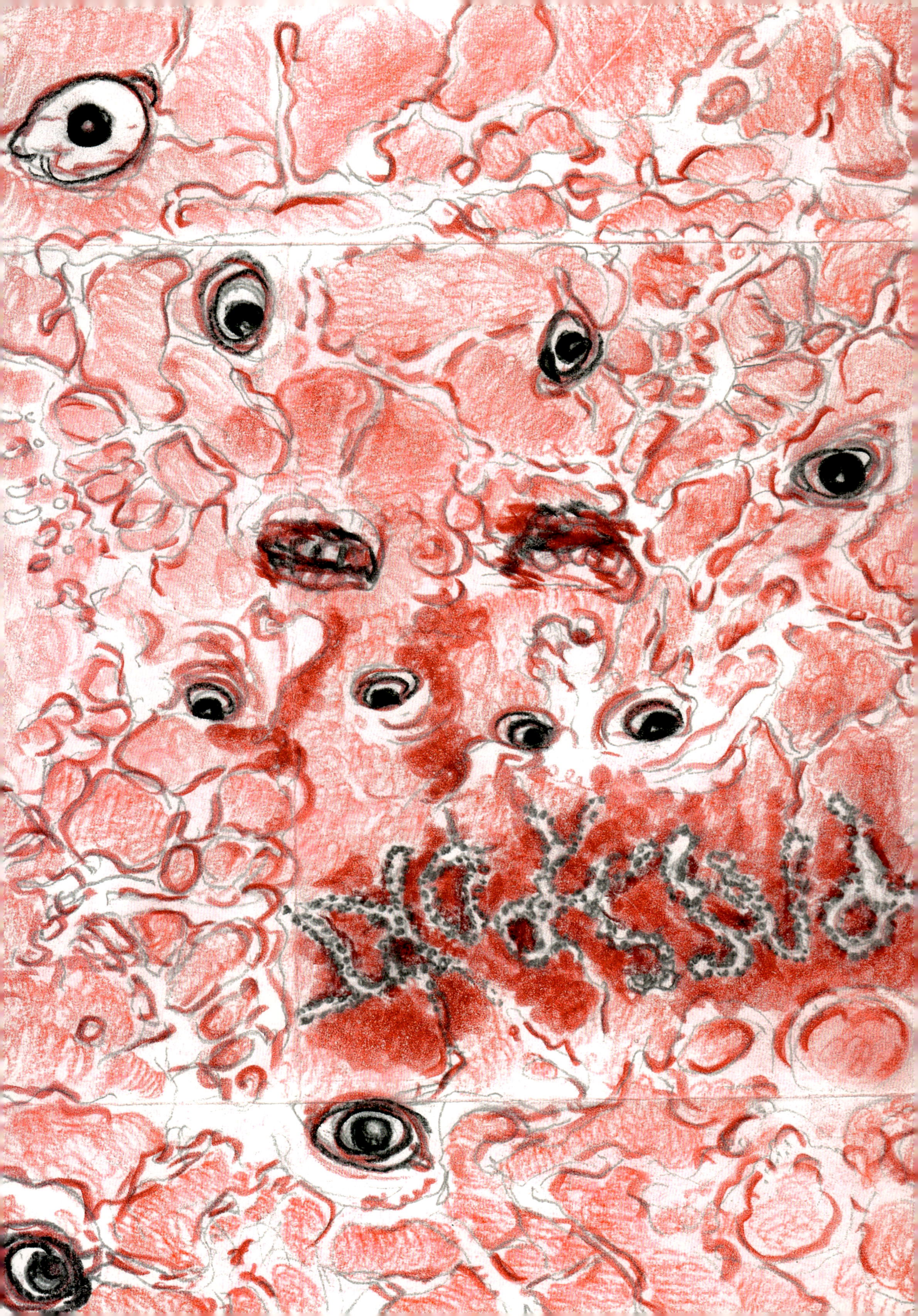
yokosvb

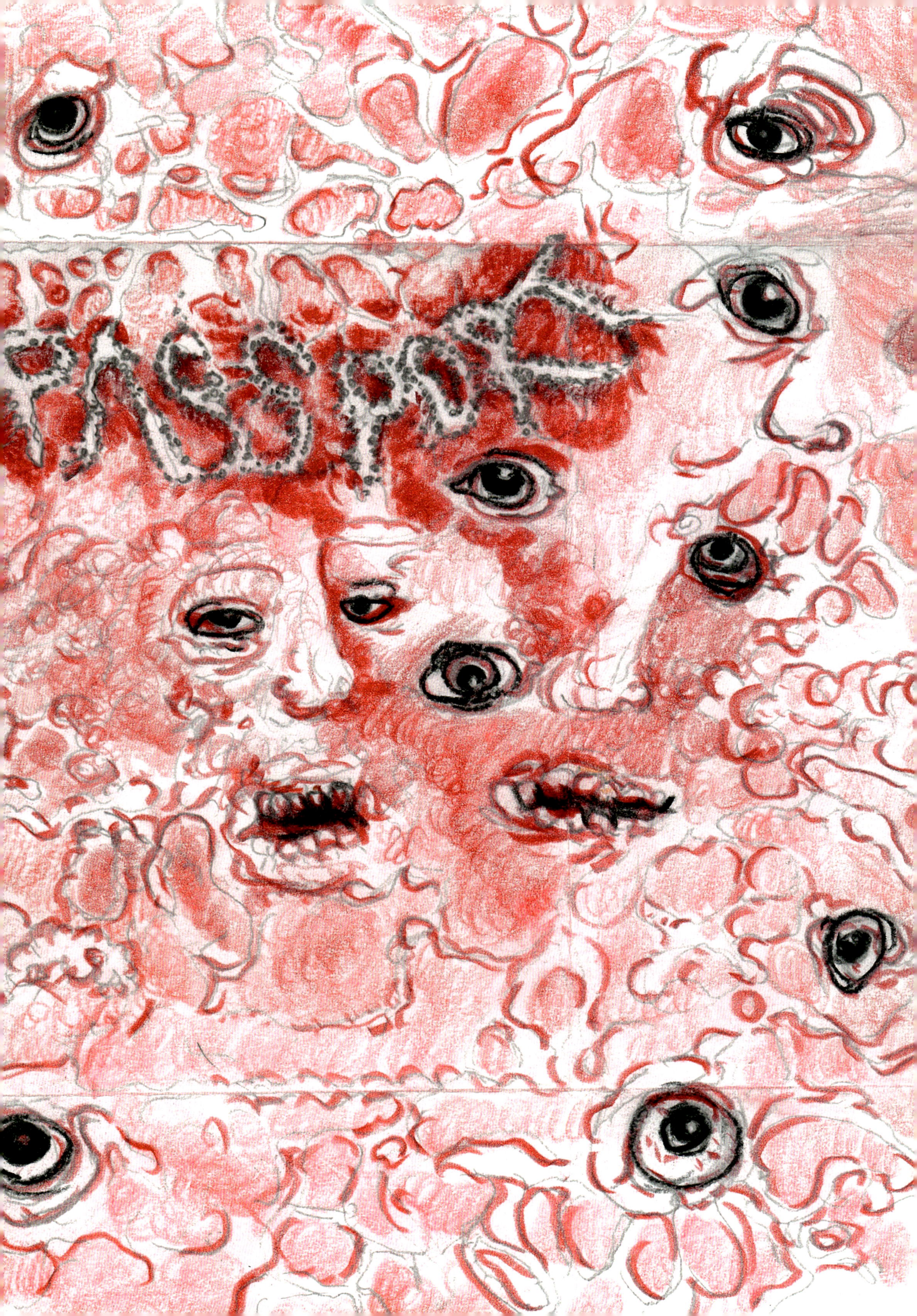

Anarchist Image Index¬

- ## Laura Poitras and Henrik Moltke

Anarchist is the code name of an operation run by the British Army for the UK's Government Communications Headquarters (GCHQ). From the top of the Troodos Mountains on the island nation of Cyprus, two antennas operating twenty-four hours a day intercept signals from satellites, drones, and radars in the Mediterranean region.

Collected through Anarchist, the images on the following pages show various stages in the processing of the collected signals. The snapshots of signals comprise data feeds with Doppler tracks from a satellite, Israeli drone video feeds, air traffic control signals, unidentified signals from an Israeli source, data feeds from a French satellite as well as data burst and commercial satellite feeds. The images are from GCWiki, an internal British intelligence wiki disclosed to Laura Poitras and other journalists by Edward Snowden.

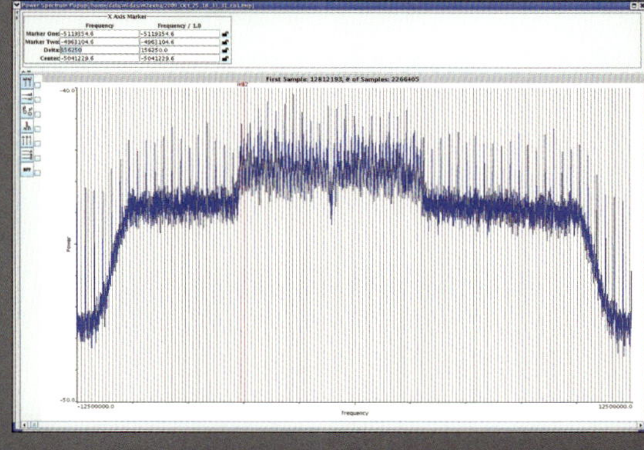

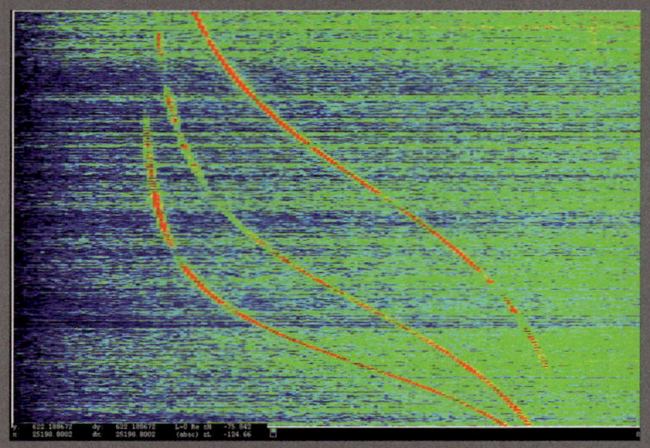

#1

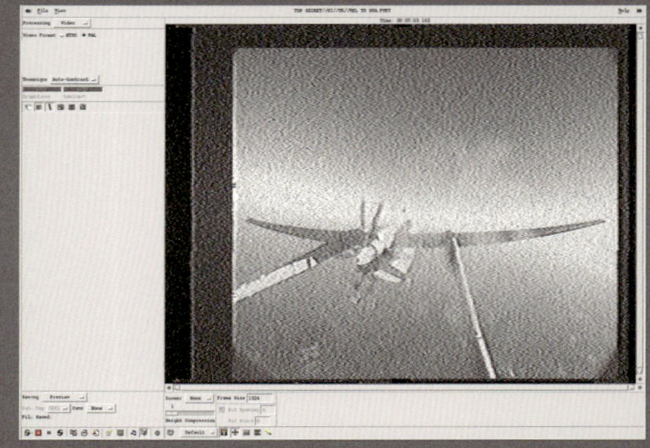

#2

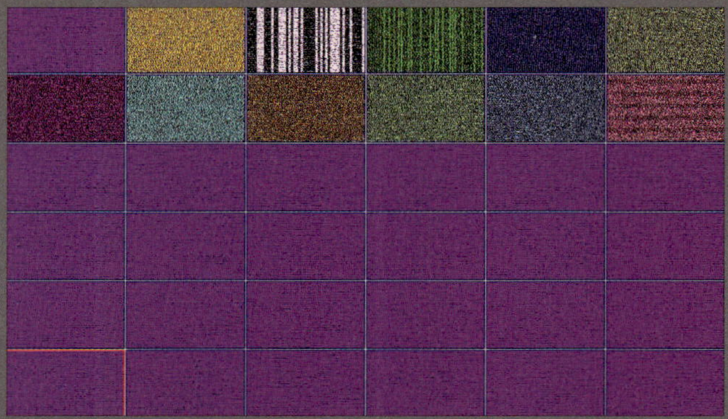

#3

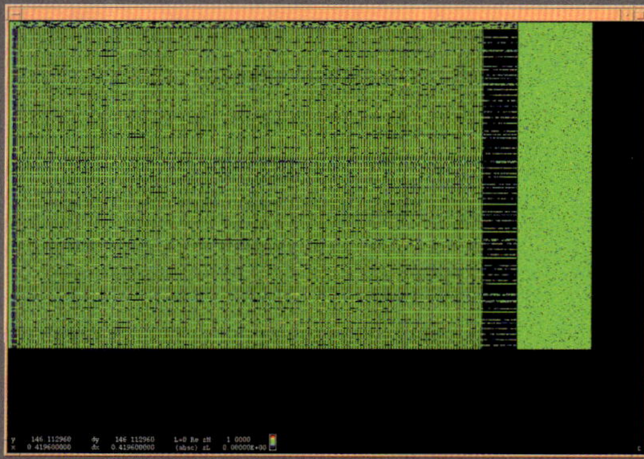

#4

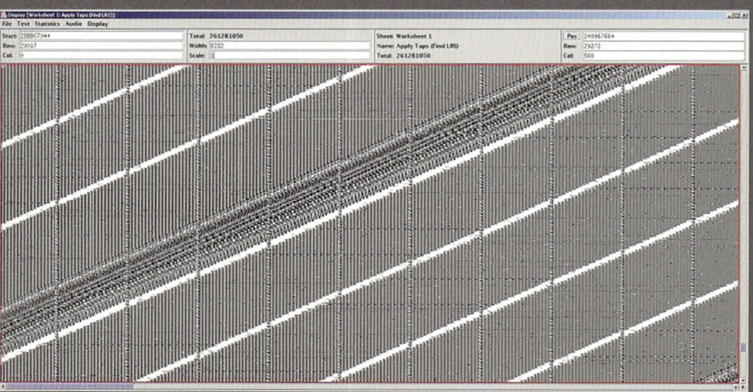

#5

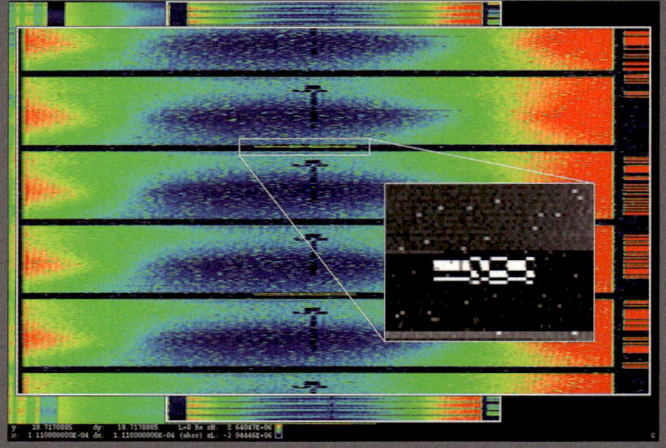

#6

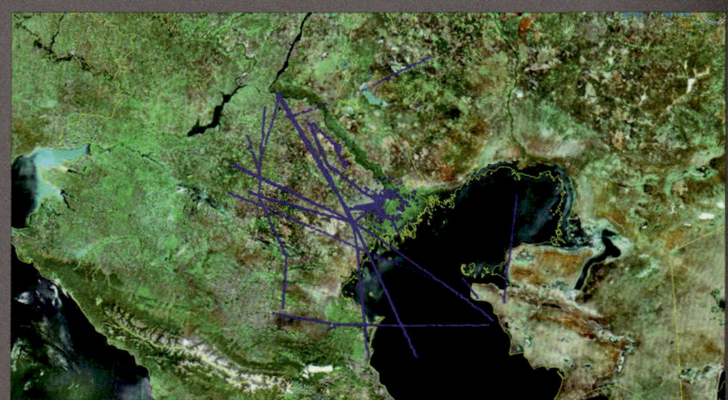

#7

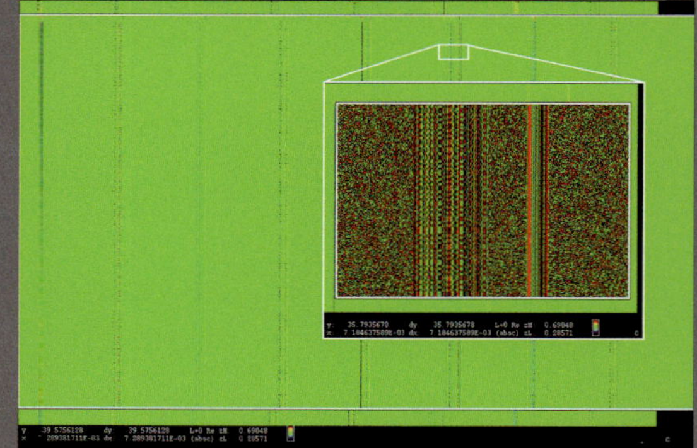

#8

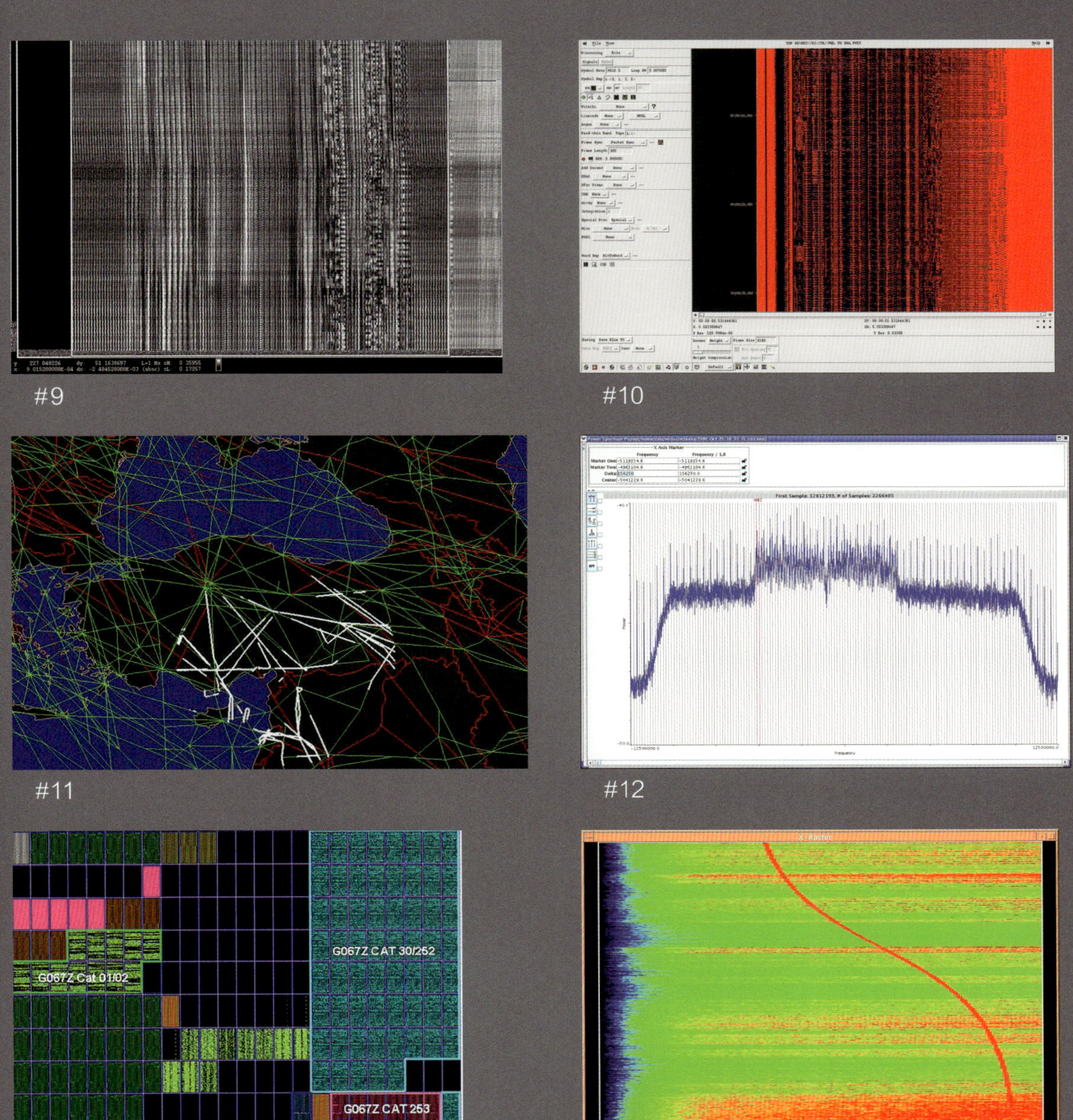

Image #1:   Data feed with Doppler tracks from a satellite, intercepted May 27, 2009.
Image #2:   Israeli drone video feed, intercepted June 10, 2009.
Image #3:   Air traffic control signals, intercept date unknown.
Image #4:   Israeli drone feed, intercepted February 24, 2009.
Image #5:   Unidentified signal from an Israeli source, intercepted January 23, 2009.
Image #6:   Air traffic control data plots near Astrakhan, Russia, intercepted date unknown.
Image #7:   Data feed from a French satellite, intercepted March 30, 2009.
Image#8:   Unidentified signal from an Israeli source, intercepted April 15, 2009.
Image #9:   Signal from an unidentified source, intercepted April 5, 2009.
Image#10:   Data feed from a drone, intercepted July 7, 2009.
Image#11:   Air traffic control data plots near the Turkish-Syrian border, intercepted date unknown.
Image#12:   Data burst, intercepted October 25, 2009.
Image#13:   Commercial satellite feed, intercept date unknown.
Image#14:   Satellite feed with Doppler track, intercepted May 28, 2009.

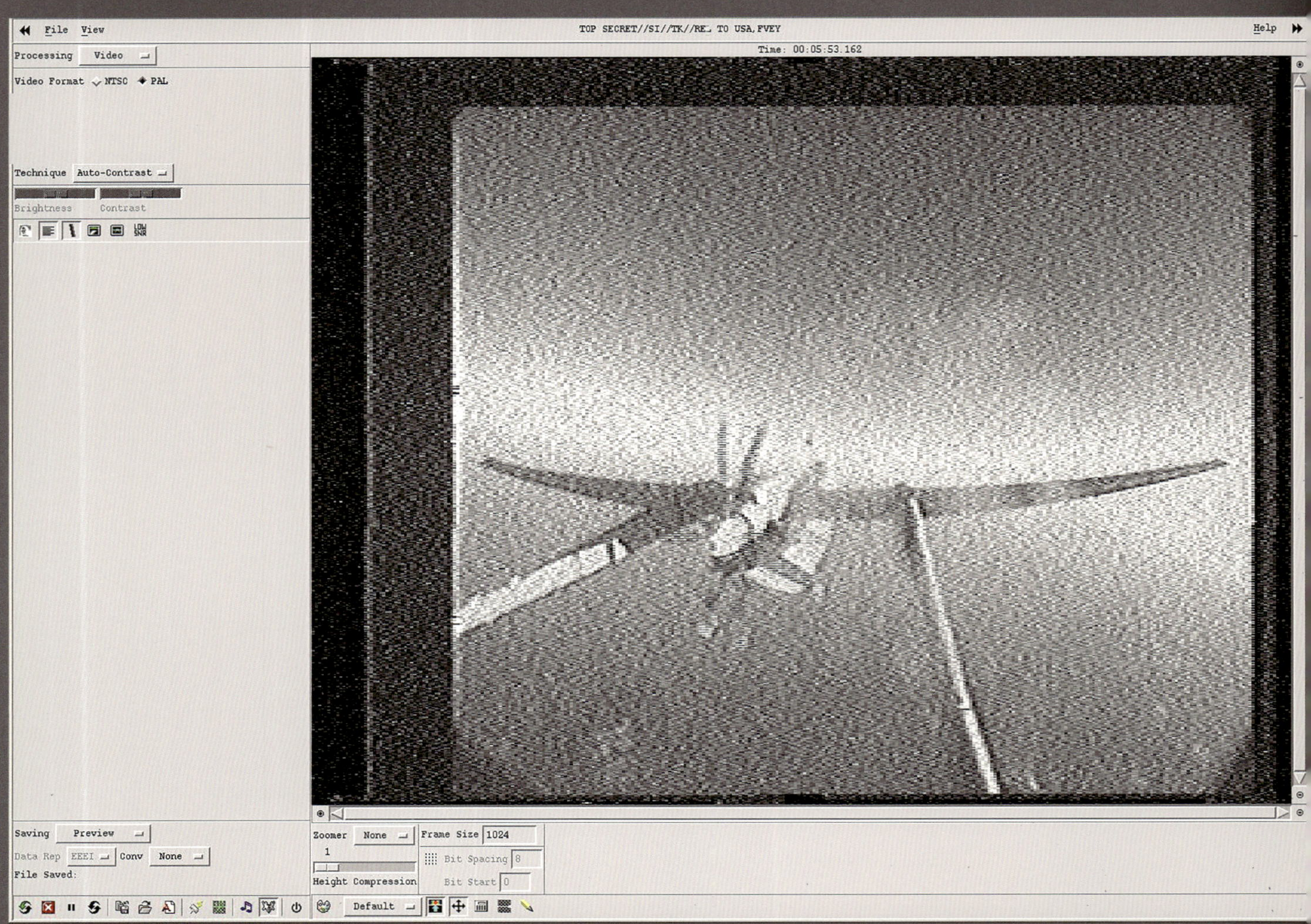
File View
Help
TOP SECRET//SI//TK//REL TO USA,FVEY
Time: 00:05:53.162
Processing Video
Video Format NTSC PAL
Technique Auto-Contrast
Brightness Contrast
Saving Preview
Data Rep EEEI Conv None
File Saved:
Zoomer None Frame Size 1024
1
Height Compression
Bit Spacing 8
Bit Start 0
Default

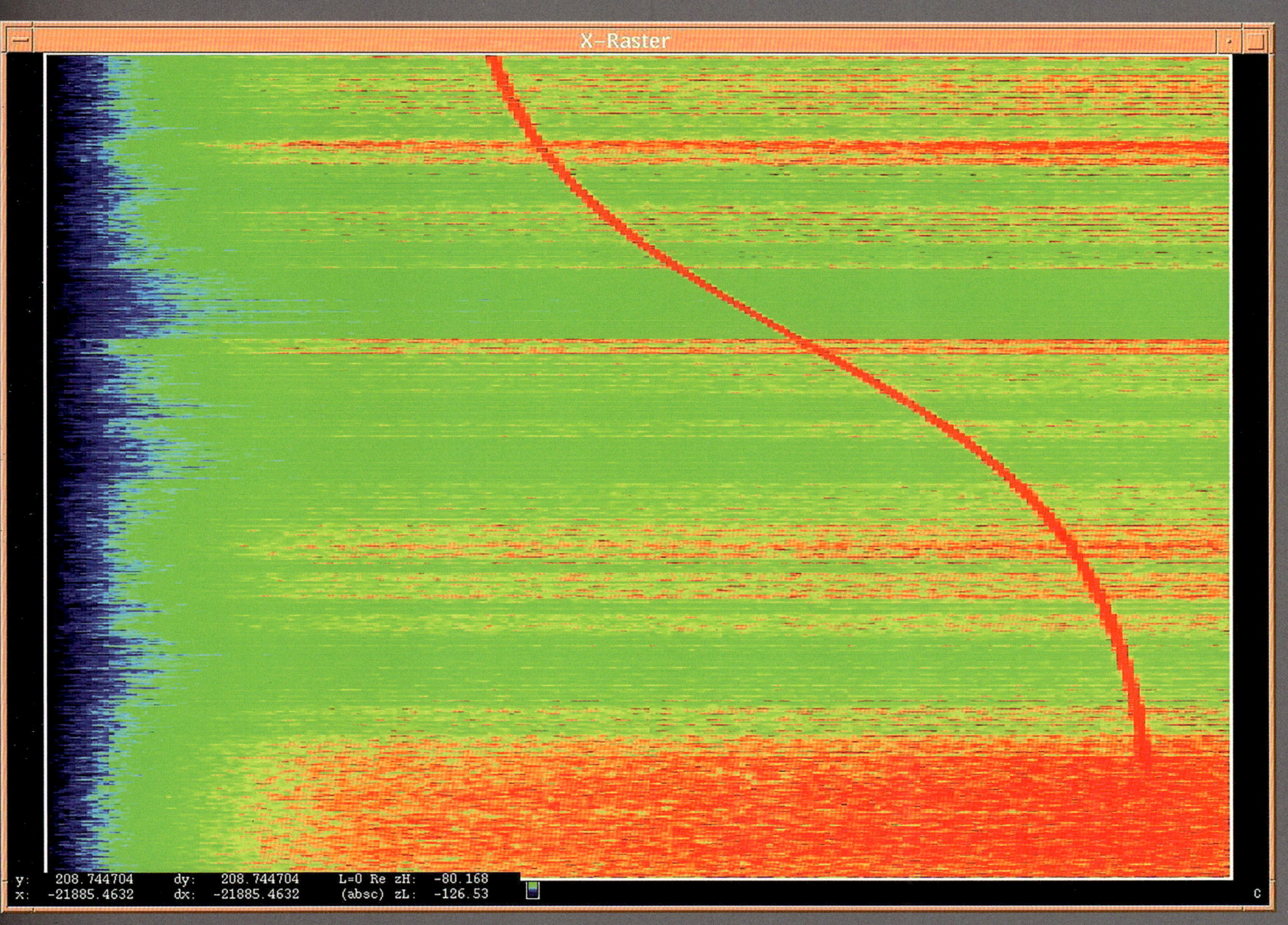

X-Raster
y: 208.744704   dy: 208.744704   L=0 Re zH: -80.168
x: -21885.4632   dx: -21885.4632   (absc) zL: -126.53

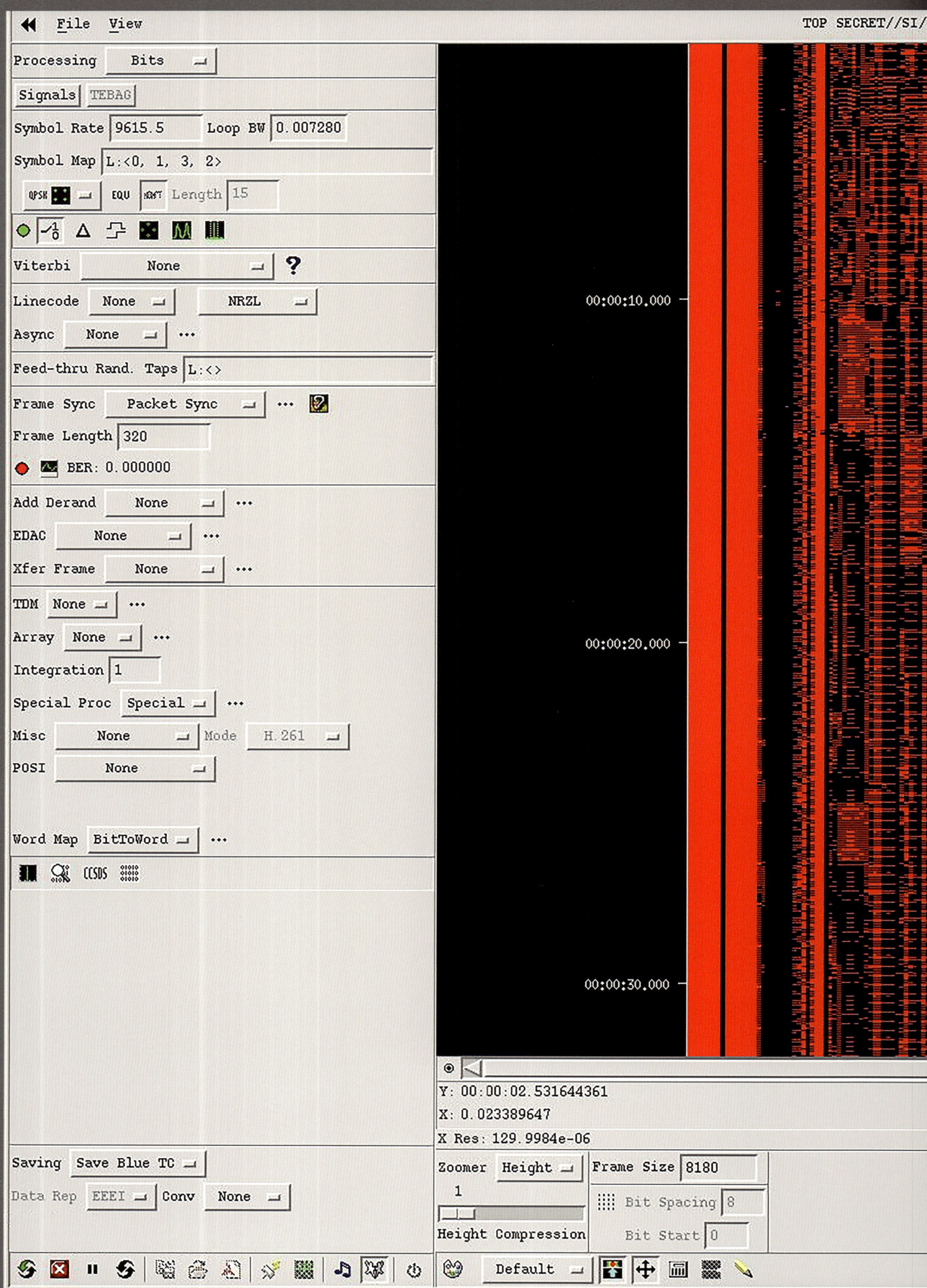

File   View
TOP SECRET//SI/
Processing   Bits
Signals   TEBAG
Symbol Rate 9615.5   Loop BW 0.007280
Symbol Map L:<0, 1, 3, 2>
QPSK   EQU   Length 15
Viterbi   None   ?
Linecode   None   NRZL
Async   None   ...
Feed-thru Rand. Taps L:<>
Frame Sync   Packet Sync   ...
Frame Length 320
BER: 0.000000
Add Derand   None   ...
EDAC   None   ...
Xfer Frame   None   ...
TDM None   ...
Array None   ...
Integration 1
Special Proc Special   ...
Misc   None   Mode H.261
POSI   None
Word Map BitToWord   ...
CCSDS
00:00:10.000
00:00:20.000
00:00:30.000
Y: 00:00:02.531644361
X: 0.023389647
X Res: 129.9984e-06
Saving Save Blue TC
Data Rep EEEI   Conv   None
Zoomer Height   Frame Size 8180
1
Bit Spacing 8
Height Compression
Bit Start 0
Default

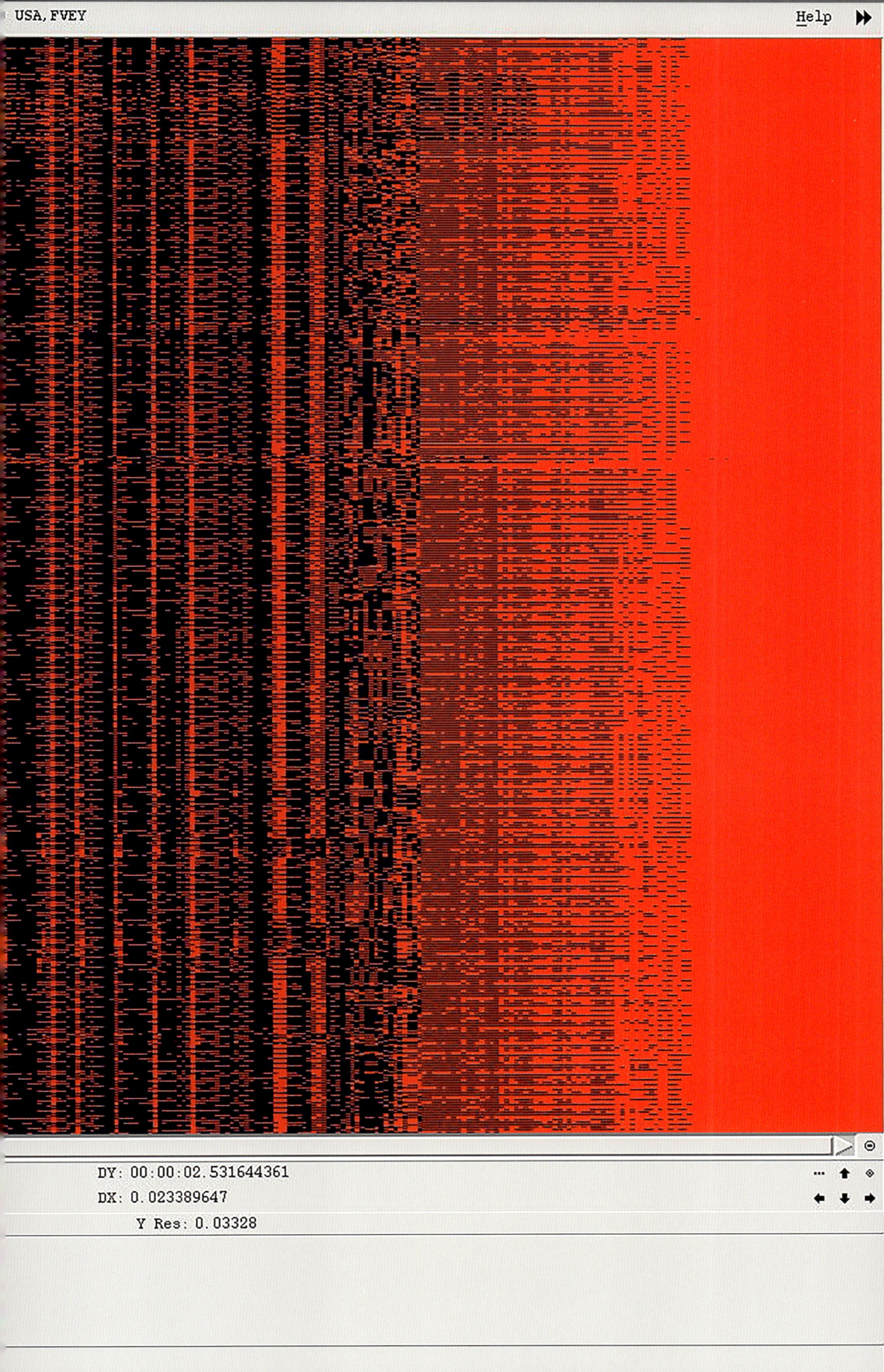
Help
DY: 00:00:02.531644361
DX: 0.023389647
Y Res: 0.03328

II —ART¬
The Snowden Templates¬

● **Julian Oliver**

This work is based on published Snowden files.
It retains the logos and graphics of the initial
NSA documents, but deletes the original text,
replacing it with a manual for do-it-yourself fill-
out. The resulting template is made available as a
writable LibreOffice document. The art work thereby
enables you to create 'your own NSA disclosure',
including descriptions of the secret bureaucratic
megastructure. It invites people to use them to irritate
journalists, testing their vigilance and integrity, or
just to feed our relentless, fist-eating paranoia that
the NSA leaks might actually be a part of a vast
and evil Alternate Reality Game designed by Glenn
Greenwald. After all, what do we know?

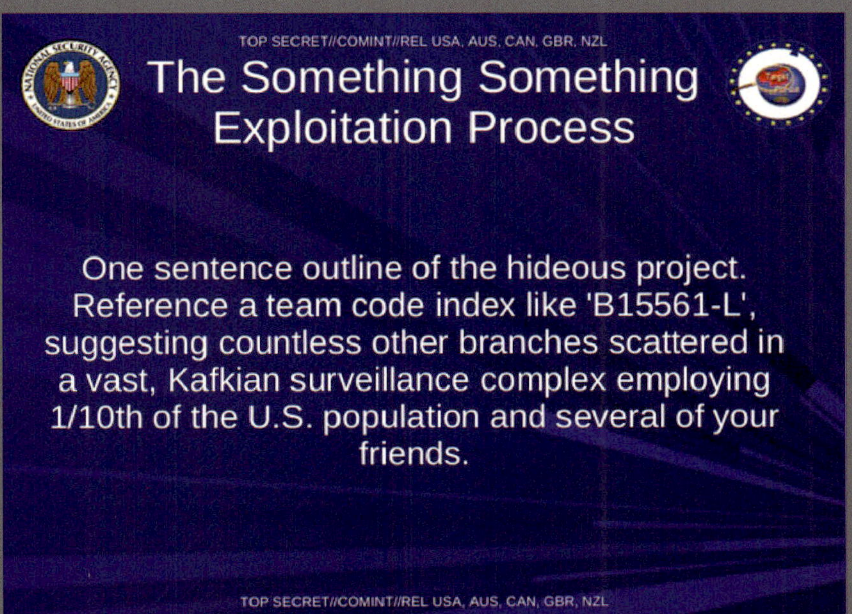
TOP SECRET//COMINT//REL USA, AUS, CAN, GBR, NZL
The Something Something
Exploitation Process
One sentence outline of the hideous project.
Reference a team code index like 'B15561-L',
suggesting countless other branches scattered in
a vast, Kafkian surveillance complex employing
1/10th of the U.S. population and several of your
friends.
TOP SECRET//COMINT//REL USA, AUS, CAN, GBR, NZL

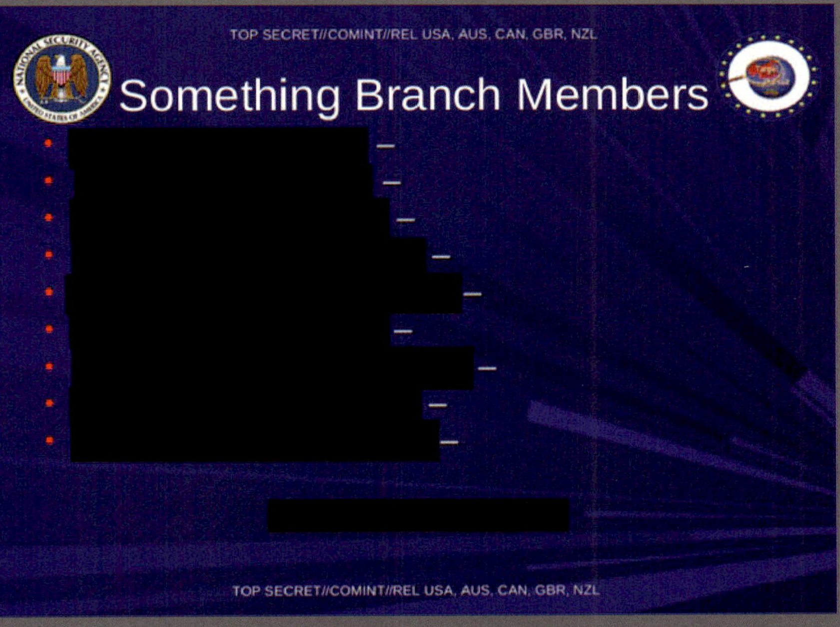
TOP SECRET//COMINT//REL USA, AUS, CAN, GBR, NZL
Something Branch Members
TOP SECRET//COMINT//REL USA, AUS, CAN, GBR, NZL

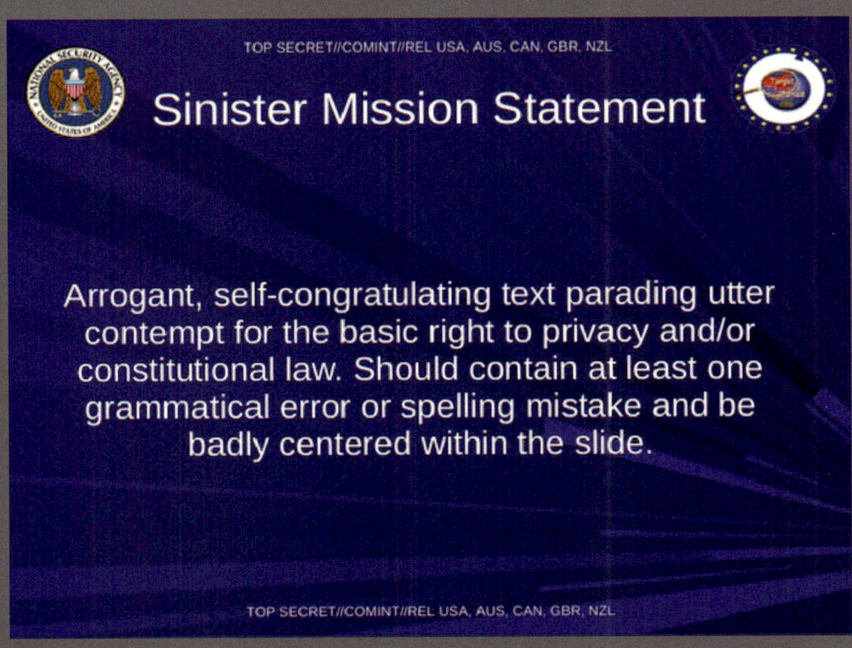
TOP SECRET//COMINT//REL USA, AUS, CAN, GBR, NZL
Sinister Mission Statement
Arrogant, self-congratulating text parading utter
contempt for the basic right to privacy and/or
constitutional law. Should contain at least one
grammatical error or spelling mistake and be
badly centered within the slide.
TOP SECRET//COMINT//REL USA, AUS, CAN, GBR, NZL

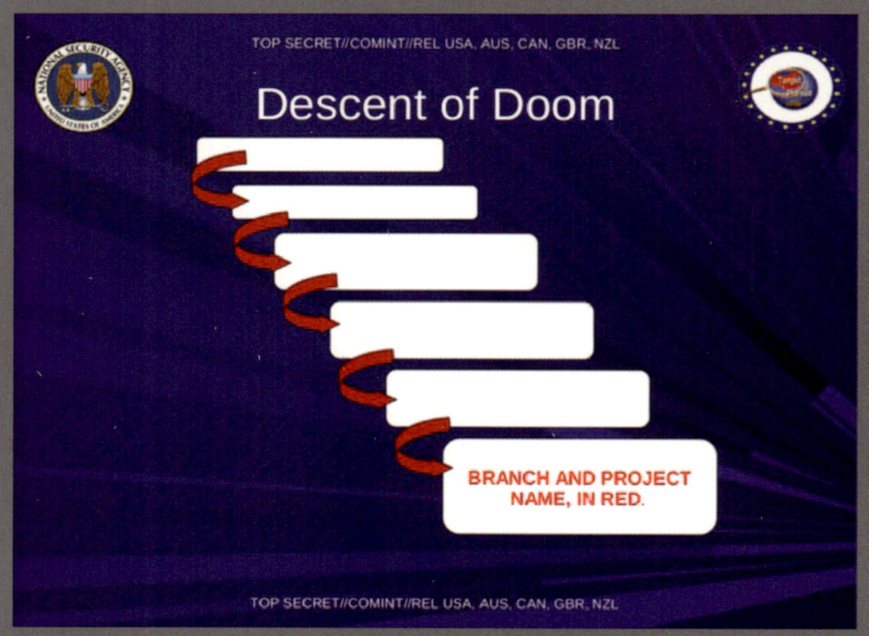

TOP SECRET//COMINT//REL USA, AUS, CAN, GBR, NZL
Descent of Doom
BRANCH AND PROJECT
NAME, IN RED.
TOP SECRET//COMINT//REL USA, AUS, CAN, GBR, NZL

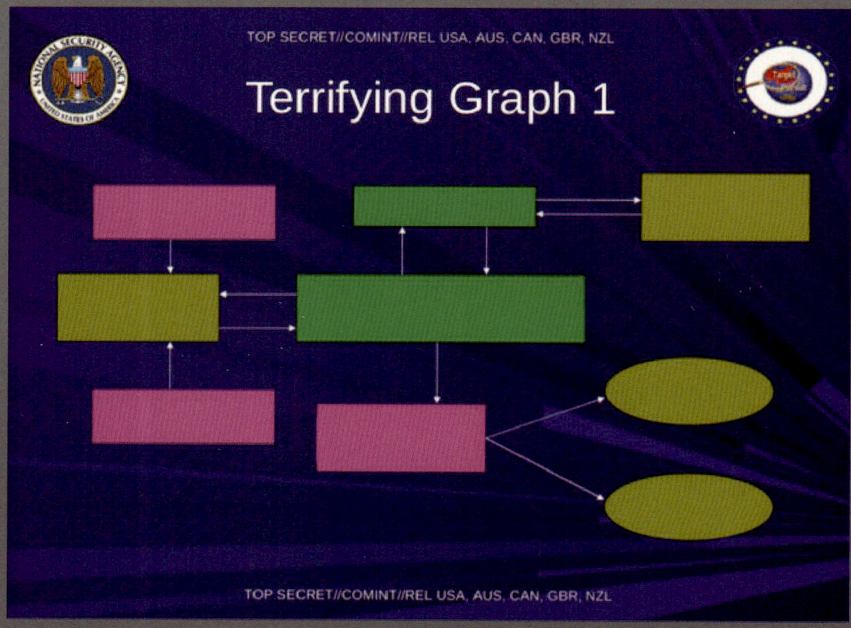

TOP SECRET//COMINT//REL USA, AUS, CAN, GBR, NZL
Terrifying Graph 1
TOP SECRET//COMINT//REL USA, AUS, CAN, GBR, NZL

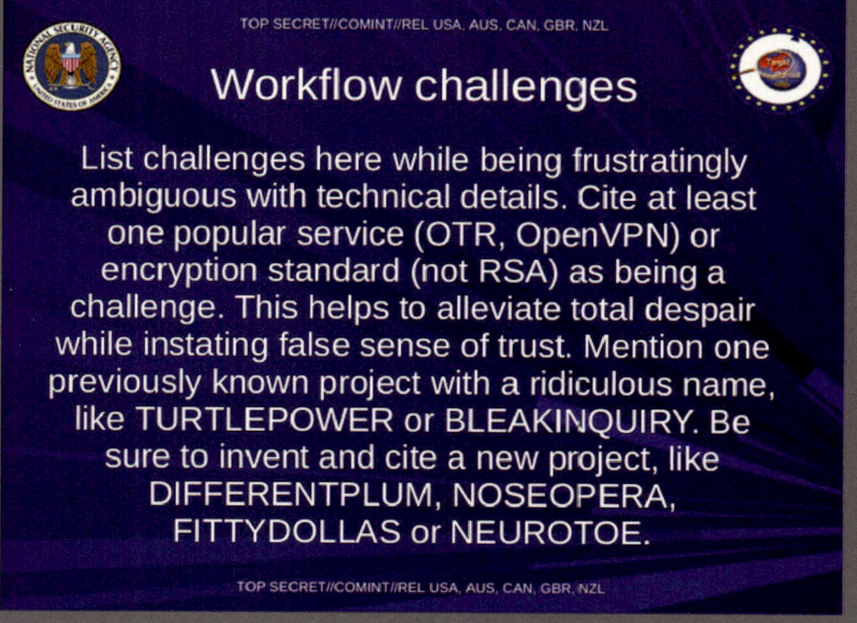

TOP SECRET//COMINT//REL USA, AUS, CAN, GBR, NZL
Workflow challenges
List challenges here while being frustratingly
ambiguous with technical details. Cite at least
one popular service (OTR, OpenVPN) or
encryption standard (not RSA) as being a
challenge. This helps to alleviate total despair
while instating false sense of trust. Mention one
previously known project with a ridiculous name,
like TURTLEPOWER or BLEAKINQUIRY. Be
sure to invent and cite a new project, like
DIFFERENTPLUM, NOSEOPERA,
FITTYDOLLAS or NEUROTOE.
TOP SECRET//COMINT//REL USA, AUS, CAN, GBR, NZL

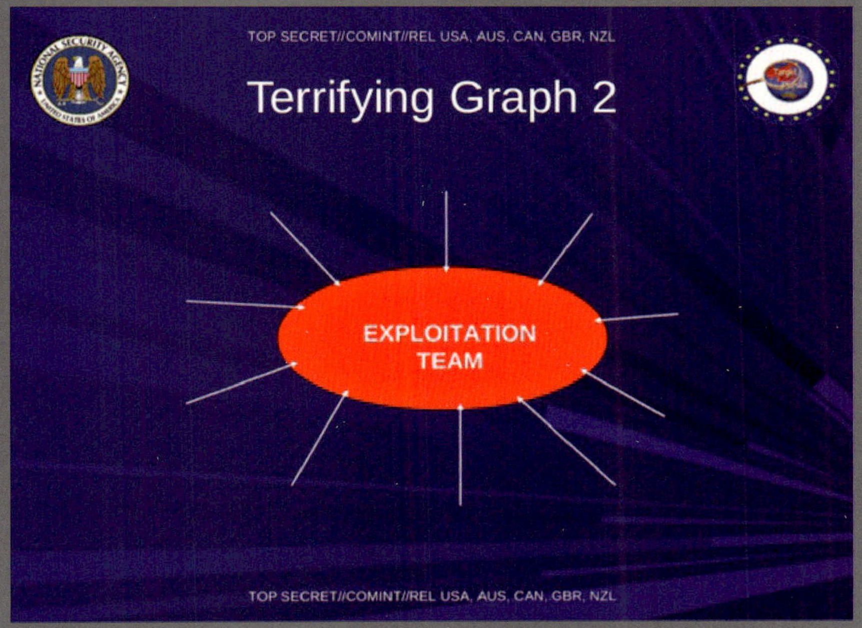

TOP SECRET//COMINT//REL USA, AUS, CAN, GBR, NZL
Terrifying Graph 2
EXPLOITATION
TEAM
TOP SECRET//COMINT//REL USA, AUS, CAN, GBR, NZL

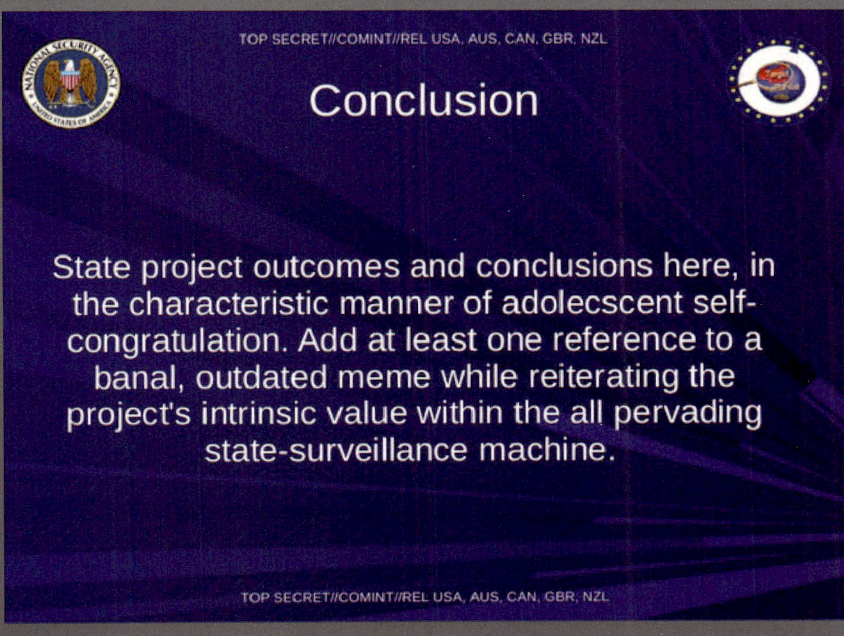

TOP SECRET//COMINT//REL USA, AUS, CAN, GBR, NZL
Conclusion
State project outcomes and conclusions here, in
the characteristic manner of adolecscent self-
congratulation. Add at least one reference to a
banal, outdated meme while reiterating the
project's intrinsic value within the all pervading
state-surveillance machine.
TOP SECRET//COMINT//REL USA, AUS, CAN, GBR, NZL

ssible to
embers
society '

ld in
mon "

TRANSFORMATION
OF THE
SNOWDEN Files
into
COMMONS

Snowden files
to public libraries

digital + analog
public records

Multi-stakeholder
Collaboration

umer
vocacy

Civil
society

Journalism
Academia
Activism
Libraries

What do actors
in the field of
... provide ?
a) files
b) other actor

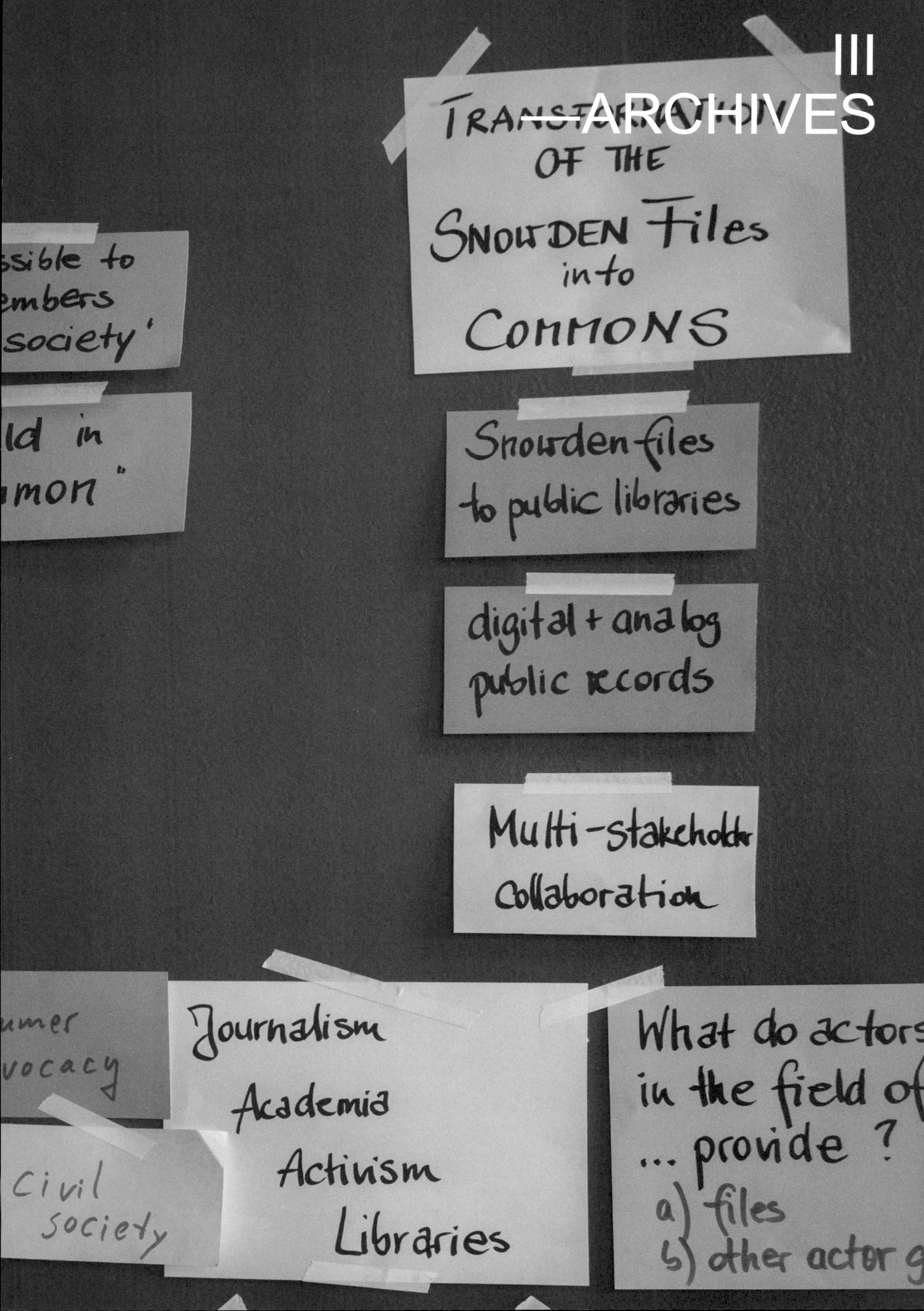

III
—ARCHIVES¬
How Civil Society Actors are Archiving the Snowden Files¬

Text
by Corinna Haas and Krystian Woznicki

Various initiatives around the world have been working doggedly to organize and archive the Snowden documents since their leak in 2013. But what are the well-thought-out approaches of each group, and how do they go about the immense task of wiring their obscure collections with the nervous system of the general public?

To begin with, Snowden's disclosures are providing proof of what many previously only guessed at. For populations that are increasingly mobile, life is being played out under a secret service microscope, with far-reaching implications for freedom and democracy. Refusing to accept the new evidence passively, various initiatives were set up shortly after the first wave of disclosures in 2013; their focus was on archiving the Snowden files that were being published by Der Spiegel, The Guardian, The New York Times, etc. Doing this has become a form of resistance to the democratic imbalance created by, on the one hand, an unrestricted intelligence service complex doing whatever it wants and, on the other, a media house network that is also not really accountable to the public.

In the early months, when the various initiatives working to archive Snowden files in the USA, Europe, and Canada were unaware of each others' activity, the Berliner Gazette organized several events at transmediale 2016 that provided the first occasion for a representative group of archiving initiatives to meet and discuss their efforts, paving the way towards cross-collaboration with the aim to better understand their own pioneering work. The question in the room was: what imperatives do we have in common? First, someone has had to preserve the files in a systematic manner. Second, someone has had to care about making them available to the public in a sustainable fashion. Third, someone has had to approach some of the pressing problems that have arisen as regards the particular method of leaking the classified files.

The method by which Snowden made the information public made it possible for it to be mishandled in some cases: Snowden entrusted the documents to a handful of selected journalists who – on this basis – created stories that in turn have been retold by a great number of media outlets all over the world. Source documents were not always disclosed or made available. Instead, it is often possible to find only the journalistic substrate of documents, not the documents themselves. But even with regard to the published files there are problems: they have been scattered across different media house platforms, which impedes systematic research. In addition to that, their status has been insecure from the outset: as we know from the past, what search engines can easily find today may by tomorrow be irretrievable from the internet. The accessibility and long-term availability of the Snowden files has not been dealt with to date.

Archive for the future

The archiving initiatives intend to counteract the blind spots of the publication process: their proponents have "recognized the political and contemporary-historical significance of the Snowden disclosures", as Geert Lovink, media theoretician and founder of the Amsterdam-based Institute of Network Cultures, highlights. They want to make the published documents available to the legitimately interested general public. They want to secure and process them in such a way that they, and all that they imply, become understandable. Journalists, teachers, scientists, activists, lawyers, and other actors should be able to browse through the documents, work with them in their own spheres, and use them to support their own forms of civil education and resistance. Not least, the archives need to be set up for the future, secured as historical evidence.

To address these goals, the grassroots archiving initiatives have taken on tasks traditionally carried out by archivists and librarians: gathering published materials and sources, offering access, providing guidance, and managing preservation – tasks which, taken together, may be referred to as "curating". The self-made archivists also bring scattered documents together and connect them with secondary sources such as media reports. They develop categories to use when classifying and indexing documents, and apply a range of search and filter options to make them browsable and searchable. They create glossaries and guides to ease access for users. They create mirror sites to safeguard the archive, and in one case an offline version is being maintained.

While the archive initiatives have similar overall aims, the very different contexts they operate in mean they cater to potentially different audiences. "Snowden Document Search" is a comprehensive Snowden document database run by the Courage Foundation, a foundation that has taken on the legal and media representation of whistleblowers. Naomi Colvin built the archive with programmer and activist M.C. McGrath. The platform maintains an ongoing listing of disclosures, allows users to find documents with the help of various filter options, and offers some of the most advanced archiving tools. A project launched by Maria Xynou, "Surveillance Without Borders", demonstrates very concretely what can be done with such an archive. Using the Snowden documents as a basis, the project illustrates how the securitization of the data sphere functions worldwide. The types of monitoring specific to each country are visualized with Google Data Maps.

WikiLeaks forerunners

The "Snowden Digital Surveillance Archive" was created in a very different context: the world of academic and journalistic organizations in Canada. The initiator is information scientist Andrew Clement, Professor Emeritus at the University of Toronto, where for more than thirty years he has been conducting so-called surveillance studies, along with pioneers of this field such as David Lyon. The archive was developed in cooperation with Canadian Journalists for Free Expression (CJFE), where it is also hosted. Published Snowden documents are added on a continuous basis and made accessible based on various search categories. A glossary facilitates the reading of documents. In this, it is actually quite similar to the "Snowden Document Search". Yet, as the context in which it has been set up differs, it not only has different political and social implications – here, it is quite evidently the institutional framework that endows the initiative with respectability, elevating it from the precarious spheres of online activism to proto-official status. It also attracts other uses: the Snowden Archive-in-a-Box demonstrates, in turn, another possible application of such an archive. It is the offline version of the Snowden Digital Surveillance Archive, under the care of Evan Light as part of a post-doctoral fellowship at Concordia University. The box offers protected and thus anonymous access to Snowden documents.

Tally Update, the third noteworthy archiving initiative, was launched by Cryptome.org. The project, widely regarded as the forerunner of WikiLeaks, can be called the mother of all digital leak platforms. John Young and Deborah Natsios, two architects from New York, have been operating the project in their spare time for more than 25 years. They are digital activism pioneers who place a strong focus on transparency requirements for intelligence services; their main medium is an online archive. Growing and expanding in scope over the past three decades, it has become one of the most important and controversial resources in the online world. Emerging from within the cypherpunk movement in the early 1990s, inspired by and inspiring the interdisciplinary art and culture scene in New York, it has a very bold and otherworldly look and feel – resembling list-based artworks more than conventional archives. This background also plays a role in the context of their efforts to collect the published Snowden files. On the one hand, they have much in common with the other archive initiatives in Canada and Europe, also seeing themselves as collectors, custodians, and guides. On the other hand, their work has a strong agenda that partly derives from the cypherpunk movement as well as transparency activism, e.g., they are vehement supporters of open access to the entire collection of documents leaked by Snowden, and they are radical mass media critics – mainly due to the fact that only a small percentage of the material that Snowden compiled has been made public.

Tally Update offers no search function but has a unique taxonomy. All documents are filed chronologically, as well as by media and publishing location. In the first years the archive has been logging new documents more quickly than others and consequently may have in that respective period the most authentic files, since it may be assumed that documents, even those already published once as a source, have been tainted by retrospective editing and re-uploading. The archive also has a number of revealing and somewhat ironic features, such as infographics that address questions like: How long will it be until all the Snowden documents become available? How old will all the participants be then? Or, who has made money with the Snowden disclosures and how much?

User guides with data protection tips

These archives represent an attempt to bring heterogeneous documents together and prepare them in such a way that they can be easily accessed and understood. Technical changes or other modifications are sometimes necessary. Because all of the archives except the Snowden Archive-in-a-Box are online, they have a common data protection problem: accessing them is impossible without risking being monitored. An important desideratum is thus the development of user guides with security tips, as well as building alternative access points including offline or even printed material. All the initiatives share the frustration of having neither reliable criteria to verify the authenticity of documents nor a feeling for the collection as a whole. Too many documents are still missing. The big question in the room is: what is still hidden in the collective unconscious of the Snowden leaks?

Since approximately one thousand documents have been published, so far it is possible to get at least a vague idea of what the complete Snowden archive may look like in twenty years. The documents are very heterogeneous; there are presentation slides, scribbled graphs, lists, text, and more. They are teeming with incomprehensible terms and abbreviations. Names of companies that worked for the NSA, the Five Eyes network and its partners are coded. In addition to search tools, a research and reading strategy is necessary to develop a real understanding of the documents. But what is the right one? Andrew Clement recommends beginning randomly: sooner or later someone will run into a document that fascinates them; they can then decrypt it using the glossary codes and gradually become more intensively engaged with the material.

The journalist and activist Sarah Harrison, one of the key figures at WikiLeaks, offers advice for deeper searches. Instead of searching first for specific topics — so-called "text mining" — it is better to develop a sense of the sorts of materials being dealt with, whether they are internal communications or correspondence between business partners, that is, the byproducts of everyday operations. They should be viewed as predecessors or updates to other documents; they have an episodic character and are always part of a series. There is much in them that is implicit because the addressee's prior knowledge is assumed. A topic that is interesting should be widely "read around" so that one becomes as conversant as possible with its context.

Indexing methods and search tools

Maintaining a critical distance is also important. Many statements are likely to correspond to a subjective worldview on the part of the authors. It is advisable to be wary of ideologically slanted statements, which include euphemisms, clichés, and the circumnavigation or omission of controversial issues. Metadata – namely, what the document says about itself according to its publication date and other data – must be taken into account to read a particular document with accuracy. Though Harrison's comments refer primarily to the Public Library of US Diplomacy (PlusD), her tips can be applied just as effectively to the Snowden documents. Perhaps the initiators of the Snowden archives will include such advice in their user guides.

We believe that such efforts are the key to the success of an archive. What is an important, indeed historical, resource worth if it is not broadly accessible? This work cannot be handed over to experts; if so, it would then have to be delegated to intelligence services, since only they understand the language deployed in the documents, and only they really understand what is being

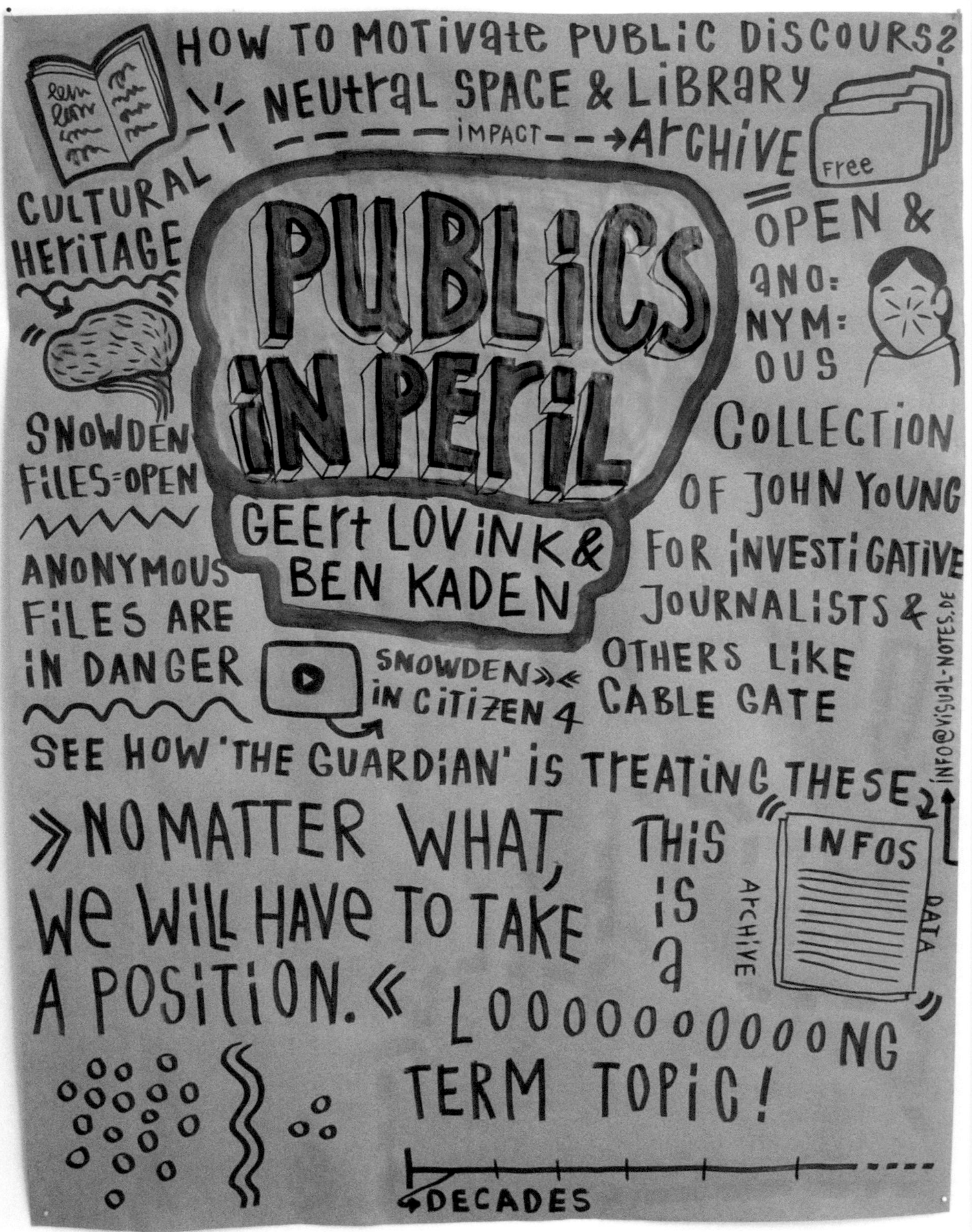

HOW TO MOTIVATE PUBLIC DISCOURS?
NEUTRAL SPACE & LIBRARY
IMPACT
ARCHIVE
Free
CULTURAL HERITAGE
PUBLICS IN PERIL
GEERT LOVINK & BEN KADEN
OPEN & ANONYMOUS
COLLECTION OF JOHN YOUNG FOR INVESTIGATIVE JOURNALISTS & OTHERS LIKE CABLE GATE
SNOWDEN FILES = OPEN
ANONYMOUS FILES ARE IN DANGER
SNOWDEN IN CITIZEN 4
SEE HOW 'THE GUARDIAN' IS TREATING THESE
INFO@VISUAL-NOTES.DE
»NO MATTER WHAT, WE WILL HAVE TO TAKE A POSITION.«
THIS IS A LOOOOOOOOOONG TERM TOPIC!
INFOS
ARCHIVE
DATA
DECADES

spoken of in each case. Thus the archive must be opened in a way that is, to a certain extent, comprehensible to the wider public, and then mediated accordingly.

Aspects of mediation include indexing methods and search tools. The archive's accessibility is improved through indexes and metadata. In addition, original documents can be linked to related news and media reports. A glossary that decrypts company code names, for example, as well as comprehensive search options, facilitates a better understanding of government monitoring programs in their entirety. In that way, the archive is aimed not only towards researchers and journalists, but also to a broader public.

Becoming a part of pop culture

The Snowden Archive-in-a-Box offers a special feature for public accessibility. As an offline archive, it provides secure access with no monitoring risk. The archive is saved on a mini computer (Raspberry Pi) and can be reproduced inexpensively. The network can therefore be installed almost anywhere and used in all sorts of places. Taken together, its research features, offline access, and mobility make it easy to shift the archive from the circles of archivists and activists to a wider public. As a piece of art, it can be presented at exhibitions, schools, political education institutes, public and scientific libraries. It can therefore become, as stated by its initiator Evan Light, a part of pop culture, or even the commons.

Visualization also plays an important role. The visual nature of Surveillance Without Borders, which provides maps showing monitoring worldwide, contributes a great deal to public accessibility. But what is particularly interesting is the organization of material. Surveillance Without Borders

classifies the documents based on groups of people who are the objects, or actors, of monitoring. Six categories were developed: "political leaders", "companies", "cooperation between companies and intelligence services", "cooperation among intelligence services worldwide", "mass surveillance of citizens", and "targeted surveillance of citizens, either groups or individual persons". All documents are assigned to one of the six categories and catalogued according to country so that targeted objects and actors can be searched for in specific states and regions. This approach makes groups of people, countries, and securitization processes visible, providing a local point of entry and the opportunity to be active at a local level. The aim of Maria Xynou, initiator of the project, is to coordinate and support such interested groups.

These approaches are inspiring because they can address a variety of specific groups, thereby contributing to the wider dissemination and popularization of the Snowden documents. Above all, they show: archives do not have to remain a passive resource. This is of particular importance for archives that deal with a type of collective unconscious, that, as in this case, is the product of secret partnerships among intelligence services and the IT industry, and with the complicity of internet users. The Snowden files potentially reveal things that society would have never known about itself or its future. By collecting and organizing, by archiving and mediating the files, civil society actors as diverse as artists, activists and researchers can establish a basis for recuperating this secret knowledge. They can thereby help create tools with which we can actively shape the future.

"Conditions are different than in 1971 when the Pentagon Papers became public."¬

Andrew Clement
Interview by Magdalena Taube

Could you introduce yourself briefly?
My name is Andrew Clement and I am a professor emeritus. I have recently retired from the University of Toronto where I was in the Faculty of Information. My background is in computer science. With a number of colleagues I initiated and built the Snowden Digital Surveillance Archive. I have been interested for a long time in questions of surveillance, particularly since 9/11, studying questions regarding surveillance within our information and communication apparatus, especially on the internet. So when Snowden's documents started coming out, in June 2013, it felt like they landed right in front of me. I was immediately really interested in them. They confirmed many of the suspicions that we had already about what was going on.

Why is it difficult yet important to archive the Snowden documents?
I think the documents that Snowden leaked and that have been published are of historic significance. Primarily in terms of what they reveal about how our states operate – particularly those of the Five Eyes countries. These include Canada, where I'm from, along with the US, the UK, Australia and New Zealand. The Snowden files show a surveillance and security apparatus that has been operating within our states' democratic institutions which is largely out of democratic control. There is a lot of evidence that it has been acting outside the law, unconstitutionally, that there is little oversight, and that they now have the capability, as well as the desire, to capture all of the electronic communication that we are now producing in very abundant quantities. Since, really, our lives depend on this communication the importance of these issues should be obvious.

Our very lives are now under the microscope. It is not just terrorists that they are after. There is a whole range of threats that secretive state agencies want to take into account. This has many consequences for people. Even if they are not doing anything wrong, they may be reluctant to speak their mind, they might be concerned about who they affiliate, associate, and even talk with. So, we see it has a 'chilling' effect generally. I think most fundamentally these agencies are operating outside of our democratic institutions and so Snowden's revelations point to a threat to the democracy that we rely on.

While you could say that my initial motivation to develop the Snowden archive was relatively personal and academic, there is something else that is also very important: Only through a major collective investigative effort drawing on multiple perspectives can we adequately come to grips with scope, consequences and remedial possibilities of mass state surveillance. An archive such as our Snowden Digital Surveillance Archive would be an essential resource in this effort.

Are there any lessons to be learnt from history?

Looking at groundbreaking leaks, especially with regard to how society managed (or not) to archive them, we can learn from history. For me the most relevant prior leak that had great social significance was whistleblower Daniel Ellsberg's publication of the Pentagon Papers. Making public authoritative internal documents about the Vietnam War that showed that officials were routinely lying about the motivations and state of the war played an important role in public opposition to the war and the eventual US withdrawal.

The Snowden documents have potentially a similar power because they too show in detail shocking government activities and bald lying by public officials. Conditions are of course different than in 1971 when the Pentagon Papers became public. There was already a strong social movement opposing the Vietnam war to which the Pentagon Papers added fuel. At present, while there are vigorous civil society organizations fighting for privacy, transparency and other human rights, a broader social movement opposing state surveillance is relatively nascent, and still quite weak. The potential value of the Snowden leak is to help in coalescing and broadening this social movement.

Furthermore, there appears to be have been more dissent in 1971 among the upper political strata than is the case now, making the challenge of changing direction even more formidable. With Donald Trump becoming US President, the urgency is greater, but fortunately it appears that resistance movements are emerging and uniting. However, to achieve sustainable reforms around mass state surveillance, we need to promote and inform the public debate around the Snowden leak and what it reveals about the secret mass state surveillance.

What is the challenge for the general public?

Now that we know our state security agencies are conducting fine-grained surveillance of everyone's electronic activities, we as a society have very serious choices to make about the appropriate role for secretive security agencies in a democracy.

If we do nothing, then we will have accepted de facto that our everyday lives are open to scrutiny by unaccountable government agencies. This I believe is inimical to the foundations of democracy and we run a high risk of becoming police states. Reining in these agencies and eliminating those aspects which are not justifiable is a very difficult, but necessary task. It can only be accomplished when substantial numbers are well enough informed about the existing surveillance practices and the threats they pose, to take effective remedial action.

Given the secrecy and complexity of the practices involved, public education about mass surveillance is vital. This is something that I have been pursuing in my research for several years, especially around the IXmaps.ca project that seeks to show people the paths their data takes across the internet and where it may be intercepted by the NSA.

Let us come back to the initial idea of developing an archive for the Snowden documents. Could you elaborate on the impetus behind it?

Firstly, I wanted a searchable archive of the Snowden documents for my surveillance research, so I could better locate and identify surveillance sites of the NSA and its Five Eyes partners that I could include in the on-going IXmaps work. It seemed like a pretty obvious idea, so I was surprised I couldn't find such an archive already available. I had some research funds, and looked for someone in my Faculty's Archive and Records Management specialization who was interested in the subject matter that I could hire.

I was fortunate to find George Raine, a trained archivist who had recently graduated from our masters program. George was keen to be involved in the project, had many of the necessary skills and was up for learning what else was needed. Jillian Harkness, another student in the program, also contributed to building the archive.

More generally it struck me that many other opportunities were opened up by the Snowden documents that could lead to academic and journalistic research and reporting that weren't addressed by the media coverage to date. Apart from Glenn Greenwald's book "No Place to Hide", reporting has consisted almost entirely of (rightfully) sensational stories based on a relatively small handful of documents newly released with the article. The ability to see an individual document in a wider context and to pursue threads across the whole range of documents makes a more penetrating inquiry into the driving forces and overall nature of mass surveillance possible.

Why is it difficult to build these kinds of archives? When you built yours did you encounter any specific problems?

Well, there are several difficulties in creating the archive. First, the documents are scattered across the sites of various media publications, so they all have to be tracked down and stored. As is typical of collections of heterogeneous documents, they are in varied formats, and some have to be converted to standard formats suitable for both readable presentation as well as automated character recognition to enable indexing and text searching.

But I think the really challenging issue is how to make the documents available in a way so that people can make sense of them – they are often difficult to understand. Security intelligence is a very complex area, filled with arcane language and codenames that hide the important actors, e.g. the telecom companies that collaborate with the NSA to enable interception of the traffic on their networks.

The archivist helps with this by providing aids to both finding and comprehending information – such as classification schemes, keywords, a brief description of each document and a glossary of commonly used terms. This requires learning some basics about the subject matter, but there are obvious limits to what an archivist can do in this regard. There is still much more to deciphering the complex, arcane and coded language of security intelligence, and then there is making the connections between documents and drawing inferences. So that is where I think the difficulty is; it is not so much getting the documents out there into an archival form, but rather, what do we do next with them.

Could you describe the archive's architecture?

Given my primary goal of promoting an open, informed public debate, I intended from the beginning to create a widely accessible on-line archive under free/ open licenses.

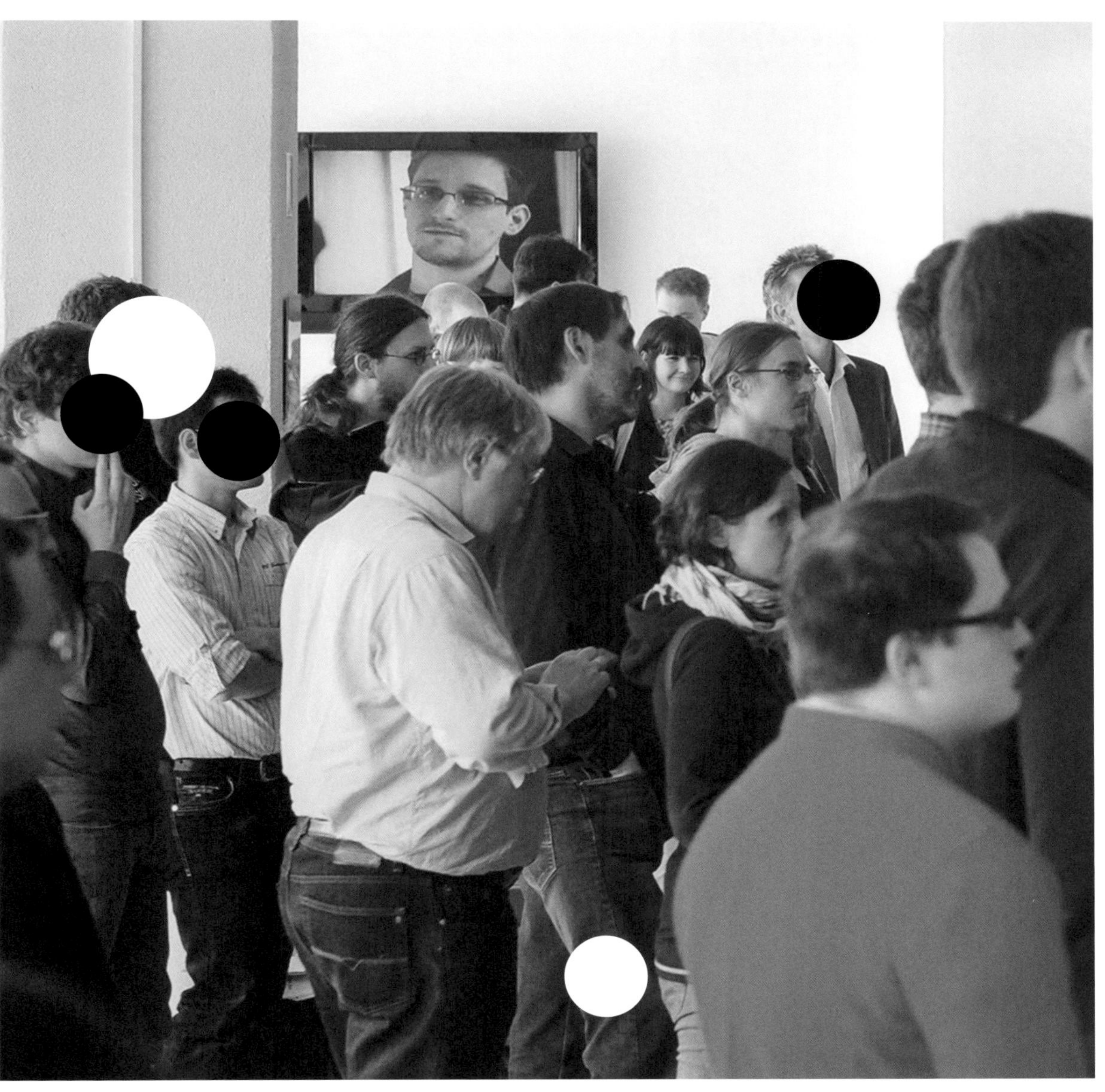

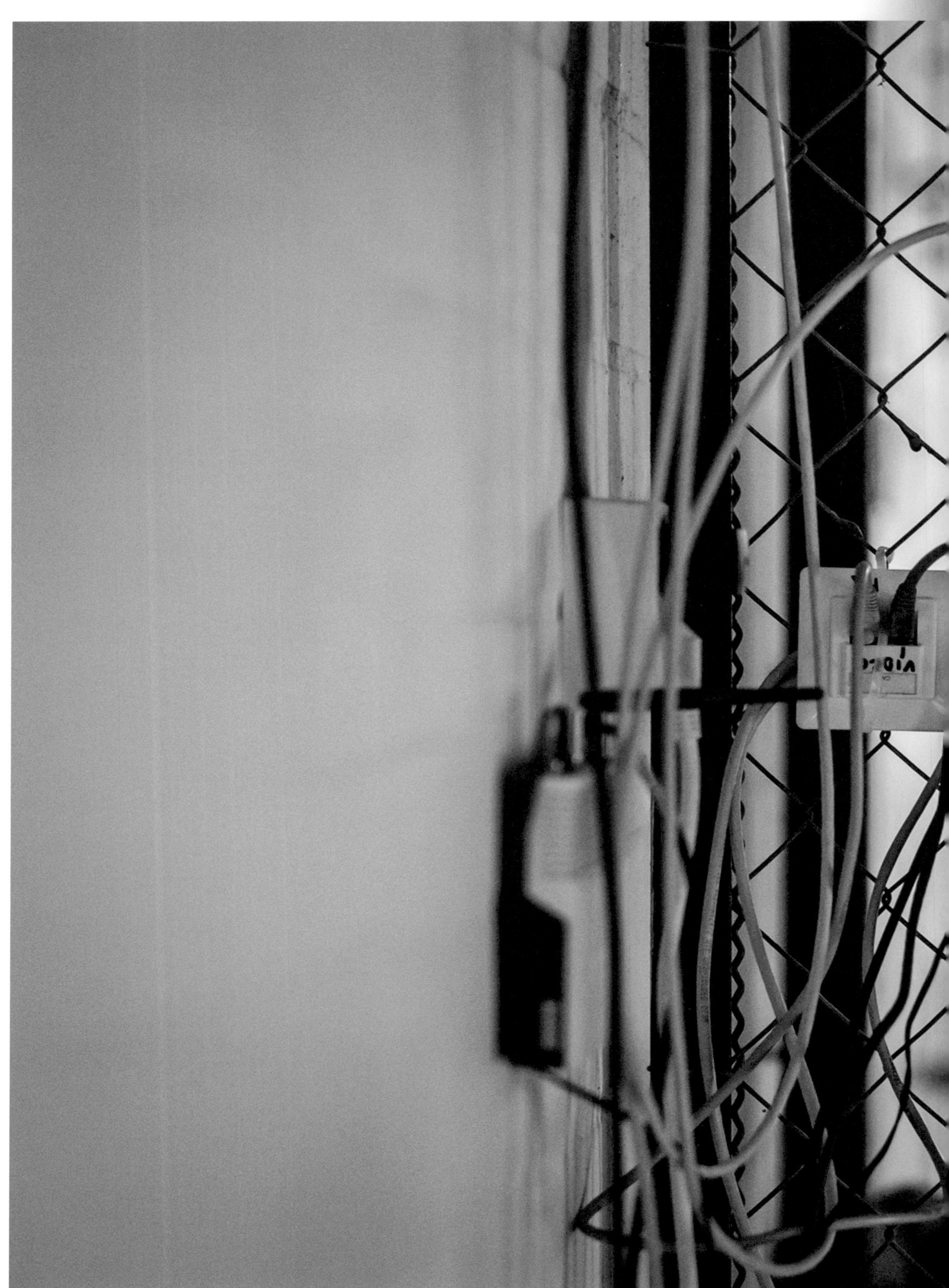

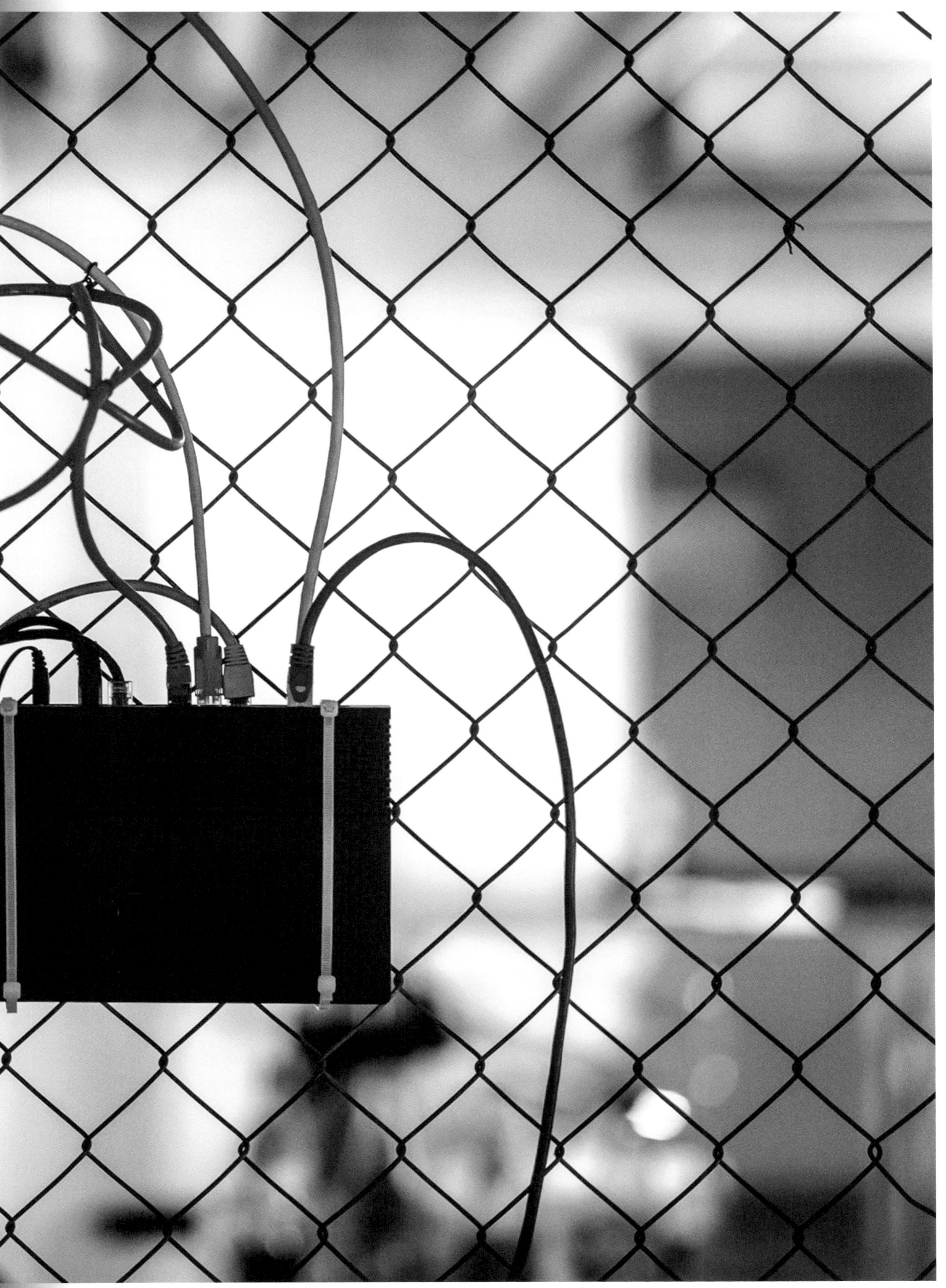

The Snowden Digital Surveillance Archive is built using Greenstone, a suite of open source software for building and distributing digital library collections. It is produced by the New Zealand Digital Library Project at the University of Waikato, and developed in cooperation with UNESCO and the Human Info NGO. It is widely used around the world for digital library initiatives, especially in developing countries. We recognize that Greenstone does not have many of the features of more recently developed digital archive platforms. Once we get a better sense of the needs of archive users we may consider porting to another platform.

The Snowden Digital Surveillance Archive that is available on the Canadian Journalists for Free Expression (CFJE) website has been highly customized. Documents are described according to a custom metadata schema that is sensitive to contextual elements of the Snowden documents that are not present in most other document collections, such as security classification codes and distribution markings. The look and feel of the collection, including the format of the document descriptions have also been very heavily modified from the standard Greenstone template.

The vast majority of documents released by the media are PDF files. In their original form, there were a lot of PowerPoint files and other proprietary formats. The newspapers did work for us by releasing them in PDF and PDF/A, which are both very widely used, open-source formats. We determined that there was little likelihood that PDF files would become obsolete in the foreseeable future. If they do, it is easy to retrieve the documents from the collection and re-upload them in a different, more widely used format.

What can people actually do with these kinds of documents?

Since there are so many documents it is hard to generalize. But one of the things that you might do with these documents is to identify the main actors – the companies, the organizations, and government partners – in your own country or region that have been working with these spy agencies, and to draw public attention to them. Asking them what they are doing with your data, why they are collaborating with these agencies and generally call them to account. They need to tell us and we need to know. We need to strip away some of that veil of secrecy and hold them to the norms and rules of law and constitutionality.

What about linking the online archive to offline archives?

Actually there is an initiative to develop an offline Snowden Archive-in-a-Box, led by Evan Light, now an assistant professor in Communications at York University in Toronto, where he works on privacy, surveillance and telecom issues.

The Snowden Archive-in-a-Box is an autonomous version of the fully text-searchable Internet-based archive Snowden Digital Surveillance Archive. It is a stand-alone wifi network and web server that enables anyone within reach of the wifi signal to research all the same documents available through the on-line version in the same way. The main purpose of the portable archive is to provide end-users with a secure, off-line method for individuals to use this database without the threat of exposing their activities to mass surveillance.

The Snowden Archive-in-a-Box began as part of a touring European project called Performigrations, which focuses on migration/immigration and was launched in Montreal at the Blue Metropolis literary festival in April 2015. An evolving project in its own right, a current version of the portable archive also includes a surveillance demonstration apparatus that monitors wifi traffic around it and plays it back to the public. In June 2015, it was showcased at the

Biografilm festival in Bologna, Italy – in partnership with Performigrations – and at the Citizenship and Surveillance Conference in Cardiff, Wales. A Snowden Archive-in-a-Box was built for Cambridge University and used in teaching by their sociology department and there are on-going discussions to develop installations in Canadian university libraries.

What is the role of public libraries in this context?

I would like to see the Snowden Digital Surveil Archive become more than a passive resource, namely also a site for collaborative research and deliberation. Libraries certainly have an important role to play, especially public libraries as they go beyond their more conventional role of making materials accessible and devote more attention to facilitating discussion and deliberation within the communities they serve based on these materials.

My own university library contacted me about conserving materials related to our Snowden archive (specifically saving the media articles that published the documents to the Internet archive). We are also hoping that libraries will host a mirror of the entire Archive. Establishing mirroring sites is desirable in several ways. Besides improving accessibility and technical stability through redundancy, it also provides local users like students access to the collection without exposing their search traffic to internet interception as well as expresses solidarity with the ideals of open access to controversial but socially relevant materials.

We have approached other universities as potential mirror sites, but so far this has been stymied by the concern that the documents may represent 'stolen goods' and so possessing them could be a criminal violation – at least in Canada. While the chance of prosecution is very small and a case in favor of hosting the documents could be made, legal departments in several universities have balked. Going directly through the libraries themselves looks to be a better prospect. They both have the necessary technical capabilities and appear more oriented than university administrations to preserving academic freedoms around contentious holdings.

How could the Snowden documents be transformed into knowledge commons?

Our current focus is on ensuring that the archive is accessible to all, reliable, easy to use, accurate and updated as new documents are published. However, to realize its potential as a 'knowledge commons' around the issue of state surveillance, it also needs a community of engaged users who will conduct research based on the archive and give wider public meaning to its contents. Ideally this would include people who can provide insightful annotations, contribute additional relevant documents, host mirror sites, stimulate conversations, initiate collective research ventures, etc. While extending the software to support such distributed collaboration and animating the wider conversation is beyond our abilities at the moment, hopefully there are others who are willing and able to take this on.

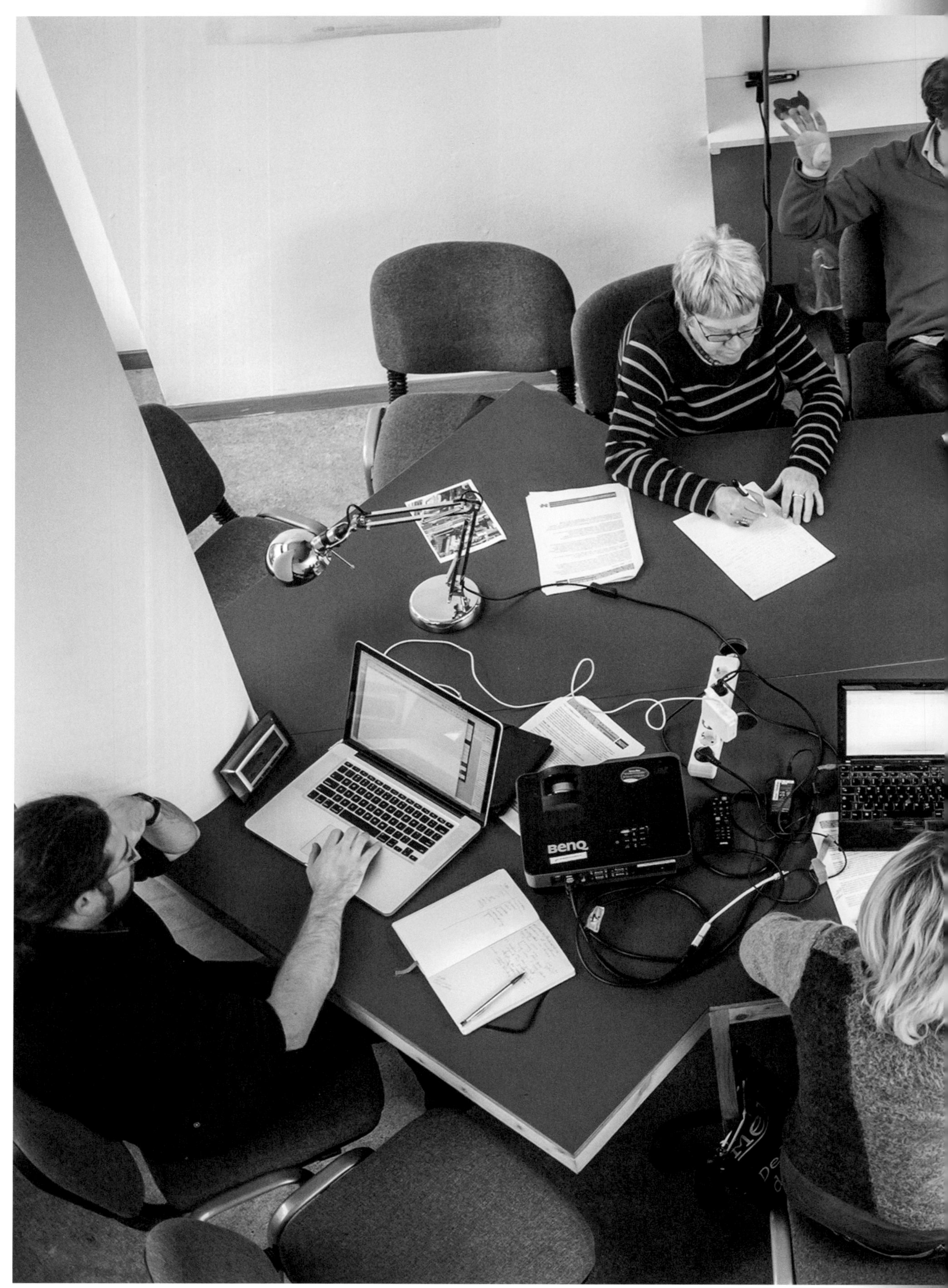

BenQ

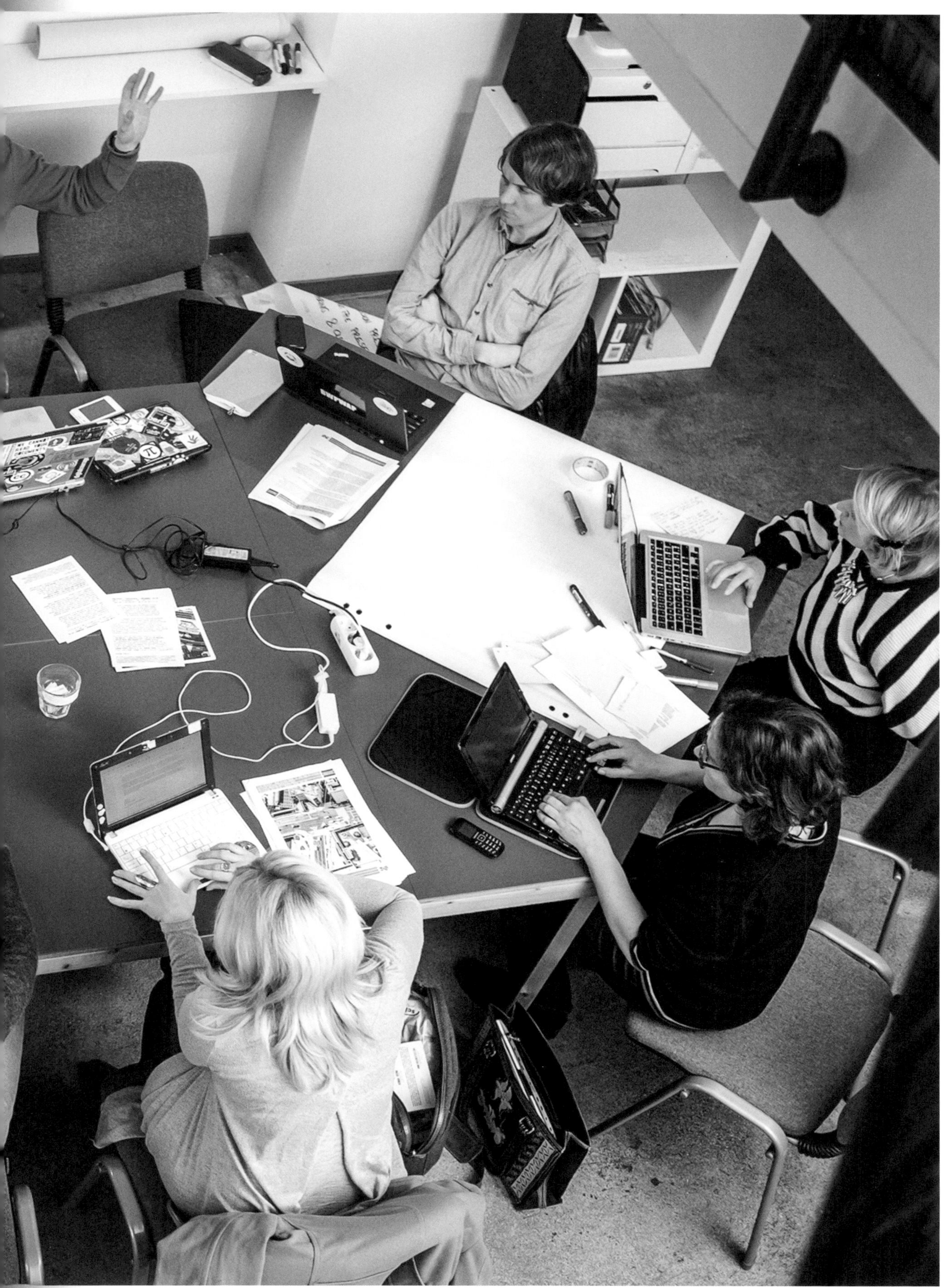

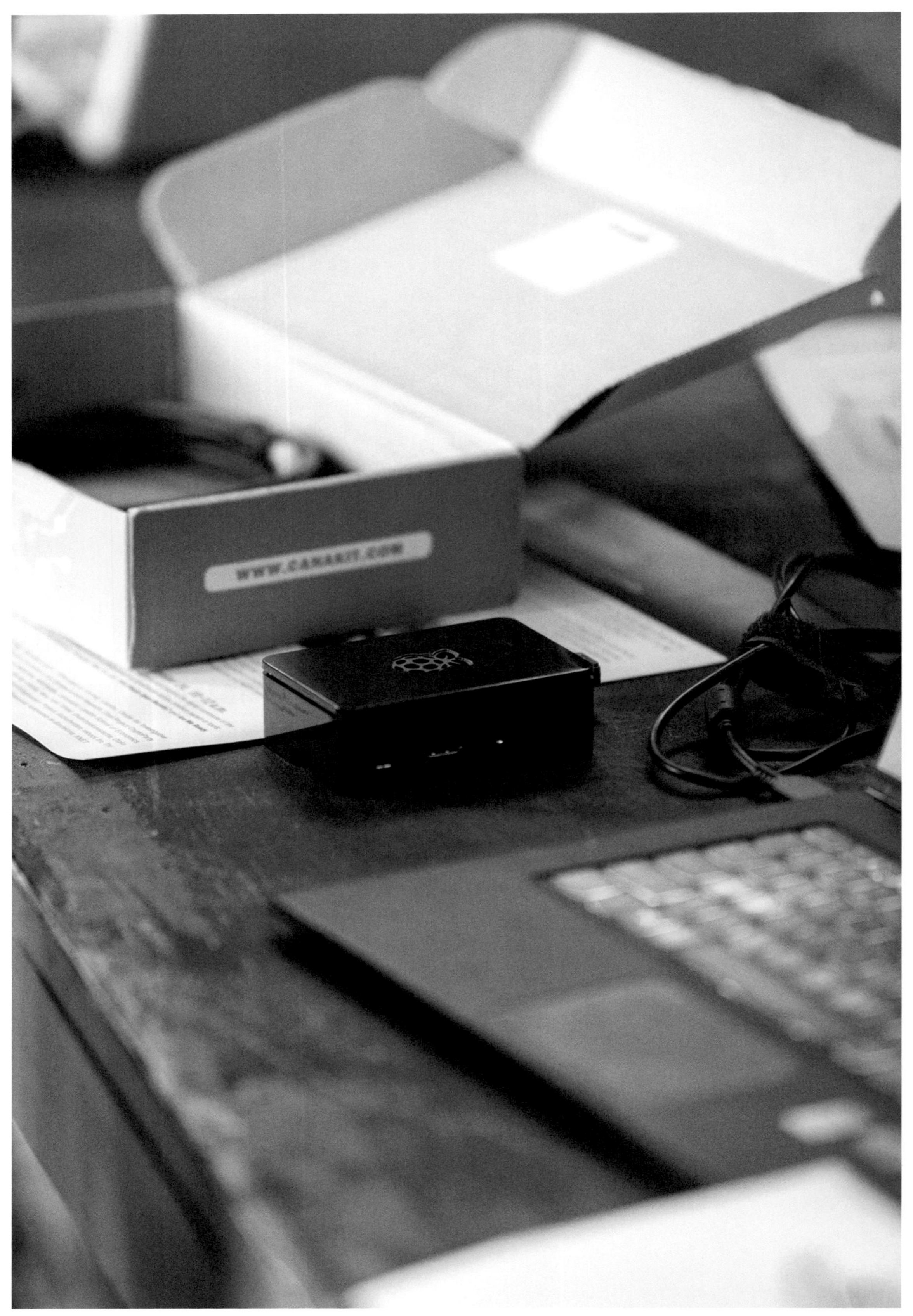
WWW.CANAKIT.COM

III
—Archives¬
"Our archiving will hopefully lead to direct social and political action"¬

Naomi Colvin, M.C. McGrath and Maria Xynou
Interview by Magdalena Taube

Could you briefly introduce yourself?

NC: My name is Naomi Colvin. I work for the Courage Foundation – an organization that protects and defends the interests of truth tellers who put themselves at risk to make significant contributions to the public record. We run Edward Snowden's defense fund and part of the work we do for him is maintaining a list of the revelations which have resulted from his incredibly brave act. Because of that I have been working with the people of Transparency Toolkit on creating the Snowden Document Search.

Why do you think it's important to have an archive?

NC: I think it's important to have an archive because these are documents of considerable historic and public policy importance. We hope that they will lead to direct social action and political action. In order for that to happen, you really need to have them in one place

where people can search through them. Now, people can browse through them in many different ways. If you think about the method by which the documents were published, basically you have odds and ends, which accompany particular articles. The actual documents that have been released, have been released in fragments all over the place and they are angled toward making a particular point.

When you look into it closely, you have a situation like this: a section of a document is initially released and then more and more sections of the same document follow over time. The user has to look at all of these sections and put them together. On a very broad level, these are the kind of problems we have been dealing with. This kind of fragmentation has been the biggest challenge for us on a conceptual and technological level.

What can people actually do with your archive and what do you hope people will do with it?

NC: It's supposed to be a way that people with an interest in a particular issue can easily find the source documents. There might be many different source documents, related to that particular issue. Our document search helps you to go through all of the Snowden documents that have been released so far by using key words. You can also use particular code names. For example you can easily find all the documents that related to the PRISM program. We also have coded them regarding topics, so you can see all the documents that relate to encryption and beating encryption, for example. It would be great to know a little more about how the search has been used so far, we haven't been concertedly keeping those records. But, from anecdotal evidence, we know that people from NGO's have been using it, people making legal cases challenging aspects of surveillance have been using it and it has been of interest to researchers as well, as well as journalists. But there is certainly a bit more work to be done on that front.

*

Could you briefly introduce yourself?

MMG: I'm M.C. McGrath and I work on Transparency Toolkit. We focus on helping journalists, researchers, and activists collect information and then make software to help them understand that information. And one of the projects that we are working on as part of this, in collaboration with Courage Foundation, is the Snowden Document Search. The aim is to make it easier to go through all of the Snowden documents in one central location.

What is your personal relationship to the Snowden findings? Do you remember how you came across them?

MMG: I came across them shortly after they launched. I started following and just kept following them for about a year. I was interested in them but I didn't really do much with them. And then I thought it would be nice if there was a central repository for all of this – I assumed there must have been one already – since this is one of the most important sets of documents available today. I went looking for it and I didn't find anything, which was a huge surprise.

A number of journalists working on the Snowden story were talking to me about how there wasn't any central repository and it was really difficult for them in their work because they couldn't simply go find a document that they knew had been published. They had to go searching all over the internet to find it and it might not have been the right version. Because of this they said it would be nice if there was a central place for all of them. That is how I started working on this project.

And from a technological perspective, what were the difficulties that you encountered in building the archive?

MMG: The first thing we did was try to get a set of documents. This was before we started to work with Courage Foundation and we were working with the best lists available. We looked at the compilation that the Courage Foundation had put together, we looked at the EFF (Electronic Frontier Foundation) lists, and the ACLU (American Civil Liberties Union) list and we made a compliance set of documents. For some of the content we did some manual tagging, though a lot of it was automatic extraction.

We had to get all the documents and we had to get them into a machine readable form. We had to get the text of the documents, which is difficult to do. Then we had to figure out which fields to extract and how to extract them. After that we had to build the software so that people could search through the data. We initially built this search software for this project but we have since turned it into something that works with any data set, or multiple data sets.

Why do you think it's important to have a searchable archive of the Snowden documents?

MMG: If there is not a central, searchable archive then it's difficult to do anything with the documents that goes beyond what the initial revelations were in the article. And it's not possible to foresee the applications that a data set might have in the future. The context is constantly changing, new information is coming out all the time and we need to be able to refer back to the documents easily. There are many use cases that might not have been considered.

To have a central repository allows people to build legal cases, it allows programmers who are building tools to protect against certain attacks, by going to get the technical details from a certain location. It allows the journalists who are trying to look at the documents in a new light based on new revelations and legal changes to go back to the relevant material. It is impossible to do that unless the information is all in one central location.

Do you have ideas or suggestions how journalists or activists could work with the archive you built?

MMG: That really depends on the person that works with the archive and the documents. People could go and look at things relevant to their country if there is a particular topic they are interested in. And programmers who are interested in building privacy tools could go and look for different attacks that the NSA uses, and try to find the ones that aren't well defended against, or that the current tools might be vulnerable to. Lawyers could use it for legal cases, they could see how information in the documents matches the laws in different countries and possibly find areas where legal cases could be built. Journalists could go and

find news stories. I think there is a wide array but it depends on who the person is who is looking at it and what they are interested in doing with it.

*

Could you briefly introduce yourself?

MX: My name is Maria Xynou. In general I work with Tactical Tech but I have been working on this independent project called Surveillance without Borders. We used the Snowden Document Search by Courage Foundation to build our project. It is a resource that essentially tries to show how surveillance is being carried out based on the Snowden revelations. As part of this project, I have classified all the documents, I have done a lot of data collection based on them, and the final point was a visualization of a global data map which illustrates which revelations are more specific to each country around the world.

What kind of difficulties did you encounter when you set up your project?

MX: To be honest, the main difficulty was the data collection. In the beginning it was very exciting, but a lot of it can't be done automatically, it has to be done manually. When you are collecting data like intelligence agencies and country codes and things like that, you can automate that process. But then there are a lot of different types of data which you can't automate; like what kind of surveillance has been carried out, what type of data has been collected, why this is happening, and so on. For the various types of data that I wanted to collect but which I couldn't automate, the process was a little bit painful. Simply because there was so much but, at the time, it was all very exciting and interesting.

I can't say I have faced many other challenges because this is such a new project and it is also a work in progress. I don't see this as a final step, I see this as the beginning. Creating a resource that helps people to go through the documents and try to understand them in context. This is just one building block, just the beginning. And then I feel the next stage is to do contextual analysis, to match patterns and to put the pieces of the puzzle together, so to speak. And finally to take action based on the findings. I feel like the next stages are probably going to be much more challenging.

What would you wish that people would do with the resource that you have built?

MX: My first wish would be that people actually find it useful. Both in the sense of them understanding the data's relevance to the revelations and them using this data to take action. The reason why it is called 'Surveillance without Borders' and the reason why I focused on a global data map as a visualization is simply that I was hoping to encourage localized global efforts to increase transparency and accountability. Hopefully journalists all over the world in, for example, Gambia, Zimbabwe and Malaysia will be able to understand the documents even better based on their local context. And, based on that, if they have the right to a freedom of information request, maybe they will send more of those, maybe they will eventually get access to more information which they will be able to cross-reference. Maybe they can do campaigns, they can check the legality of these systems and take appropriate legal action. In short, the hope is that the information will actually be useful to researchers, academics, journalists, activists, and the public at large and that action will come out of this.

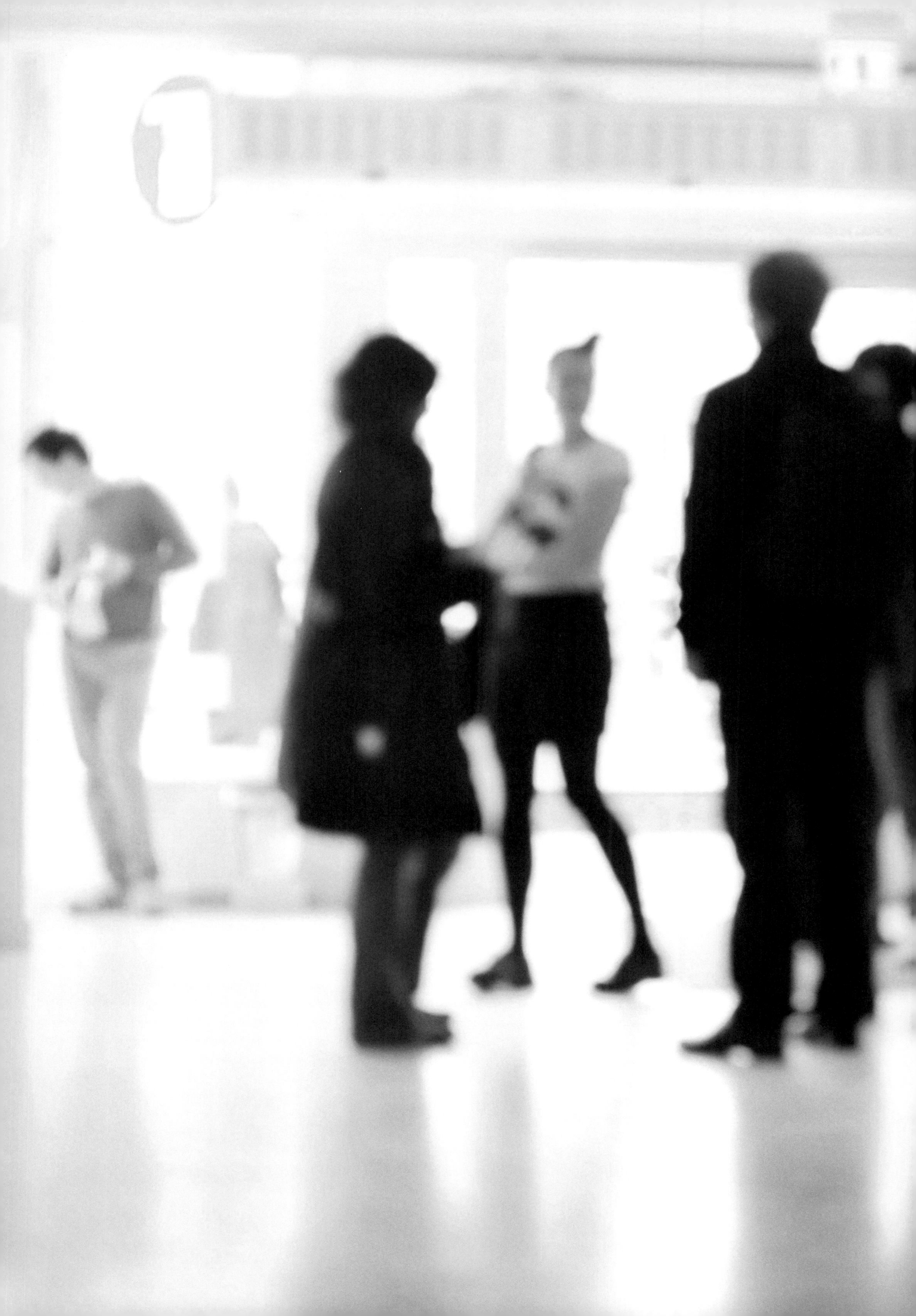

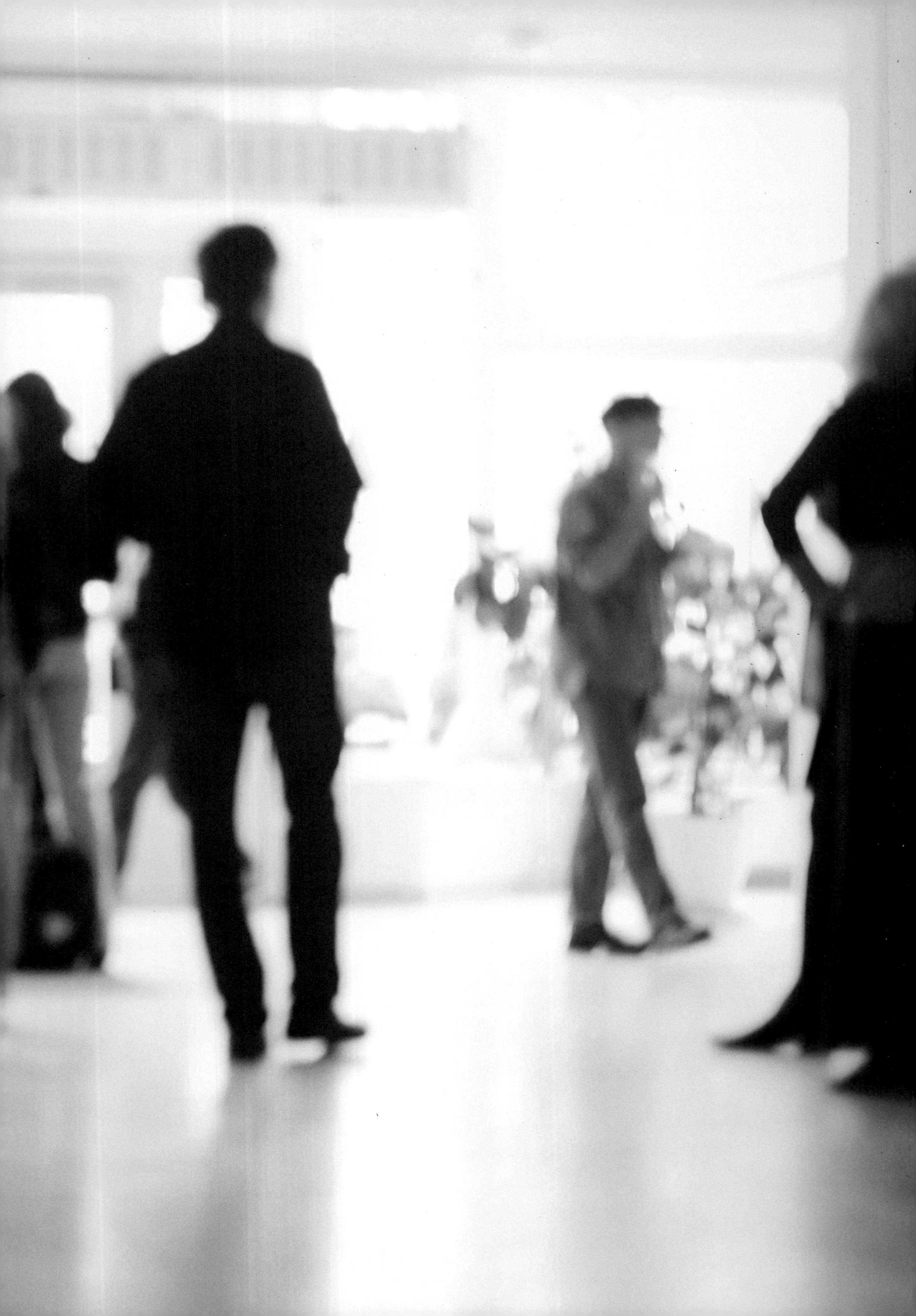

III
—Archives¬ "We allow the documents to speak for themselves"¬

Deborah Natsios and John Young
Interview by Magdalena Taube

Could you briefly introduce yourself?

JY: My name is John Young and with my partner Deborah Natsios we operate the website Cryptome.org. The name refers to cryptography, also called communications security or information security. Our original remit was to publish documents on these topics. Documents that certain people had access to but which had not yet been made public. We decided to start publishing documents because the people who had access, did not want to be associated with the documents. We set up our website in 1996 and continued to publish documents. We don't make comments or write stories, we just publish the documents. Thus it is more like a library than a news media. In fact, we have been rejected by the news media as being unworthy. To us, that is good news.

Could you also introduce yourself and talk about the relationship between Cryptome.org, the Snowden documents and the revelations related to them?

DN: My name is Deborah Natsios. We are both practicing architects in New York City, in the old sense of brick and masonry architecture. Since Cryptome's founding twenty years ago – a founding which came out of our involvement with the cypherpunks and crypto-wars group – our role has shifted. Now we are hybrid systems architects as well as architects in the classical sense. Our cultural perspective provides a framework for evaluating events as they occur. The Snowden moment was on the heels of many topics that we have dealt with and addressed over the years.

We keep quite an even keel about the Snowden material because we see it in a continuum of active response that we have provided over twenty years to a series of issues, that end up being quite interrelated. The Snowden material – which titillated the public and was sensational and lurid and was mined in the mainstream media for its sensual outrageousness – was something to which we took a more taciturn attitude. Because we had anticipated it. We had been close to the material for many years and it was not a surprise to us, though we were grateful for the validation that it brought.

So, in our Cryptome fashion we started making a tally. That is a presentation of the material for public consumption, without commentary. One without any form of ornamental narrative designed to provide a context which, often, is quite superficial. We allowed the documents to speak for themselves. And allowed our readers to struggle with them. Because the passivity of the public after the Snowden revelations, especially in the US, shows that these spoon-fed narratives are enjoyed by the consumers while they eat. But once the meal is over they wander off. Somehow it has not engaged their ontological sense and so our strategies are quite different from those consumer-driven, and market-driven ones which the media use.

Could you explain a little bit further why you do it that way? Maybe in order to do this, you could describe the Cryptome architecture further?

JY: It is the principle of the library: you make the document available, and then there are many uses that can be made of the document. Now, uses are being made other than what the media has done. With our approach we also want to show, that the documents actually cannot speak for themselves because so few have been released. In fact, there has been censorship by the media in order to sensationalize material.

We know that because we have been covering NSA material for many years before this and what is missing from this topic is information about the technical field. There is very little information about the machinery with which this surveillance is being carried out, the technology concerned. This is the case because journalists are not interested in dealing with that side of things. They are interested in news making which relies on lurid information – alluring as well as lurid. Thus they make it sensational.

Out there, there are also other people who handle the information in other ways. You go to a library and people can do what they like with the material they are handed. We think it is the most neutral way to make the information available. Of course it is only a tiny amount of the documents that we have on Cryptome. It is not a big deal. The media has made a big deal of it. But what they have, it is actually not large in size. The material is heavily edited, heavily redacted, highly selective. And it is a terrible distortion of what the NSA does. We know that from many years of publishing on them.

There has been such a rush-on to monetize this sensationalism. We feel that we should probably say more about that. But it is too early for that. We think they will wind up shooting themselves in the head by making too much of it all. The Snowden archives are being done by the people that will help with that. But I think we need to make it more widely available. People should be able to use the library. And also, we should demand the rest of the documents.

98 percent of them have not been released. Right now there is a growing swell amongst scholars and technicians and other people to say, 'we want the rest of the material, we know you are tampering with it'. In a way the journalists are lying to us. We find that very interesting because they are getting away with it. But when people take time to look at the archives they will see the gaps within it. And smart people will find more gaps and get something else going. At least, that is our hope, because that is what Cryptome does. We want all sorts of information available so that interpretations can be made. But not our own interpretations. Of course, we have got our own sneaky interpretation, but we are not going to tell you what that is.

Do you see setting up these archives as important with regards helping journalists do their work? You stated that you feel journalists are not actually prepared for reading these documents and knowing what is inside them. Having accessible archives will help with future leaks – would you agree with that?

JY: It could. We need more people than just journalists to look at it. We need to make it more accessible because they have their own constraints on what they can do – they are not courageous people, despite what they say. They are commercial people and they cannot risk their financial security. But scholars and other individuals will actually go further than journalists. Then the journalists can follow behind the courageous people as they are doing here and now. You can see there has been fairly conservative reporting. There needs to be more reporting on what the NSA does besides what Snowden allegedly released. Snowden released a lot more than has been published and he knows that. He is in something of a jam now, to not talk about what else he released. Maybe there was some arrangement between him and the journalists, which meant that they would run the show. But they have run a very poor show. But you would not know that if you had not followed the topic. So, they are taking advantage of people's ignorance with regards what the NSA actually does.

Because the NSA has the tools that the public once had access to. Tools to protect ourselves against people like the NSA. Half of their organization deals with protection of information, rather than seeking information. And that second half is not what is being covered by the press. The technology of both – aggression and counterintelligence – has not been covered. The NSA is expert in all of that. Now, there are scholars who know this and as we get more into it they will actually provide a much better and more trustworthy picture than what we have seen so far. So far we have seen titillation, exaggeration and misinformation.

The journalists who are covering it, are incompetent in technology. They are strong in civil liberties and aggressive litigation in favor of their behalf. Greenwald, the attorney, is heavily biased. The reason why Snowden chose that group is partly that he was turned down

by others. We don't know who turned him down and so the folks who did this, did it their way. We need to see more ways of doing this and I hope that will come out of our efforts.

DN: There is also a disturbing ethical issue about journalists having written themselves into this story to the degree that they have. Making themselves the heroes and the subjects of this story and perpetuating this as a crowning glory of independent journalism. There has been altogether too much self-congratulation, prize awarding, and focus on the journalists when there were clearly issues of conflict of interest. They should have sought to distance themselves from the story. That is why we look to other kinds of researchers having access to the material and working with it. The journalists' mandate to educate to provoke, how successful has it been? Well, the American public is pretty much dormant in this matter now – what can we say about that outcome? It is not a very good outcome. We cannot blame the journalists. But if there is a public obligation to wake up the polity – has it been successful? I don't think so.

JY: One of the most damning things they have admitted to – and they said that Snowden set it up – is that they must consult with the United States government before they publish something. We know that the press has long known that and freely admit it because Snowden says: "I don't want you publish anything that would harm the United States of America, you must check with the government." We think that is corrupt. Scholars on the other hand, don't do that. But that is the relationship between the sacred media and the sacred government. They work closely together and we think that is why it is a poor representation. This is government approved information. The media say they make the final editorial decision but they do check. And we have actually tried to find out who they checked with and how it was done, but they won't tell you that. Why? Because these are 'classified documents'.

Basically the journalists are inside the government now. This is unfortunate. They say that is how Snowden wanted to do it but they won't actually reveal how he actually did it. And he just says: "I gave it to them, and they can do what they like with it." There are actually quite a number of ethical issues, as Deborah said, that are just not being touched and that is because the press covers its ass. The press will not attack the press, they glorify the press, and that is a good business decision. And we need people to look at this other than the press. The press in America is deeply corrupted despite what they say and that is because they have been coddled for so long that they are used to it. We think there are better alternative ways of handling this information and that is why we run our website.

APPENDIX¬
Snowden Commons

APPENDIX¬
Public Records!
Knowledge Commons!¬

Text and compilation
by Magdalena Taube and Krystian Woznicki

Have civil societies actually learned anything from the Snowden disclosures? Did civil society actors eventually create a basis for change? Or has the political potential of this historical leak yet to be realized?

To a historically unprecedented extent, the disclosures of the NSA whistleblower Edward Snowden allow insights into an excessive control apparatus operated by the biggest superpower of our time, the USA. In that sense they mark a new era: we are now living in a post-Snowden world. Yet we as civil societies are not allowed to be actively involved in this rupture. Most of the time we passively witness well-orchestrated scoops – if we are paying attention at all. How can we overcome this dilemma? How can we co-create the post-Snowden world?

When asking these questions, it seems pressing that we hold a debate about the value of democracy and public structures that is currently not taking place in mass media. In the course of doing so, we need to reset the agenda. Until today, the narratives of the Snowden disclosures revolve for the most part around individual/private problems rather than communal/public ones. For instance, they foreground privacy (a private matter after all, rendering also a private choice, whether related to the disclosures or not). In contrast to that, a debate about the value of democracy and public structures can bring issues of collective empowerment to the fore – and thereby options and strategies for co-creating the post-Snowden world.

A crucial basis for this is open and sustainable access to the Snowden files. Right now, there is no public archive for the documents compiled by Edward Snowden. Instead, the files remain privatized, stored by a few journalists/media houses. At least some initiatives have begun collecting and archiving those files that have been publicized by the media houses. However, the situation is far from ideal, not only impeding free access to public information, but also obfuscating how we could collectively transform the leaks into actual knowledge – that is: into a commons that might serve us as a basis for changing the state of affairs.

Against this backdrop, the Berliner Gazette launched an initiative called "Snowden Commons". This initiative makes a simple proposal: let us design a model for the Snowden files to become public records, thereby creating a basis for the general public to turn these files into commons. Since autumn 2013 we have been creating many spaces for debate and reflection, e.g. in our online newspaper, where we have set up a special section, and in the context of our events, where workshops and panels have been dedicated to the theme, not only in Berlin, but also in Sapporo and Bucharest. For instance, in spring 2014 a one day event with five parallel tracks inquired into possibilities of "collaboration after Snowden", while the entire workshop section of our 15th annual conference UN|COMMONS explored the "commons in the post-Snowden world". Our findings have been presented at various fora such as universities and libraries, including a workshop at the conference "Surveillance and Citizenship: State-Media-Citizen Relations after the Snowden Leaks" that took place at the Cardiff University in June 2015, as well as lectures at various events of the library community, including the gathering of One Person Libraries, the German Annual Librarian's Congress and the Berliner Arbeitskreis Information at the University Library of the Technical University of Berlin.

 In its first phase, the initiative has focused on interventions in the form of public statements (in the media and at events) that have aimed to stimulate public debate at the juncture of knowledge production and democracy.

The following section gathers some data on our interventions as well as public responses related to this issue. In an attempt not to overload readers with information, we are providing a selective overview of our efforts, thereby omitting the details of many inspiring and relevant activities. The data section is augmented with photos by Norman Posselt and Andi Weiland that they have taken at various stages of the Berliner Gazette initiative. Their image series "The Many Faces of the Snowden Commons" presents a representative group of civil society actors who have joined us over the years: librarians, researchers, coders, curators, journalists, activists, artists, entrepreneurs, architects, campaigners and policy consultants.

Ours is perhaps a unique moment in history. We are facing many uncertainties as in our digital age notions of publicness and accessibility are undergoing a profound upheaval. The digital avant-gardes and traditional public institutions alike are challenged by the same situation: how can we nurture and maintain cultures and forms of knowledge as commons? Dealing with this question since it was founded in 1999, the Berliner Gazette uses its experience to focus on this issue in the context of the Snowden disclosures. Looking at it anew, we propose to rediscover the meaning of the commons by examining those forms of knowledge, technology and life that today operate under privatized conditions, but which in the future we might transform into commons.

INTERVENTION #1

Title: Open the Snowden Files!
Format: Essay (EN/GER)
Author: Krystian Woznicki
(berlinergazette.de)
Date: 7/9/14
Site: Berliner Gazette

Open the Snowden Files!
URL (Text/EN): http://berlinergazette.de/
wp-content/uploads/Open-the-Snowden-
Files_KW_E.pdf
URL (Text/GER): http://berlinergazette.
de/open-the-snowden-files

Extract: *"Should the Snowden files remain privatized – stored by a few journalists and media houses? Or should they be in the hands of the public? I think that we need to raise the question. Most importantly because processes in the public service should be designed to be as inclusive as possible in order to live up to the challenges of this specific obligation."* This quote stems from the essay written by Krystian Woznicki, published in Berliner Gazette in July 2014, initiating an international debate.

PUBLIC RESPONSES #1

Reader comments:

Reader comments in Berliner Gazette
(98):
URL (Text/GER): http://berlinergazette.
de/open-the-snowden-files/#comments

Reader comments in netzpolitik (10):
URL (Text/GER): https://netzpolitik.
org/2014/diskussion-ueber-den-umgang-
mit-den-snowden-dokumenten-alles-
veroeffentlichen-oder-portionierte-
neuenthuellungen/#comments

Press comments:

Gesa Ufer: "Snowden documents: 'A little bit strange.' Journalist criticizes exclusive media access to the documents. Interview with Krystian Woznicki" In: Deutschlandradio Kultur, Program: Kompressor, 7/15/14
URL (audio/GER): https://soundcloud.
com/snowdencommons/kompressor-
journalist-kritisiert-exklusiven-
medien-zugang-zu-den-snowden-
dokumenten-15072014
URL (audio transcription/GER): http://
berlinergazette.de/wp-content/uploads/
SC_Transkribierung_Kompressor.pdf
Anna Biselli: "Discussion about how to handle the Snowden documents: Publish everything or bit by bit?" In: netzpolitik.org, 7/15/14
URL (text/GER): https://netzpolitik.
org/2014/diskussion-ueber-den-umgang-
mit-den-snowden-dokumenten-alles-
veroeffentlichen-oder-portionierte-
neuenthuellungen
Detlef Borchers: "What has been. What will be." In: heise online, 7/13/14
URL (text/GER): http://heise.de/-2258088

Republished:

In: Cryptome.org, 7/15/14 (early draft)
URL (text/EN): http://cryptome.
org/2014/07/open-snowden-files.htm
In: Carta.info, 7/11/14
URL (text/GER): http://www.carta.
info/73546/open-the-snowden-files
In: Exberliner, Issue 130, September
2014, p. 13
URL (text scan/EN): http://bit.ly/2kiLhT2
In: Netzpolitik Jahrbuch 2014, epubli
Berlin, December 2014, pp. 172–180
URL (e-book/GER): http://www.epubli.de/
shop/buch/42451
In: Tecno|Grafía[s], 2016
URL (text/SP): http://www.tecno-grafias.
com/abran-los-archivos-de-snowden.htm

INTERVENTION #2

Title: Publics In Peril:
Snowden Files For All?
Format: Panel Discussion (EN)
Guests: Ben Kaden (libreas.eu) & Geert
Lovink (Institute of Network Cultures)
Moderation: Janet Merkel (Centre for
Cultural Policy at the Hertie School
of Governance)
Date: 11/15/14
Site: Berliner Gazette annual conference
SLOW POLITICS at Supermarkt Berlin

URL (video/EN): http://vimeo.com/
album/3135535/video/112157789

Extract: *"Like so many of the historical info leaks of recent years, the published Snowden files remain unsheltered, roving around the net, while those which have not been published yet are stored under precarious circumstances on some private USB sticks. This is not a sustainable condition! We need a public archive! I therefore support strongly the efforts being made in Berlin with regard to that issue. The archiving or 'librarization' can start in Berlin – in exile, so to speak. Ultimately, the public archive for the Snowden files should be erected in Washington D.C.!"* This quote stems from Geert Lovink, Director of Institute of Network Cultures (Amsterdam), a panelist at the Berliner Gazette annual conference SLOW POLITICS in November 2014.

PUBLIC RESPONSES #2

Press/public comments:
Stefan Krempl: "The call for publishing the Snowden Documents gets louder" In: heise online, 11/16/14
URL (text/GER): http://heise.de/-2457781
Patrice Riemens, Waag Society, Amsterdam
URL (quote/EN): http://nettime.org/Lists-Archives/nettime-l-1411/msg00031.html

"Speakers at the Berliner Gazette conference stated that the paradigm shift following the disillusionment with mass surveillance has had comparatively little resonance among the broader public. With regard to this they criticized the gradual disclosure of individual facets of the NSA scandal, as this procedure disregards the limits of the attention economy. In contrast to this, they advocated for a neutral public platform that allows collective administration and collaborative processing of the files leaked by NSA whistleblower Edward Snowden." This quote stems from Stefan Krempl.

"What is really important is what is to be done, how to act on the knowledge we already have." This quote stems from Patrice Riems.

Material:
List discussion in nettime.org (9):
URL (thread archive/EN):
http://nettime.org/Lists-Archives/nettime-l-1411/threads.html#00030
Photos from the panel discussion:
URL (photo album):
https://www.flickr.com/photos/berlinergazette/sets/72157650082796220

INTERVENTION #3

Title: From the Snowden Files to the Snowden Commons: The Library as a Civic Hub
Format: Position Paper (EN)
Author: anonymous
Date: 12/3/14
Site: Berliner Gazette

From the Snowden Files to the Snowden Commons: The Library as a Civic Hub
URL (text/EN): http://berlinergazette.de/wp-content/uploads/Snowden-Commons.pdf

Extract: *"Where, other than the library, could migrants come together with hackers, could poor people (who cannot afford computers or internet access) come together with journalists, could researchers come together with students? We envision the library as a unique and vital space where multiple communities and individuals can work together on shared concerns, with the support and facilitation of librarians and other staff. In any case, such hopes will depend on robust public financial support for public libraries, such that they can become the hubs of citizenship, political engagement and autonomy in our troubled but promising digital age."* This quote stems from the position paper that a group of anonymous citizens collaboratively produced at the Berliner Gazette annual conference SLOW POLITICS (November 13–15, 2014), including representatives of library studies, librarians, net activists, social and political scientists, curators and artists.

Press comments:

Anja Reinhardt: "The 'Slow Politics' conference in Berlin. Interview with Krystian Woznicki" In: WDR 3, program: Mosaik, 11/14/15
URL (audio/GER): https://soundcloud.com/slow-politics-press/slow-politics-wdr-3
URL (audio transcription/GER): http://berlinergazette.de/wp-content/uploads/Transkribierung_Mosaik_Auszug.pdf

Anna Biselli: "Will there be a printed version of the Snowden documents? – Results of the 'Slow Politics' conference in Berlin" In: netzpolitik.org, 12/3/14
URL (text/GER): https://netzpolitik.org/2014/wird-es-eine-gedruckte-ausgabe-der-snowden-dokumente-geben-ergebnisse-der-slow-politics-konferenz

Vladimir Balzer/Axel Rahmlow: "What should happen with the Snowden leaks? Interview with Ben Kaden" In: Deutschlandradio Kultur, program: Studio 9, 1/5/15
URL (audio/GER): https://soundcloud.com/snowdencommons/studio-9-was-soll-mit-den-snowden-leaks-geschehen-05012015
URL (audio transcription/GER): http://berlinergazette.de/wp-content/uploads/SC_Transkribierung_Studio-9.pdf

"Everybody has the right to unrestrictedly access information from public sources. Traditionally, the library is an institution that makes sources accessible in an unrestricted manner. Now we need to ask: the Snowden files, that have been published so far in the context of newspaper reporting – how can they become sources that are publicly accessible in an unrestricted manner?" This quote stems from Vladimir Balzer and Axel Rahmlow.

Republished:

In: LIBREAS. Library Ideas, 26 (2014).
URL (text/GER): http://libreas.eu/ausgabe26/08anonym
Uniform Resource Name: urn:nbn:de:kobv:11-100222989

Title: Snowden Files For All?
Format: Workshop (EN)
Guests: Eva Babalona (kiathess.gr), Diani Barreto (Courage Foundation), Branka Curcic (Kuda.org), Kristoffer Gansing (transmediale), Patricia Hoeppe (Frankfurt University of Applied Sciences), Evan Light (Portable Snowden Surveillance Archive), Frauke Mahrt-Thomsen (Kritische Bibliothek), Diana McCarty (reboot.fm/faces), Morana Miljanovic (Hertie School of Governance), André Rebentisch (meshcon.net), Maria Tengarrinha (O Espelho), Caleb Waldorf (apubliclibrary.org)
Moderation: Sabrina Apitz (berlinergazette.de) and Corinna Haas (ICI Library)
Date: 10/22/15 – 10/24/15
Site: Berliner Gazette annual conference UN|COMMONS at Volksbühne at Rosa-Luxemburg Platz Berlin

Extract: *"The Snowden disclosures have caused a global debate. What could a responsible handling of the leaked documents look like? How can they be archived in a way that makes them accessible to the public for a long period of time? How can they become part of a national archive? The workshop 'Snowden Files For All?' discusses existing projects and will come forward with a position paper. This paper will introduce an idea about how to create a Snowden archive collectively."* This quote stems from Corinna Haas, head of the ICI Library, who co-moderated the workshop with Sabrina Apitz at the Berliner Gazette UN|COMMONS annual conference.

PUBLIC RESPONSES #4

Position paper:
Why the Snowden files should be made accessible through public libraries.
A position paper.
URL (text/EN): http://berlinergazette.de/snowden-files-public-library-position-paper

Warum die Snowden Dokumente in eine öffentliche Bibliothek gehören.
Ein Positionspapier.
URL (text/GER): http://berlinergazette.de/snowden-files-positionspapier

"When the files are accessible to the general public, and when communities gather and collaborate around them, the Snowden files will constitute a commons. This condition entails not only increasing the accessibility of the files as such, but developing interpretations, interfaces and platforms that encourage discourse by a broad cross-section of society, not just specialists or experts." This quote stems from the position paper that was developed by Berliner Gazette as well as participants of the workshop "Snowden Files For All", which was held at the Berliner Gazette annual conference UN|COMMONS, October 22–24, 2015 in Berlin.

Material:
Video about the workshop:
URL (video/EN): https://vimeo.com/146362950
Photos from the workshop:
URL: https://www.flickr.com/photos/berlinergazette/albums/72157656391907159/page3

INTERVENTION #5

Title: Diving into the Snowden Archives
Format: Panel discussion and workshop (EN)
Guests: Andrew Clement (The Snowden Digital Surveillance Archive), Naomi Colvin (Couragefound.org), Evan Light (Snowden Archive-in-a-Box), Geert Lovink (Institute for Network Cultures), M.C. McGrath (The Snowden Document search / Transparency Toolkit), Frauke Mahrt-Thomsen (Kritische Bibliothek), Deborah Natsios (Cryptome.org/The Tally Update), Pit Schultz (nettime.org), André Rebentisch (meshcon), Maria Xynou (Surveillance without Borders), John Young (Cryptome.org/The Tally Update).
Moderation: Sabrina Apitz, Corinna Haas, Krystian Woznicki (all Berliner Gazette)
Date: 02/04/16 – 02/05/16
Site: Berliner Gazette kick off event for its annual project TACIT FUTURES at transmediale, Haus der Kulturen der Welt Berlin
URL (audio/EN): https://soundcloud.com/berliner-gazette/tacit-futures-panel-transmediale-snowden-archives

Extract: *"Interpretations of the published documents remain unfinished due to their cryptic language and specialized information. And only a small percentage has been published. The question of how to turn them into commons is more critical now than ever."* This quotes stems from an introduction given by Krystian Woznicki, founder of the Berliner Gazette, Berlin, at the Berliner Gazette kick off event for its annual project TACIT FUTURES at transmediale, Haus der Kulturen der Welt Berlin

PUBLIC RESPONSES #5

Press comments:

Joachim Scholl: "How can we read the Snowden documents? Interview with Corinna Haas". In: Deutschlandradio Kultur, program: Lesart, 02/04/16
URL (audio/GER): https://soundcloud.com/berliner-gazette/tacit-futures-interview-dradio-snowden-archive

Max Biederbeck: "Why you should access the Snowden documents yourself". In: WIRED, 02/05/16
URL (text/GER): https://www.wired.de/collection/latest/schaut-die-snowden-dokumente-am-besten-selbst-durch

<u>Florian Fricke:</u> "Snowden archive: Only a fraction of the documents has been published." In: DeutschlandRadio, program: Fazit, 02/06/16
URL (text/GER): http://www. deutschlandradiokultur.de/snowden- archive-erst-ein-bruchteil-der- dokumente.1013.de.html?dram:article_ id=344882
URL (audio/GER): https://soundcloud. com/berliner-gazette/tacit-futures- reportage-dradio-snowden-archives

<u>Annabelle Georgen:</u> "Des millions de documents inexploités: comment gérer l'héritage de Snowden?" In: Les Inrocks, 02/22/16
URL (text/FR): http://www.lesinrocks. com/2016/02/22/actualite/comment- gerer-lheritage-de-snowden-11807369

<u>Andrea Liu:</u> "Report Transmediale: Festival for Art & Digital Culture".
In: afterimage, Vol. 23, No. 6, 2016
URL (text/EN): http://vsw.org/afterimage/ 2016/04/29/reporttransmediale-festival- for-art-digital-culture

<u>Pit Schultz:</u> "Interview with John Young and Deborah Natsios of Cryptome. org". In: reboot.fm, program: Nettimes, 03/27/16.
URL (audio/EN): http://reboot.fm/2016/ 03/27/nettimes-3-interview-with-cryptome

"There are seminal initiatives in Europe, the U.S. and Canada that are archiving the Snowden documents. By doing this, the documents are made accessible for academic research and also for an appropriation by civil society." This quote stems from the interview with Corinna Haas conducted by Joachim Scholl in February 2016.

Material:
Video interviews with participants of panel discussion and workshop:
URL (Vimeo album): https://vimeo.com/ album/3785772

Photos from the panel discussion and workshop
URL (Foto album): https://www. flickr.com/photos/berlinergazette/ albums/72157662038932563

The Many Faces of the Snowden Commons¬

Portraits by Norman Posselt
and Andi Weiland

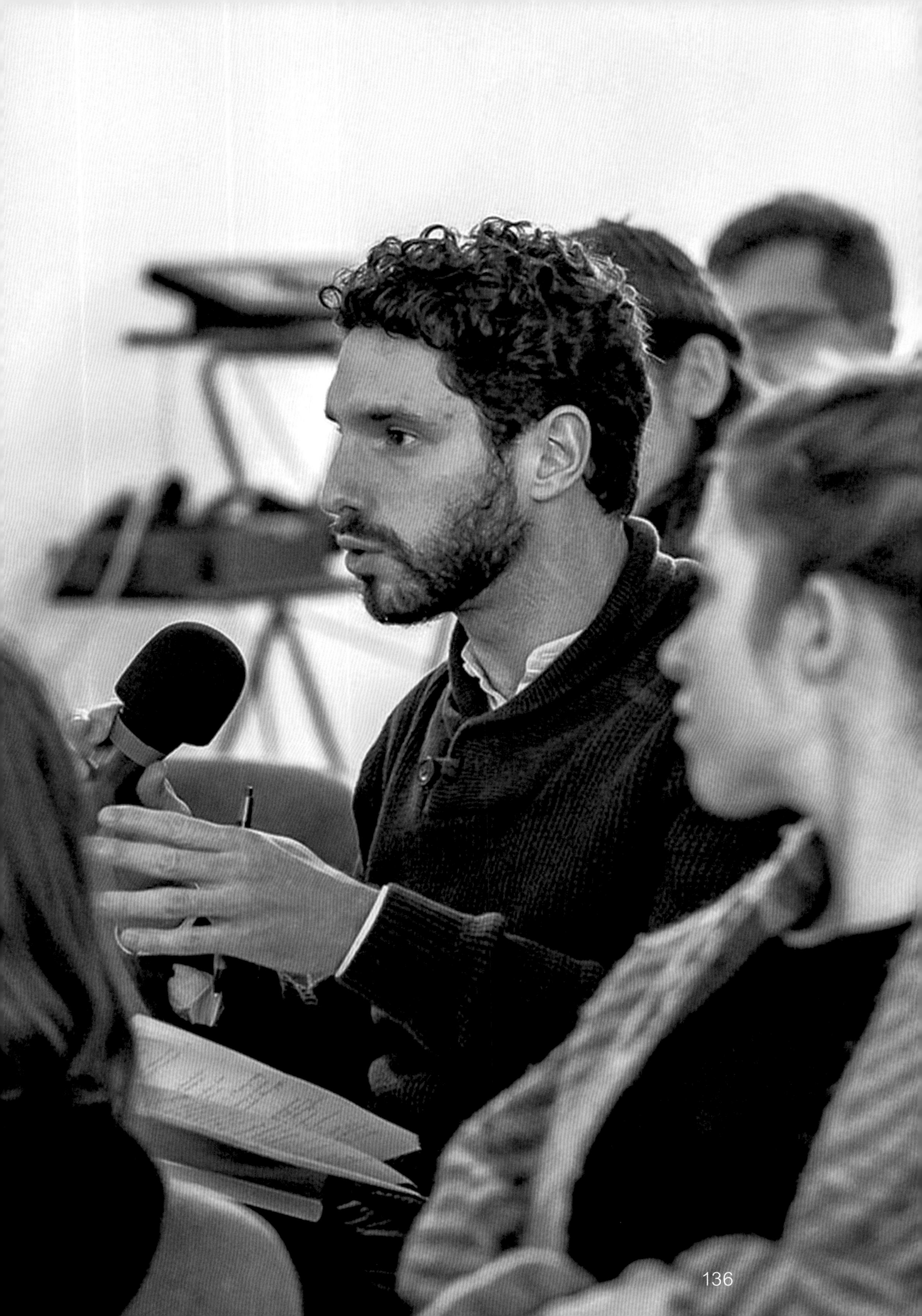

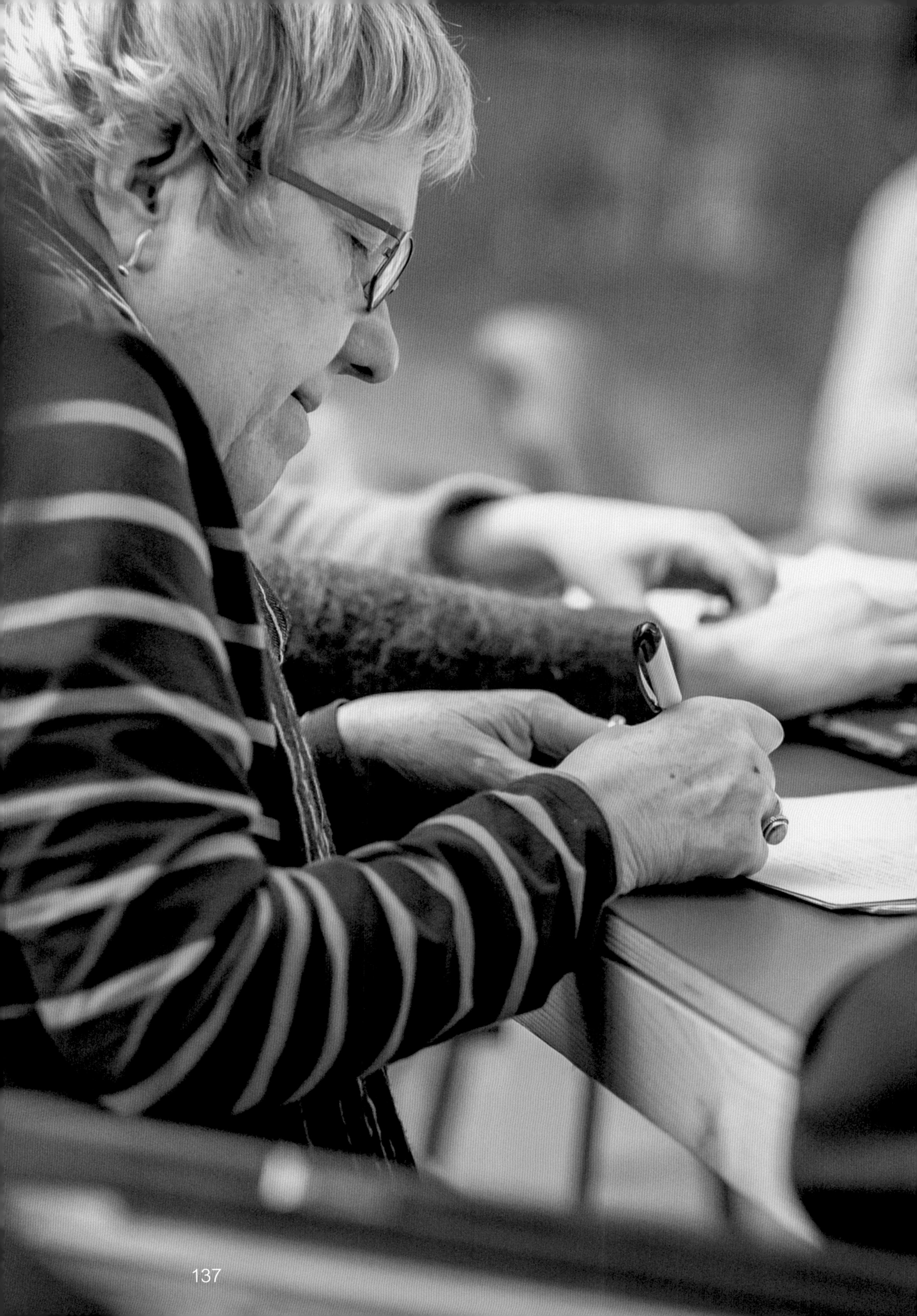

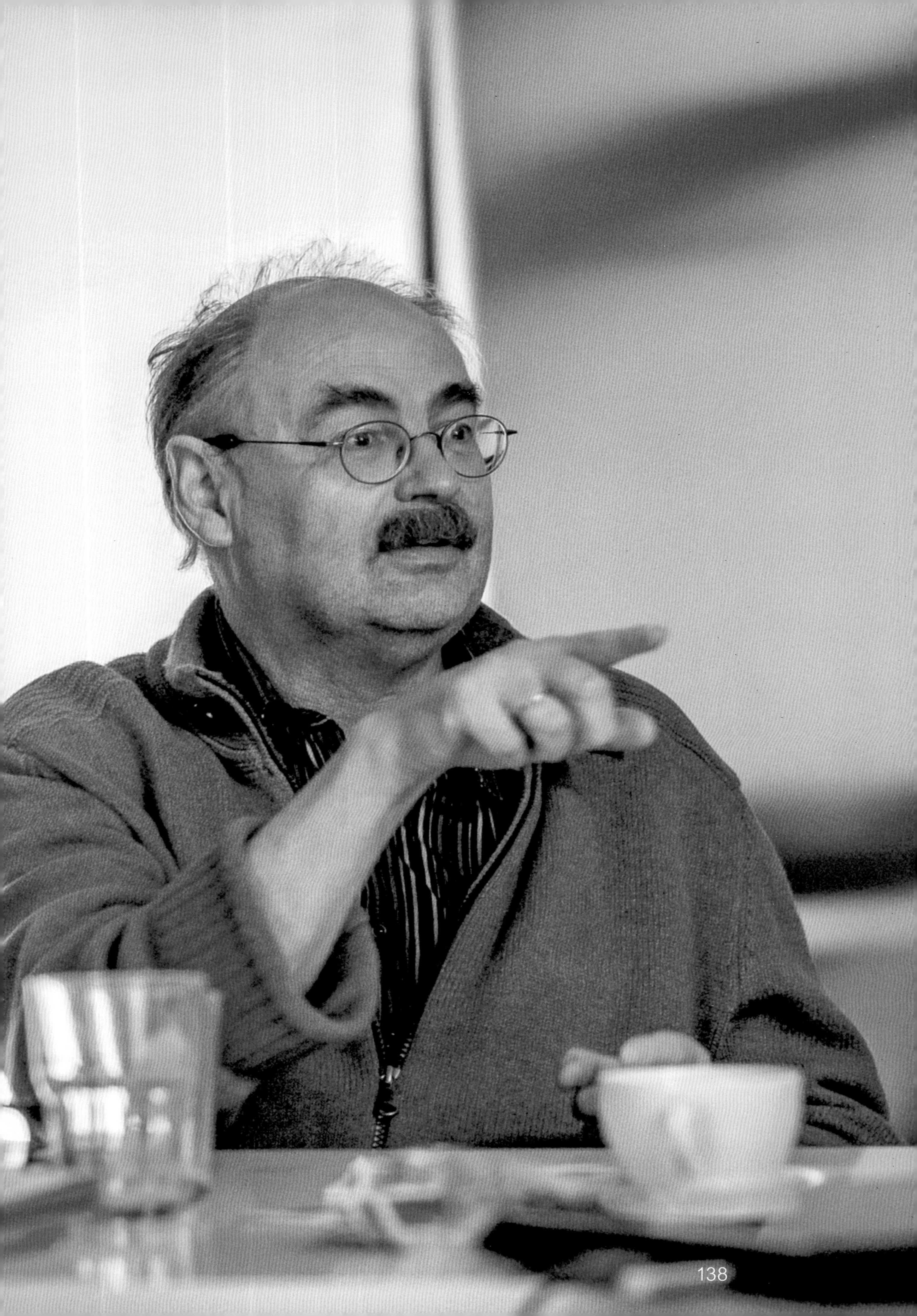

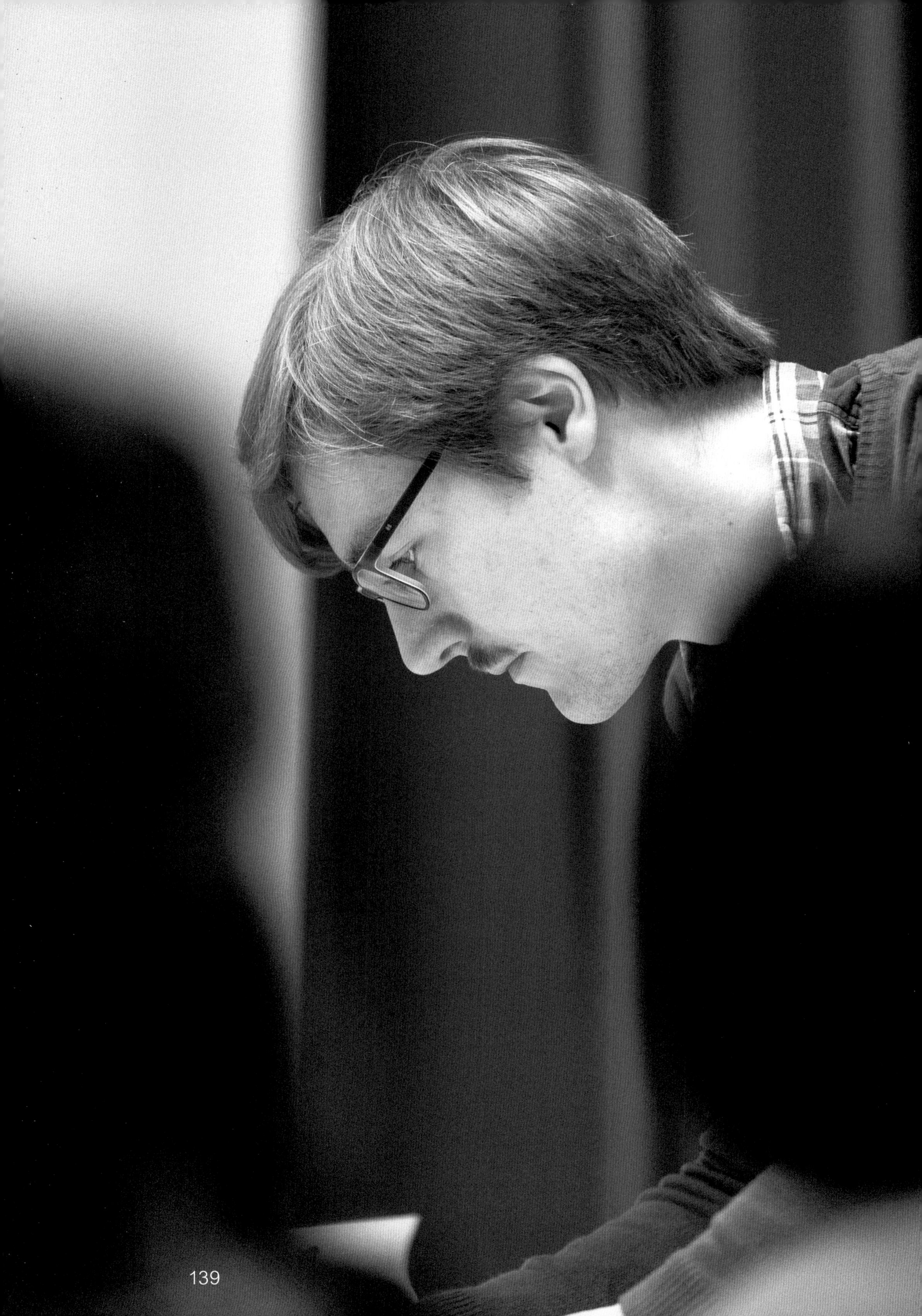

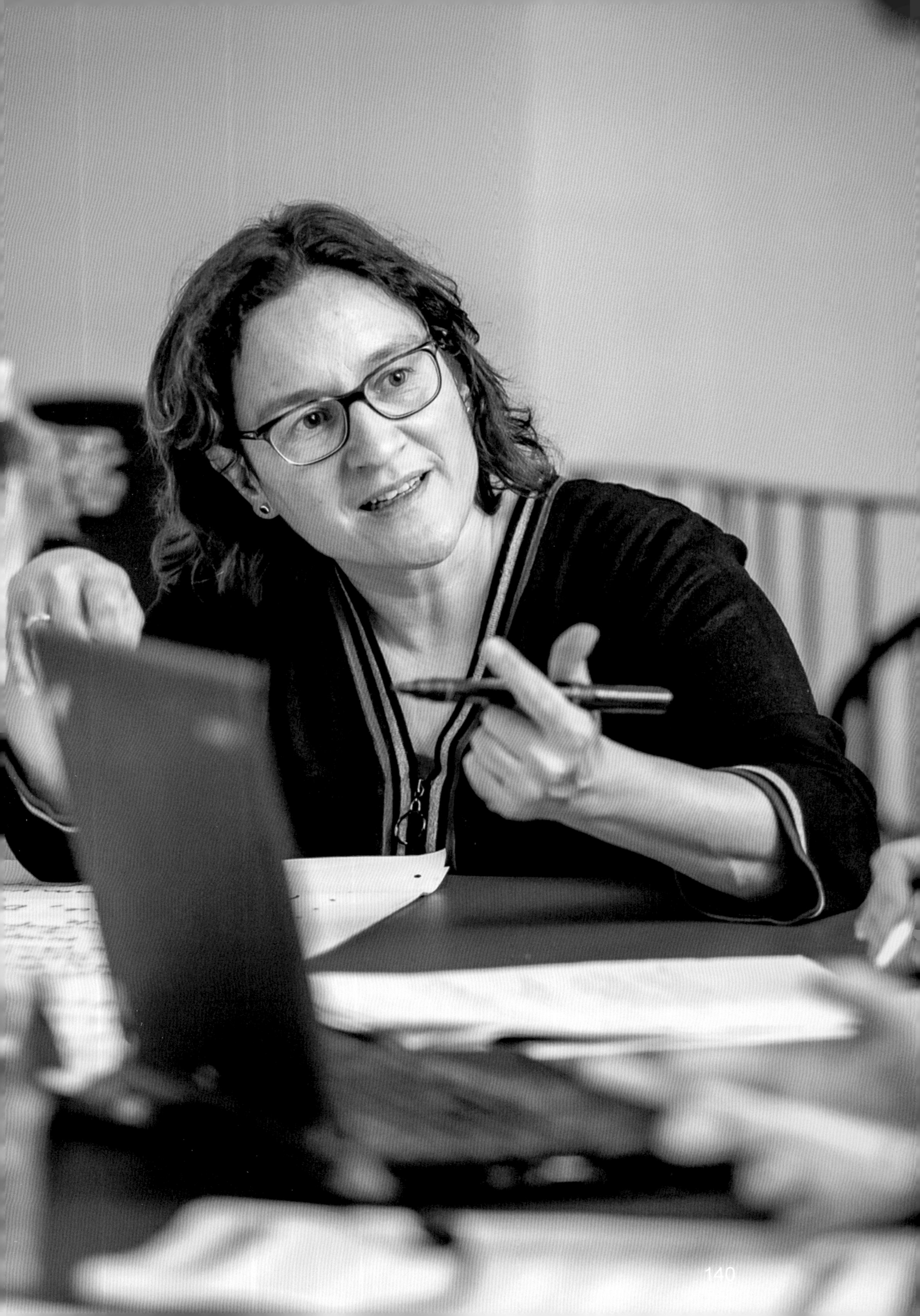

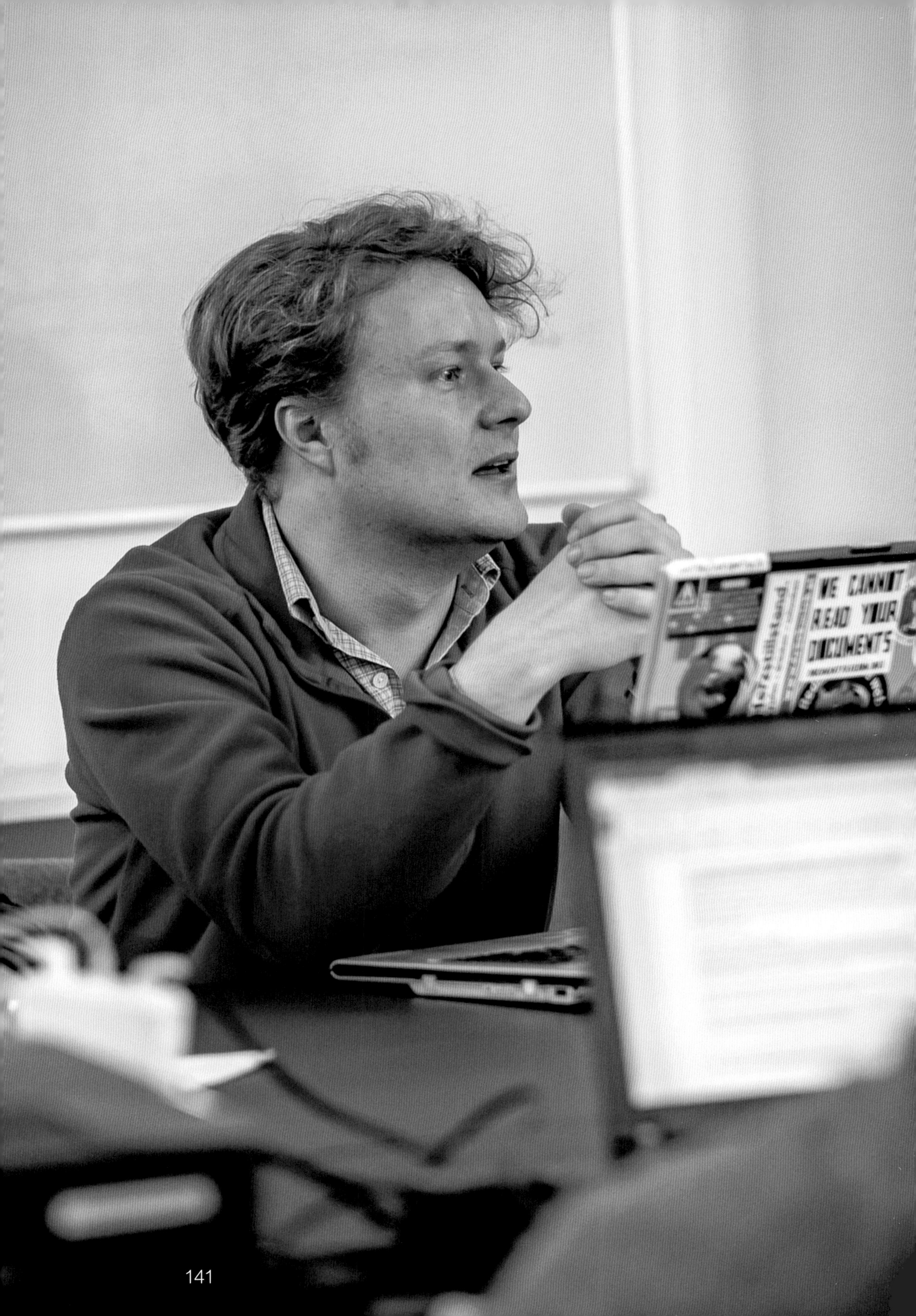
WE CANNOT
READ YOUR
DOCUMENTS

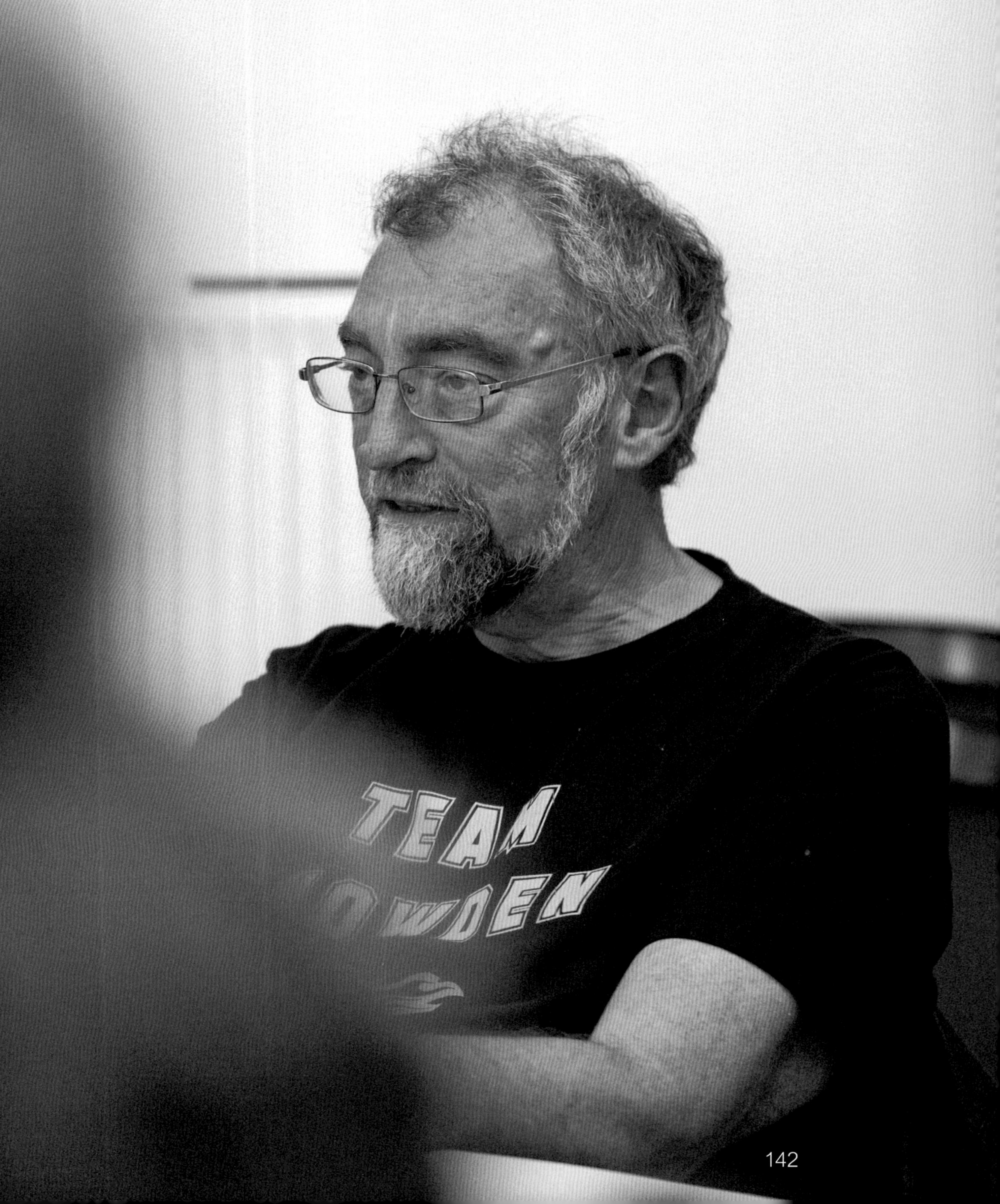

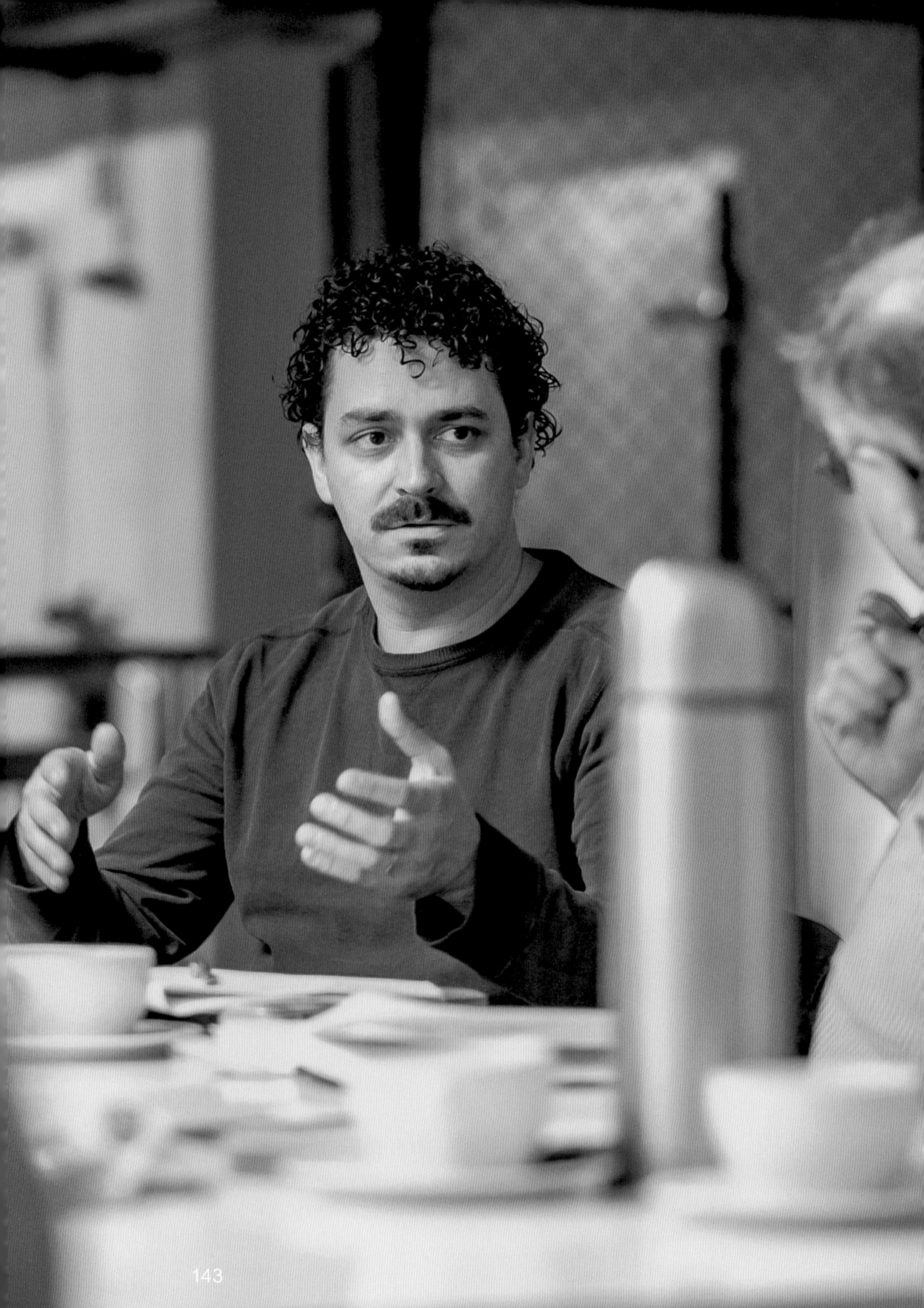

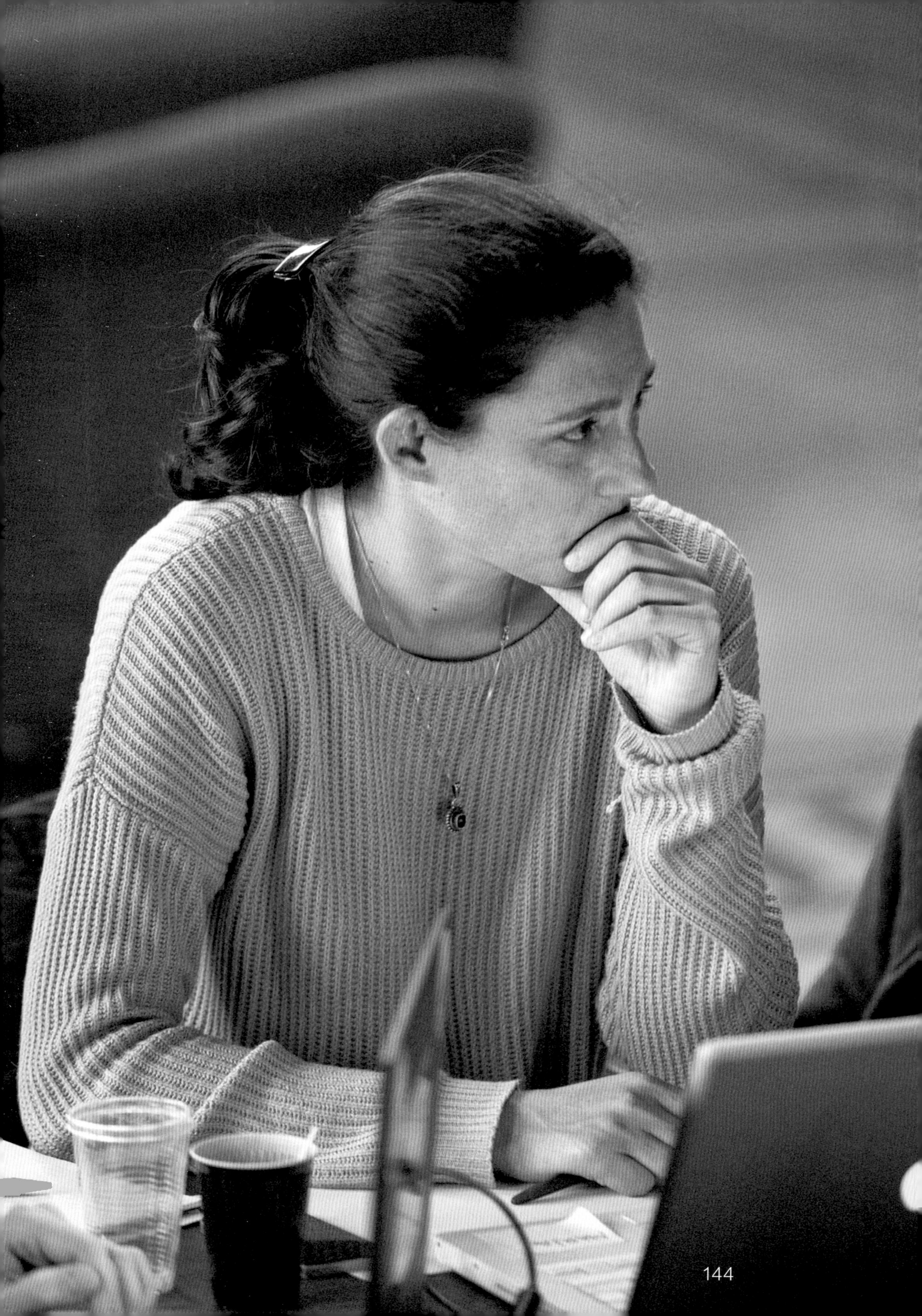

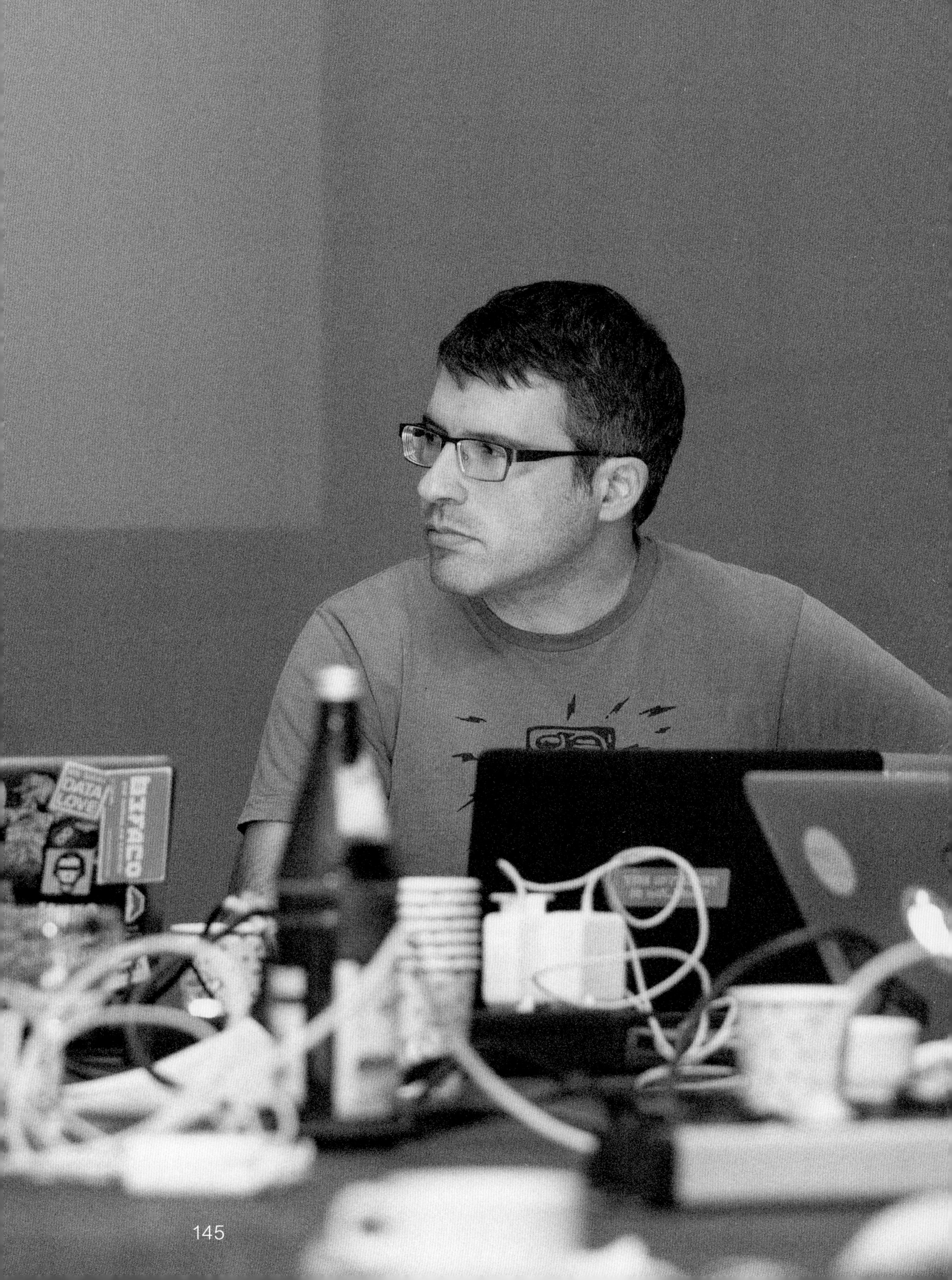

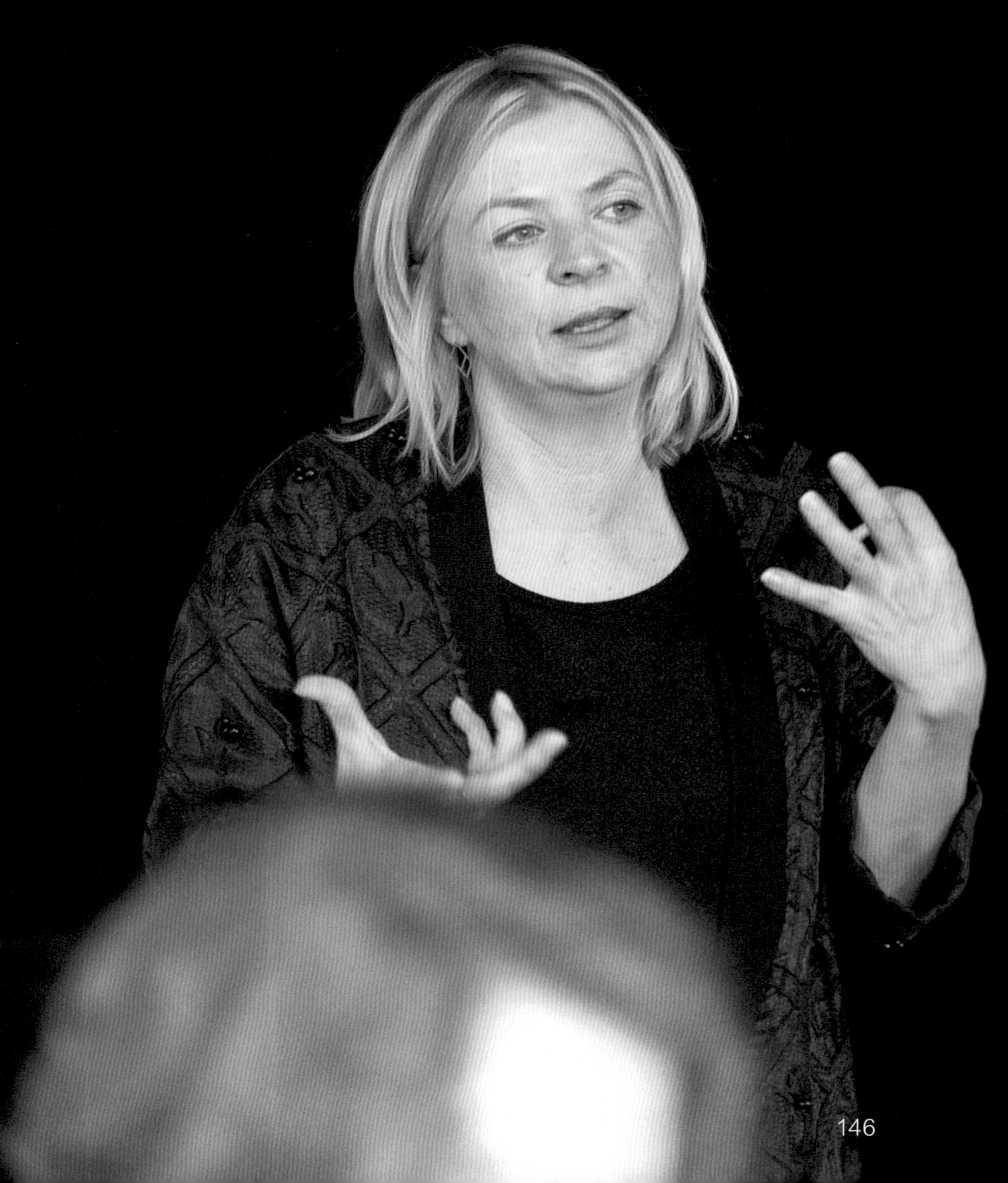

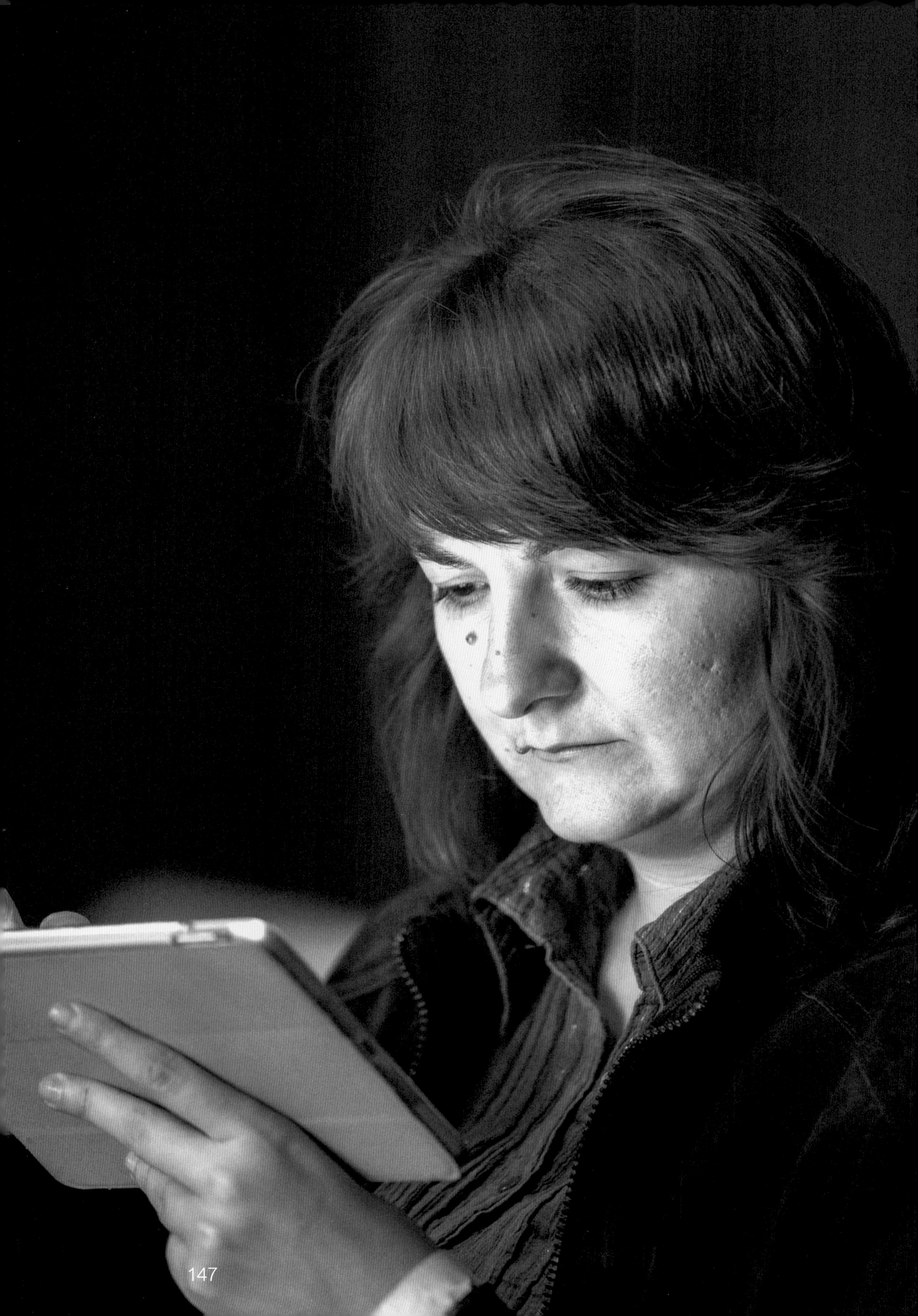

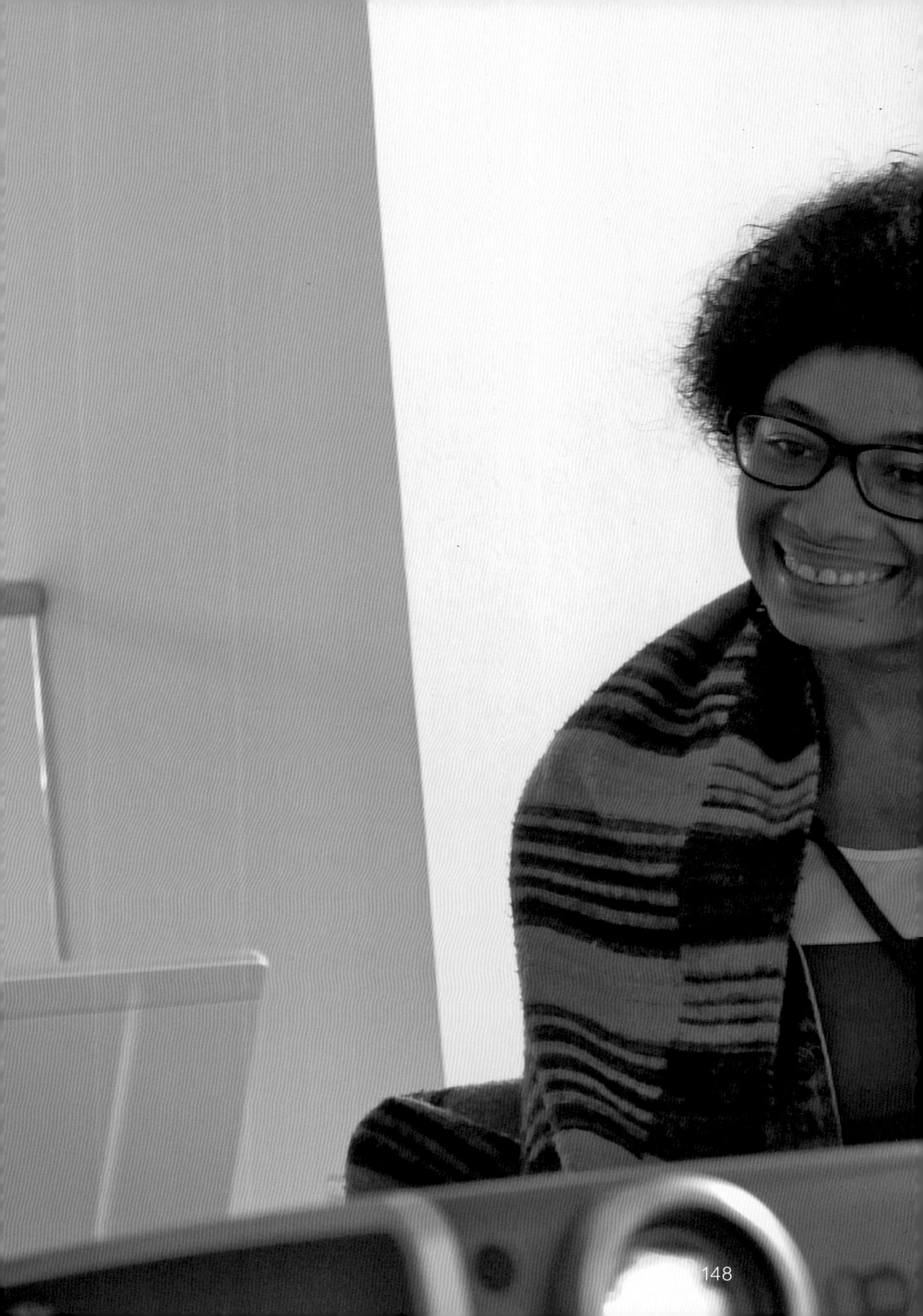

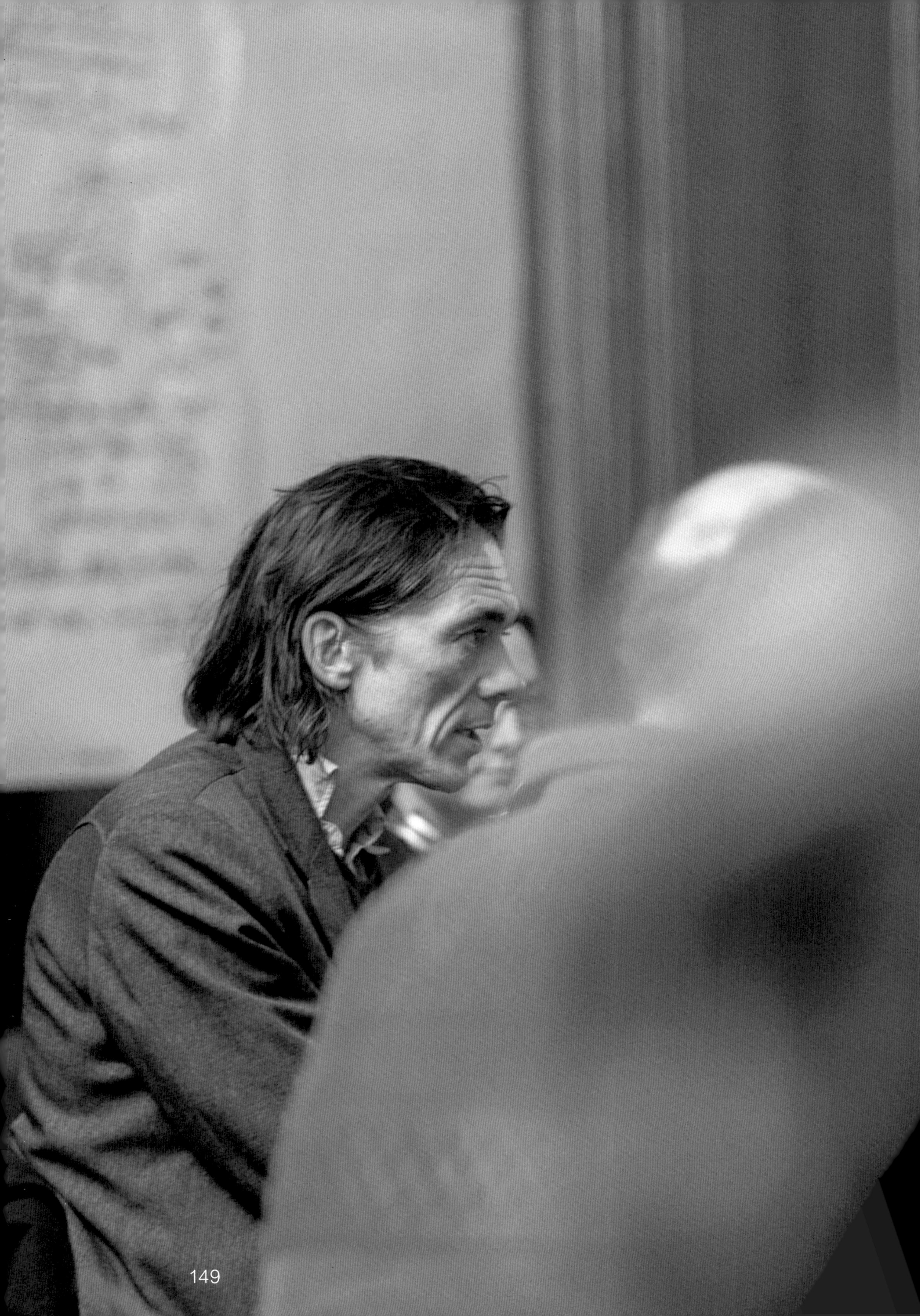

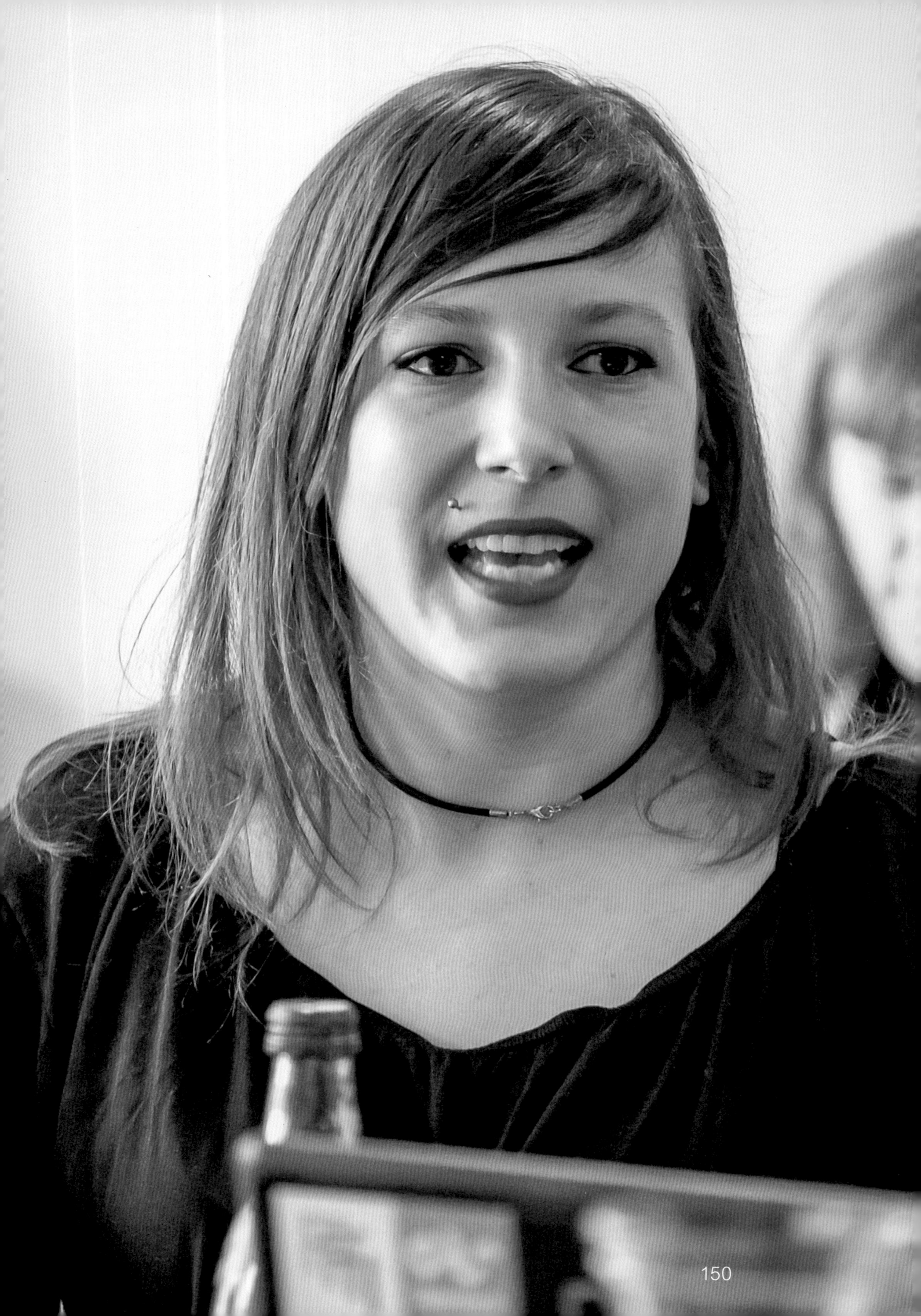

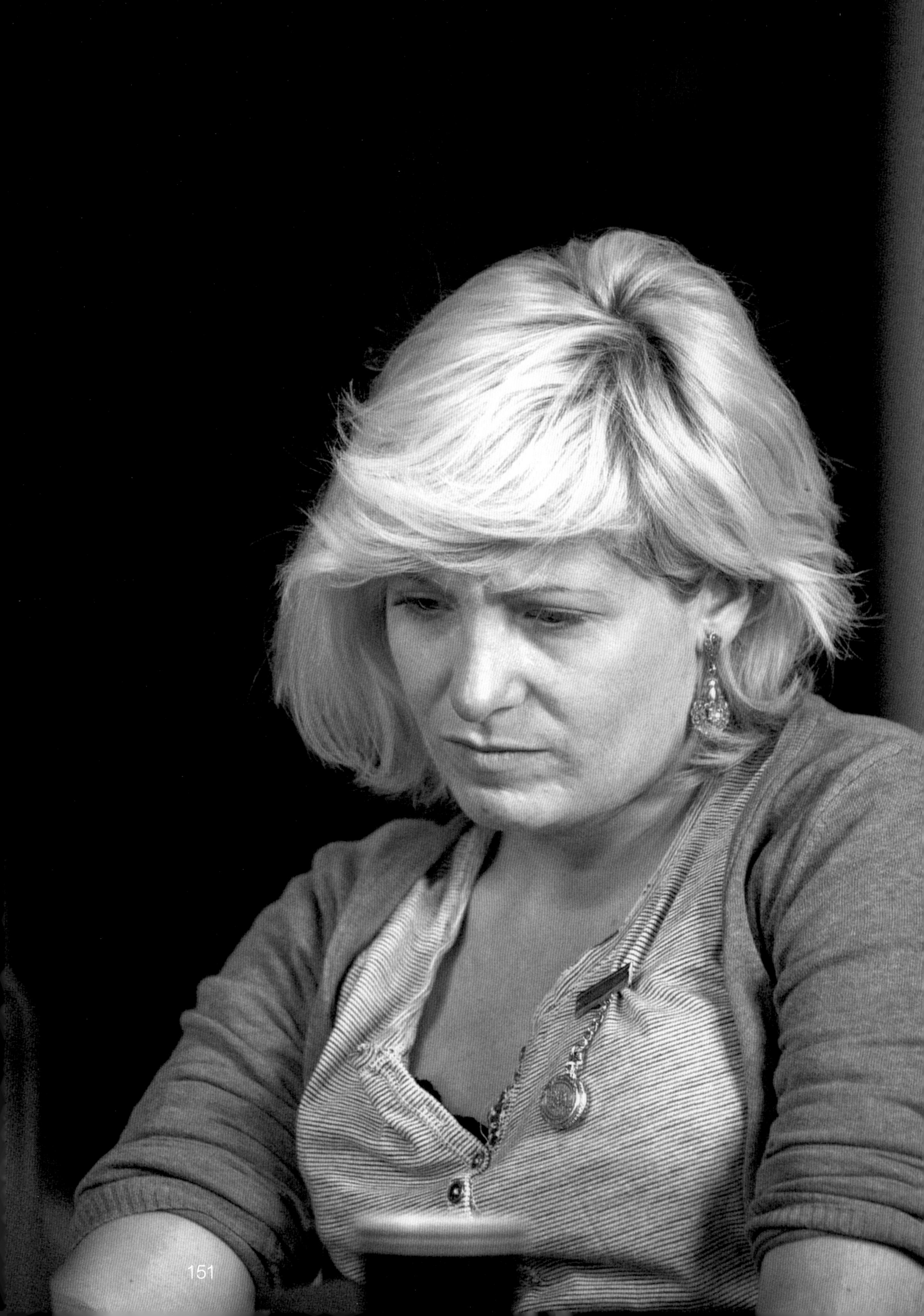

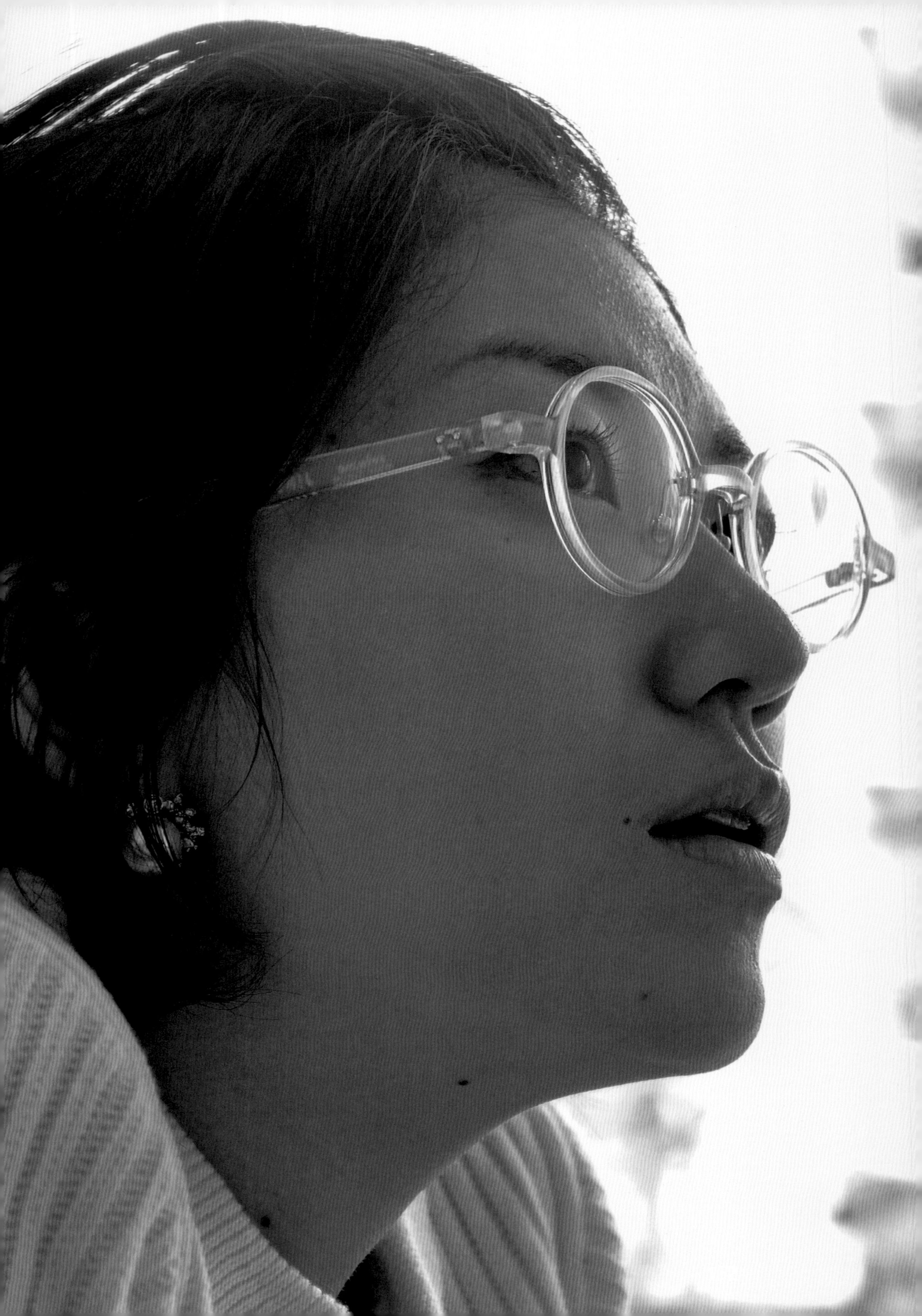

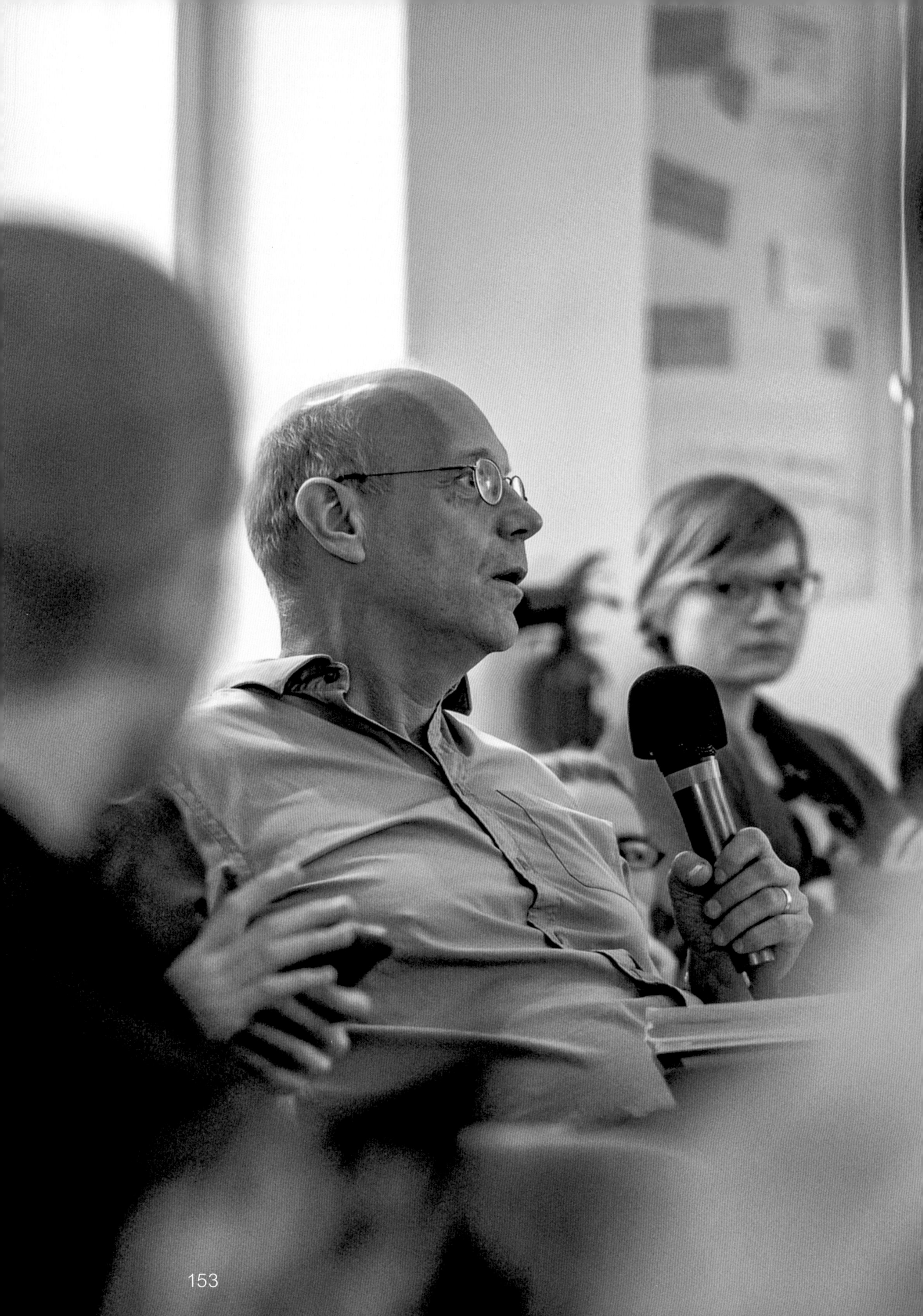

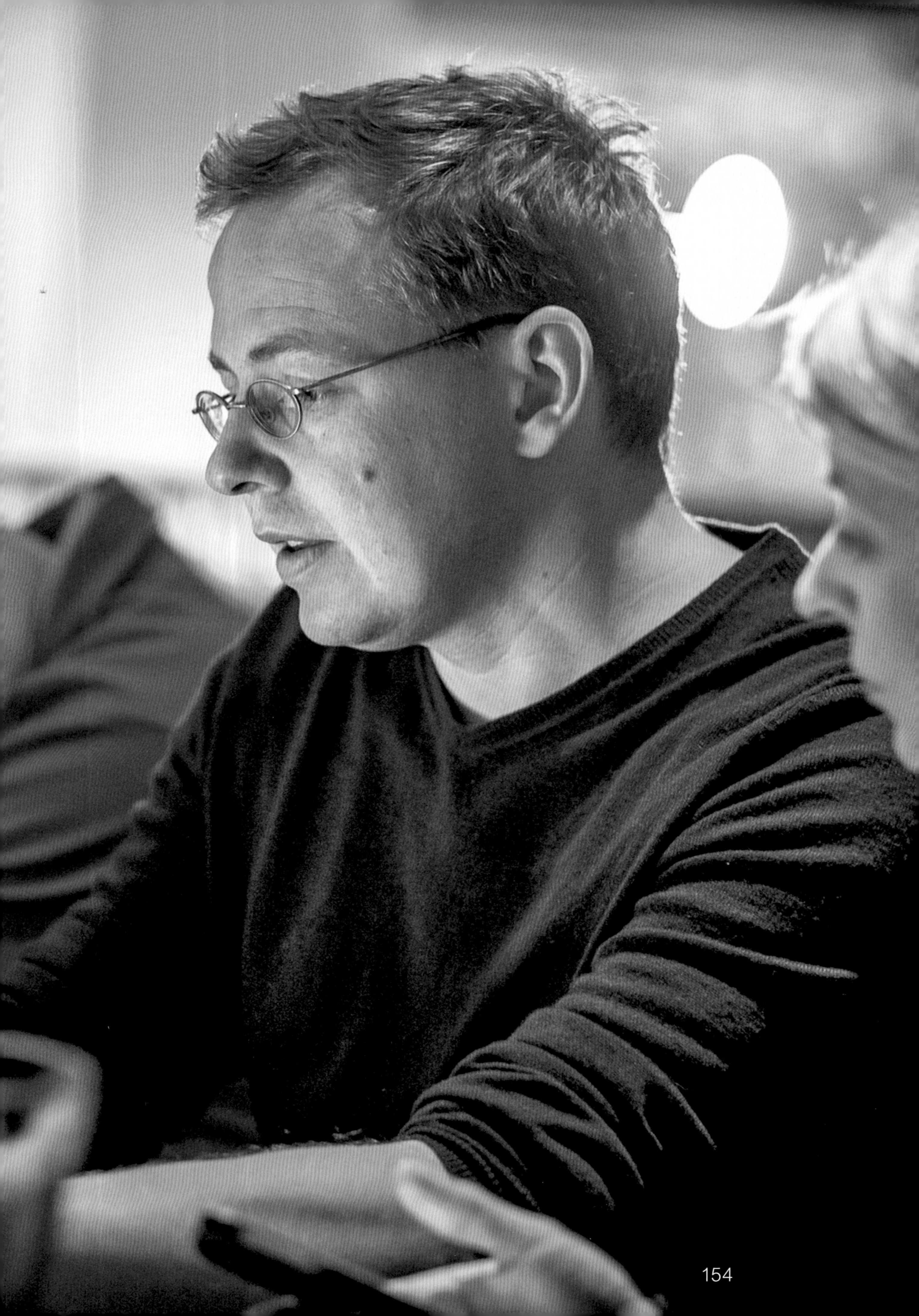

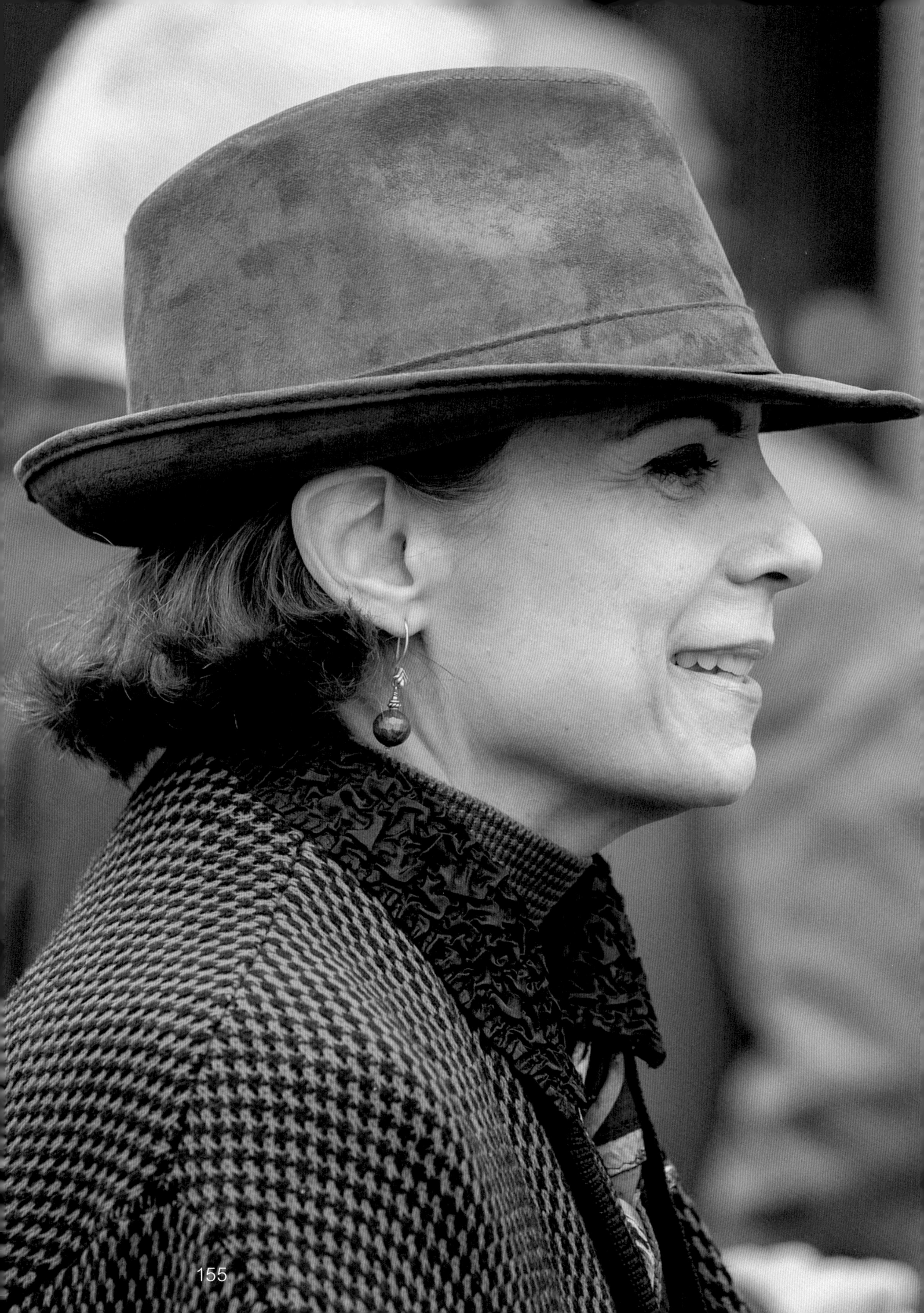

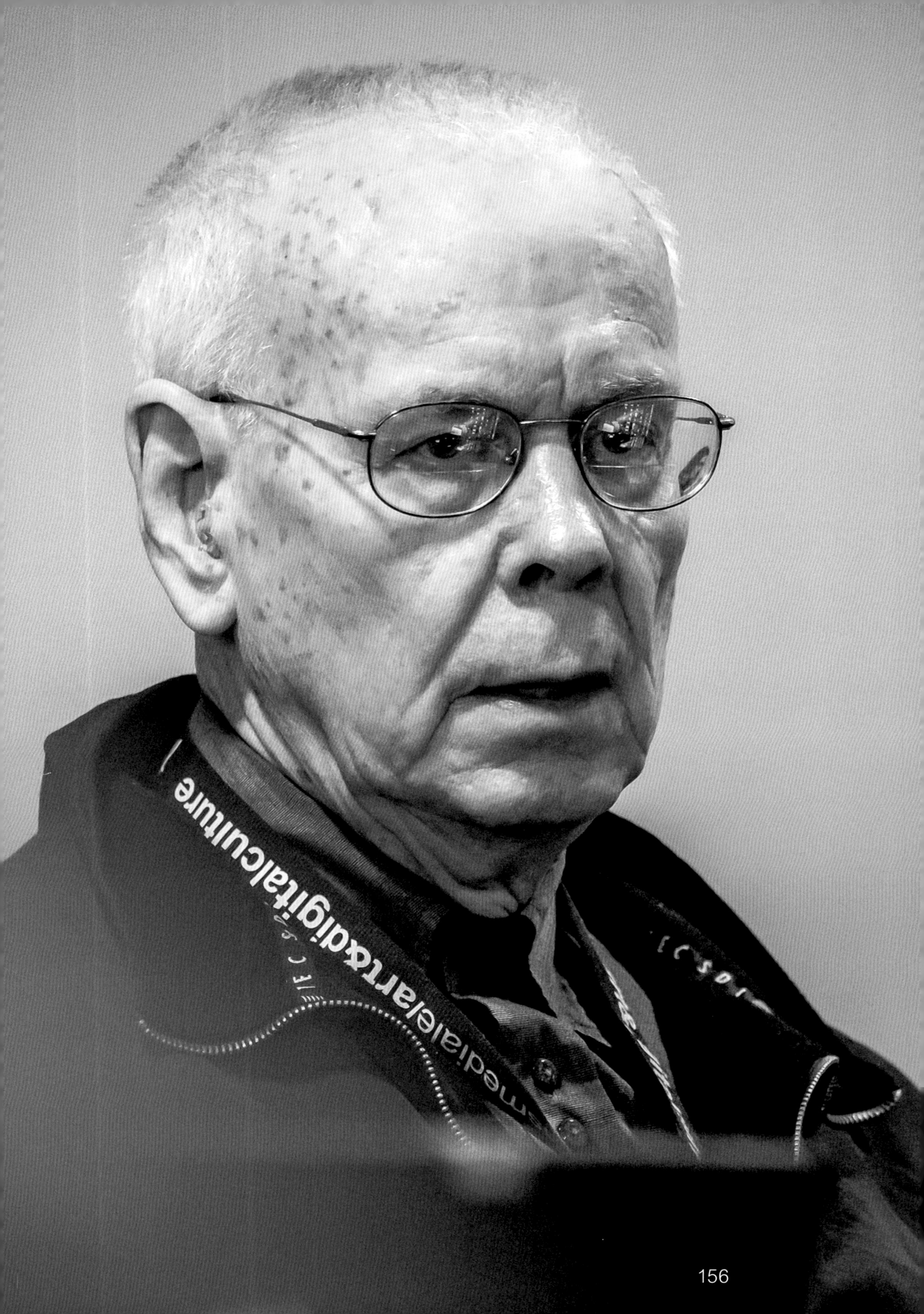

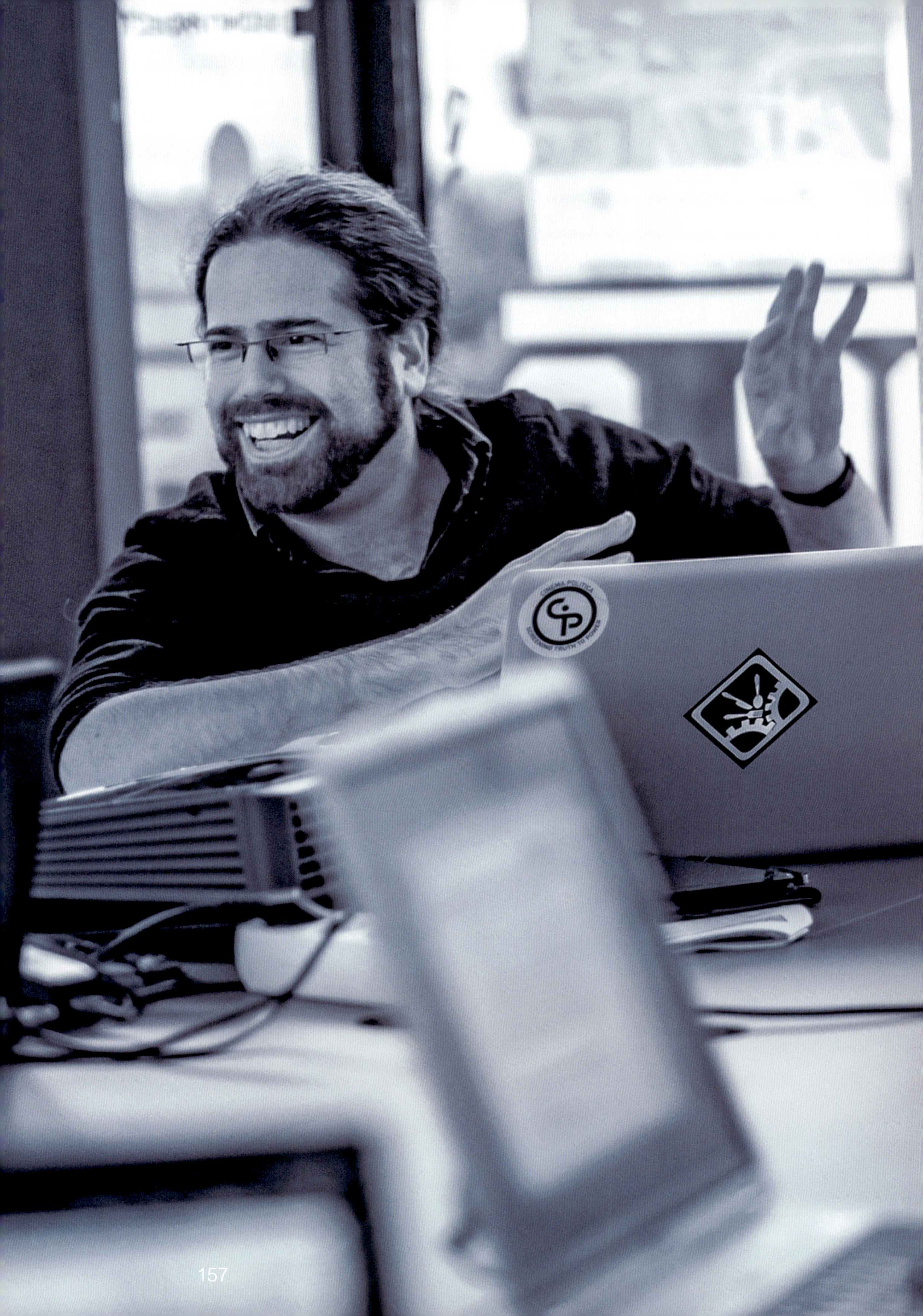

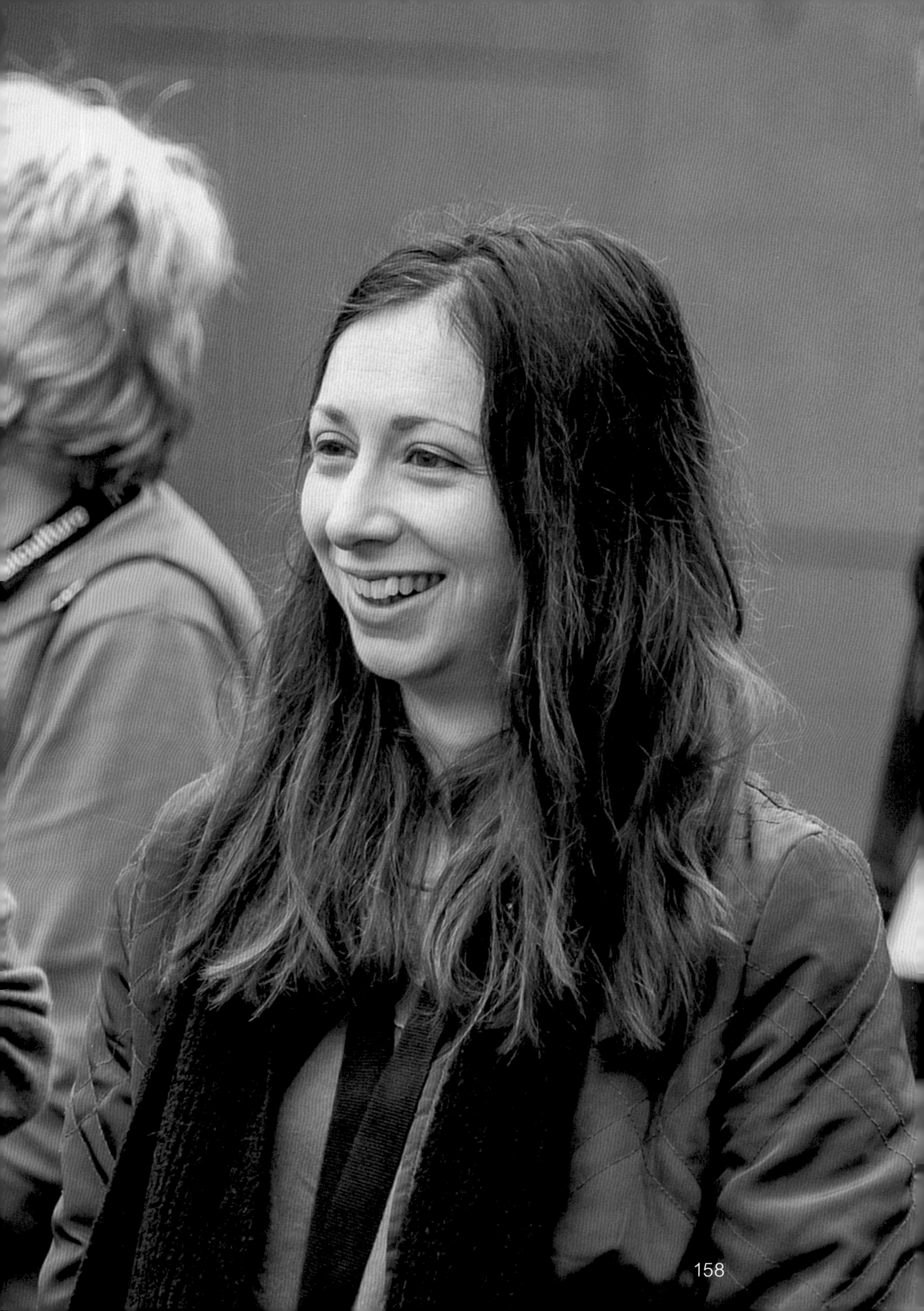

Further Reading / Print and online / Indexed according to this book's chapters

PREFACE

Keywords: Civil Resistance / Democracy / Future / Infrastructure / Migration / Preemption / Security Politics / Social Motion / Snowden / War on Terror

Elmar Altvater: Controlling the Future. Edward Snowden and the New Era on Earth. (German-language). In: Blätter für deutsche und internationale Politik, 4/2014.

Markus Beckedahl and Andre Meister (ed.): Überwachtes Netz. Edward Snowden und der größte Überwachungsskandal der Geschichte. epubli, 2013.

Lloyd C. Gardner: The War on Leakers. National Security and American Democracy, from Eugene V. Debs to Edward Snowden. The New Press, 2016.

Monica Horten: The Closing of the Net. Polity Press, 2016.

Brian Massumi: Ontopower. War, Powers, and the State of Perception. Duke University Press, 2015.

Angela Richter: Supernerds. Conversations with Heroes. Alexander Verlag, 2015.

Saskia Sassen: Expulsions. Brutality and Complexity in the Global Economy. Harvard University Press, 2014.

Florian Sprenger: The Politics of Micro-Decisions. Edward Snowden, Net Neutrality, and the Architectures of the Internet. Meson Press, 2015.

Bernhard Taureck: Überwachungs-demokratie. Die NSA als Religion. Wilhelm Fink Verlag, 2014.

William Walters: Putting the Migration-Security Complex in its Place. In: Risk and the War on Terror. Louise Amoore and Marieke de Goede (ed.). Routledge, 2010.

Krystian Woznicki and Brian Massumi: After the Planes. A Dialogue about Movement, Perception and Politics. Diamondpaper, 2017.

WEBSITES

Chaos Computer Club
http://www.ccc.de/en

Electronic Frontier Foundation
https://eff.org

German Parliamentary Committee investigating the NSA spying scandal at Netzpolitik.org https://netzpolitik.org/tag/nsa-untersuchungsausschuss

PRISM Break https://prism-break.org

Transparency Toolkit
http://transparencytoolkit.org

CHAPTER 1: MEDIA

Keywords: Journalism / Leaks / Mass Media / Participation / Privatization / Public Interest / Snowden Files / Social Media / Surveillance / WikiLeaks

Jacob Appelbaum: Talks 2005–2013. Greyscale Press, 2013.

Benedetta Brevini et al (ed.): Beyond WikiLeaks. Implications for the Future of Communications, Journalism and Society. Palgrave Macmillan, 2013.

David P. Fidler (ed.): The Snowden Reader. Indiana University Press, 2015.

Barton Gellman: Dark Mirror. Edward Snowden and the Surveillance State. Bodley Head, 2017.

Glenn Greenwald: No Place to Hide. Edward Snowden, the NSA and the Surveillance State. Hamish Hamilton, 2014.

Luke Harding: The Snowden Files: The Inside Story of the World's Most Wanted Man. Guardian Faber Publishing, 2014.

Geert Lovink: Social Media Abyss.
Polity Press, 2016.

David Lyon: Surveillance after Snowden.
Polity Press, 2015.

Marcel Rosenbach and Holger Stark:
Der NSA-Komplex. Edward Snowden
und der Weg in die totale Überwachung.
DVA, 2014.

WEBSITES

The NSA files https://theguardian.com/
us-news/the-nsa-files

The SIDtoday files https://theintercept.
com/document

The NSA Revelations All in One Chart
https://projects.propublica.org/nsa-grid

NSA Spying Scandal http://spiegel.de/
international/topic/nsa_spying_scandal

Snowdens Deutschland-Akte http://
spiegel.de/netzwelt/web/snowdens-
deutschland-akte-alle-dokumente-als-
pdf-a-975885.html

CHAPTER 2: ART

*Keywords: Accessibility / Classified
Documents / Design / Digital Control /
Mnemotecnics / Photography / Radical
Empiricism / Secrecy / Power /
Snowden*

Olaf Arndt (ed.): Troia. Technologien
Politischer Kontrolle. Belville, 2005.

Thomas Bayerle: Rasterfahndung.
Suhrkamp Verlag, 1981.

Gregoire Chamayou: Fichte's Passport.
In: Theory and Event, 2013.

Simon Denny: Secret Power.
Koenig Books, 2015.

Jochem Hendricks and Magdalena
Kopp: Revolutionäres Archiv. Verlag
Walther König, 2015.

Metahaven: Black Transparency.
The Right to Know in the Age of Mass
Surveillance. Sternberg Press, 2015.

Trevor Paglen: Invisible. Covert
Operations and Classified Landscapes.
Aperture, 2010.

Laura Poitras: Astro Noise. A Survival
Guide for Living Under Total Surveillance.
Harvard University Press, 2016.

João Ribas (ed.): Under the Clouds. From
Paranoia to the Digital Sublime. Serralves,
2015.

Taryn Simon: An American Index of
the Hidden and Unfamiliar. Hatje Cantz
Verlag, 2012.

Louise Wolthers et al (ed.): Watched.
Surveillance, Art and Photography.
Verlag Walther König, 2016.

WEBSITES

Image Atlas http://imageatlas.org

NSA graphic designer/art director
https://behance.net/ddarchicourt

Secret Power
http://simondennysecretpower.com

The Snowden Templates
http://julianoliver.com/output/snowden-
templates/templates/1/Template1.odp

UbuWeb http://ubu.com

CHAPTER 3: ARCHIVES

*Keywords: Archive Architectures /
Classification Methodologies /
Digital Archives / Politics of Search /
Social History / Snowden Archives /
State Secrets*

Marcus Burckhardt: Archive des
Digitalen. Medienphilosophische
Überlegungen zu Utopie, Dystopie und
Realität digitaler Archivierung. In: SPIEL.
Eine Zeitschrift fur Medienkultur, Vol. 29,
Nº. 1–2, 2010. pp. 21–36.

Yann Chateigné and Markus Miessen:
The Archive as a Productive Space of
Conflict. 2016. Sternberg Press, 2016.

Georges Didi-Huberman and
Knut Ebeling: Das Archiv brennt.
Kadmos Verlag, 2007.

Wolfgang Ernst: Digital Memory and the
Archive. Electronic Mediations, 2012.

Sarah Harrison: Indexing the Empire.
In: The WikiLeaks Files: The World

According to US Empire. WikiLeaks (ed.). Verso, 2015. pp. 145–158.

Gunilla Knape: Order and Collapse. The Lives of Archives. Art and Theory Publishing, 2016.

Hamad Nasar in conversation with Anna-Sophie Springer and Etienne Turpin: Intensive Geographies of the Archive. In: Anna-Sophie Springer and Etienne Turpin (ed.): Fantasies of the Library. MIT Press, 2016.

Taryn Simon: The Picture Collection. Cahiers D'art, 2017.

Travelling Communiqué Project Group (ed.): Travelling Communiqué. Spector Books, 2016.

WEBSITES

Cryptome https://cryptome.org

Global Surveillance Disclosures https://archive.org/details/nsia-snowden-documents

Global Surveillance. An annotated and categorized overview by Oslo University Library. https://tinyurl.com/no21984

NSA Documents https://aclu.org/nsa-documents-search

NSA Primary Sources https://eff.org/nsa-spying/nsadocs

Snowden Document Search https://search.edwardsnowden.com

Snowden Digital Surveillance Archive https://snowdenarchive.cjfe.org

Snowden Tally https://cryptome.org/2013/11/snowden-tally.htm

APPENDIX

Keywords: Copyright Activism / Commons / Democracy / Knowledge Commons / Public Libraries / Social Movements / Transparency

Geoffroy de Lagasnerie: L'Art de la révolte. Snowden, Assange, Manning. Fayard, 2015.

Sherrin Frances: OWS People's Library and Jorge Luis Borges. Radical Politics,

Heterotopic Spaces, and the Practice of Hope. In: ctheory, October 7, 2014. http://ctheory.net/articles.aspx?id=733

David McDonald (ed.): Making Public in a Privatized World. The Struggle for Essential Services. Zed Books, 2016.

Melissa Morrone and Lia Friedman: Radical Reference. Socially Responsible Librarianship Collaborating With Community. In: The Reference Librarian, vol. 50, n. 4, 2009. pp. 371–396. http://eprints.rclis.org/23443

Tomislav Medak and Marcel Mars (ed.): Public Library. WHW, 2015.

Birgit Ostrom: Governing the Commons. The Evolution of Institutions for Collective Action. Camebridge University Press, 1990.

Birgit Ostrom et al (ed.): Understanding Knowledge as Commons. From Theory to Practice. MIT Press, 2007.

Lauri Rapeli: The Conception of Citizen Knowledge in Democratic Theory. Palgrave Macmillan, 2014.

Aaron Swartz: The Boy Who Could Change the World. The Writings of Aaron Swartz. The New Press, 2015.

WEBSITES

BStU Archives http://argus.bstu.bundesarchiv.de

Library Genesis http://libgen.io

LIBREAS. Library Ideas http://libreas.eu

Memory of the World https://memoryoftheworld.org

Peer to peer foundation http://p2pfoundation.net

Radical Imagination Project http://radicalimagination.org

Biographical Notes

ZELJKO BLACE works in fields of contemporary arts/culture, digital media/technologies and community sport, by cross-pollinating queer activism, media and social practices as an artist, activist, researcher, reporter, producer, designer, curator and critic. He was co-founder, coordinator and curator of Multimedia Institute/club MaMa in Zagreb 1999-04 (still contributes as a member). He curated exhibitions: GenArt 2002 @ HDLU.hr for new.media.culture.week; runtimeART in Zagreb/Split 2004 with A. Broeckmann; Silent*Observers @ MMSU.hr 2005 & @UCSD.edu in CalIT2 2006; Another Sport is possible?!. @ whw.hr/GalerijaNOVA 2012 & @MMSU.hr 2014; GenderBlending @ConstantVzw.org 2015; Contesting/Contexting SPORT @nGbK.de & KK/B 2016.
⌨ http://zeljko.blace.name

ANDREW CLEMENT is Professor Emeritus in the Faculty of Information at the University of Toronto, now living on Saltspring Island, on Canada's west coast. With a PhD in Computer Science, he has had longstanding research and teaching interests in the social implications of information/communication technologies and participatory design. His recent privacy/surveillance research projects include the Snowden Digital Surveillance Archive and IXmaps, an internet mapping tool that visualizes secret NSA internet interception sites and the routing of personal data through them.
⌨ https://ixmaps.ca

COLNATE GROUP is an anonymous art collective which has undergone many changes since its creation at the beginning of the 1990s. Their work has appeared in a variety of contexts –

often outside the traditional art world, including post cards, hotel rooms, night clubs, subway stations and the internet.

NAOMI COLVIN is Case Director at the Courage Foundation, an international organization that supports individuals who risk life or liberty to make significant contributions to the historical record. One of their beneficiaries is Edward Snowden and, in addition to ensuring his personal safety is secured, Courage has been carefully tracking the global impact of his disclosures. The organization collaborated with Transparency Toolkit to build the Snowden Document Search.
⌨ https://couragefound.org

SIMON DENNY is an artist based in Berlin. He studied at the University of Auckland's Elam School of Fine Arts in 2001-2005 and was a Meisterschüler at Städelschule, Frankfurt am Main (2007–2009). He makes sculptures and installations that take his research into the practices and aesthetics of technology companies and products as their starting point. His subject matter has included the redesign of the New Zealand passport, German technology conferences, internet entrepreneur Kim Dotcom, the Snowden files and Blockchain. In 2015 Denny represented New Zealand at the 56th Venice Biennale.
⌨ http://simondennysecretpower.com

CORINNA HAAS is an academic librarian based in Berlin. She runs the research library at ICI Berlin Institute for Cultural Inquiry. She has a background in Compared Literature and European Ethnography and does research on ethnography in libraries and the use of

library space. She is active in various professional networks and has been serving as the managing chairwoman of the Berlin section of the German Library Association. She has been actively involved in numerous events in Berlin that brought together researchers, activists, artists and librarians who were working with the Snowden documents.
https://ici-berlin.org/library

CHRISTOPH HOCHHÄUSLER is a film director and screenwriter based in Berlin. His film "Falscher Bekenner" (2005) was screened in the Un Certain Regard section at the 2005 Cannes Film Festival and his film "The City Below" (2010) was screened in the Un Certain Regard section at the 2010 Cannes Film Festival. He is co-founder and co-editor of the film magazine Revolver and a professor at the dffb, the German Film and Television Academy Berlin.

EVAN LIGHT is a media scholar and artist based in Toronto. He is Assistant Professor of Communication at Glendon College, York University, Canada. He holds a PhD in communication from the Université du Québec à Montréal. He is a member of the Algorithmic Media Observatory and the Centre de recherche interuniversitaire sur l'information, la communication et la société. His work has appeared in publications including the Canadian Journal of Communication and the Journal of Peer Production. He created the Snowden-Archive-in-a-Box, an device for enabling off-line research on surveillance. As an expert in networks and privacy, he works to challenge the social, political and economic logics of surveillance. http://glendon.yorku.ca

M.C. McGRATH is a software engineer and activist based in Berlin. He is the founder of Transparency Toolkit, a non-profit that collects open data and builds free software to expose surveillance and

human rights abuses. One of his projects is the Snowden Document Search. He is also a Thiel Fellow and an Echoing Green Fellow. Previously, he studied civic technology at Boston University and did research at the MIT Media Lab. While in school, he participated in Google Summer of Code and was a member of the hackerspace BUILDS.
http://shidash.com

HENRIK MOLTKE is a freelance journalist, researcher, and filmmaker. He is co-director of "Project X" (2016) with Laura Poitras. His recent work has appeared in The New York Times, The Intercept, and at the Whitney Museum of American Art. Moltke won the 2014 Danish Investigative Journalism Award and was nominated for the Cavling Prize, the most prestigious award in Danish journalism. He co-directed the 2007 documentary film "Good Copy Bad Copy" and has produced several award-winning long-format radio documentaries and cross-media features.

DEBORAH NATSIOS is an architect, artist and activist in New York. Together with her partner John Young she runs the website Cryptome.org. Here, they collect leaked documents about freedom of expression, privacy, cryptography, dual-use technologies, national security, intelligence, government secrecy. She received her graduate degree in architecture from Princeton University. She has taught architecture and urban design at Columbia University and Parsons The New School for Design, and held seminars at the Pratt Institute and the University of Texas. She is the principal of Natsios Young Architects.
https://cryptome.org

JULIAN OLIVER is an artist based in Berlin. His work and lectures have been presented at many museums, galleries, international electronic-art events and conferences, including the Tate Modern,

Transmediale, the Chaos Computer Congress, Ars Electronica, FILE and the Japan Media Arts Festival. He has received several awards, most notably the distinguished Golden Nica at Prix Ars Electronica 2011 for the project Newstweek (with Daniil Vasiliev). He is an advocate of Free and Open Source Software and is a supporter of, and contributor to, initiatives that promote and reinforce rights in the networked domain. ✎ https://julianoliver.com

TREVOR PAGLEN is an artist based in New York City and Berlin. His work deliberately blurs lines between science, contemporary art, journalism, and other disciplines to construct unfamiliar, yet meticulously researched ways to see and interpret the world around us. Paglen's visual work has been exhibited at the Metropolitan Museum of Art, New York; The Tate Modern, London; The Walker Arts Center, Minneapolis; The San Francisco Museum of Modern Art; the 2008 Taipei Biennial; the 2009 Istanbul Biennial; the 2012 Liverpool Biennial, and numerous other solo and group exhibitions. He is the author of five books and numerous articles. He won the Deutsche Börse Photography Prize in 2016. ✎ http://paglen.com

LAURA POITRAS is a documentary filmmaker based in Berlin. Following an early career in experimental film, Poitras turned her attention to contemporary social issues, offering insight into complex topics. Her signature work, a trilogy of feature-length documentaries about America's post–September 11 war on terror, explores the human consequences of military conflict abroad from unusual vantage points, reflecting relationships she forges over months and years of close interaction. In May 2013, she met NSA whistleblower Edward Snowden and has been reporting his disclosures for Der Spiegel, The New York Times, and The Guardian. ✎ http://praxisfilms.org

NORMAN POSSELT is a freelance photographer and photo editor based in Berlin. He studied media and communication sciences in Halle (Saale) and focuses on portraits as well as conference documentation in the field of design and typography. ✎ http://normanposselt.com

SAZAE bot is a Twitter bot based in Tokyo. It is a parody-bot avatar of the most famous Japanese manga character, Sazae-san. In 2010, SAZAE bot started as a bot on Twitter, copy and pasting phrases found from various posts around the Internet. The avatar depicts universal reality with some elements of critical thinking. The avatar itself is the continuous "incident" that occurs from mutual relationships between it and its 250.000 followers, and eventually, its activities become memes of thoughts. In 2016 SAZAE bot received the Prix Ars Electronica. ✎ http://anon.site

MAGDALENA TAUBE is a journalist and researcher based in Berlin. She earned an MA in German Literature and British/North American Studies and a PhD from Humboldt University Berlin. Her research focus is digital journalism. In 2016 Magdalena was appointed Bucerius research fellow of the ZEIT foundation in Hamburg with a work focussing on Big Data and civil society. Magdalena is managing editor of the berlinergazette. de. She has vast experience in teaching digital literacy and journalism at Humboldt University Berlin, Bard College Berlin, Leuphana University Lüneburg, Hokkaido University Sapporo and many more. ✎ http://berlinergazette.de

STEFAN TIRON is a an artist based in Bucharest. He is a member of Paradis Garaj artist collective. He studied art history at the National University of Arts in Bucharest obtaining his degree in 2001. He is founder and co-curator of a series of art and science wonder shows